Microsoft®
Exchange Server 2007
FOR
DUMMIES®

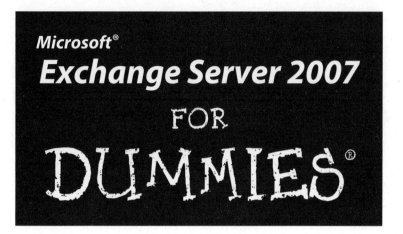

by John Paul Mueller

WILEY

Wiley Publishing, Inc.

Microsoft® Exchange Server 2007 For Dummies®

Published by
Wiley Publishing, Inc.
111 River Street
Hoboken, NJ 07030-5774

www.wiley.com

Copyright © 2009 by Wiley Publishing, Inc., Indianapolis, Indiana

Published by Wiley Publishing, Inc., Indianapolis, Indiana

Published simultaneously in Canada

For general information on our other products and services, please contact our Customer Care Department within the U.S. at 800-762-2974, outside the U.S. at 317-572-3993, or fax 317-572-4002.

For technical support, please visit www.wiley.com/techsupport.

Wiley also publishes its books in a variety of electronic formats. Some content that appears in print may not be available in electronic books.

Library of Congress Control Number: 2008936635

ISBN: 978-0-470-39866-1

Manufactured in the United States of America

10 9 8 7 6 5 4 3 2 1

WILEY

About the Author

John Mueller is a freelance author and technical editor. He has writing in his blood, having produced 81 books and over 300 articles to date. The topics range from networking to artificial intelligence and from database management to heads-down programming. Some of his current books include a Windows power optimization book, books on both Windows Server 2008 GUI and Windows Server 2008 Server Core, and a programmer's guide that discusses the new Office Fluent User Interface (RibbonX). His technical editing skills have helped more than 58 authors refine the content of their manuscripts. John has provided technical editing services to both *Data Based Advisor* and *Coast Compute* magazines. He's also contributed articles to the following magazines: *CIO.com, DevSource, InformIT, Informant, DevX, SQL Server Professional, Visual C++ Developer, Hard Core Visual Basic, asp.netPRO, Software Test and Performance,* and *Visual Basic Developer.*

When John isn't working at the computer, he enjoys spending time in his workshop crafting wood projects or making candles. On any given afternoon, you can find him working at a lathe or putting the finishing touches on a bookcase. He also likes making glycerin soap, which comes in handy for gift baskets. You can reach John on the Internet at `JMueller@mwt.net`. John is also setting up a Web site and blog at `http://www.johnmuellerbooks.com/`; feel free to look and make suggestions on how he can improve it.

Dedication

This book is dedicated to my nephew Jason, who is at childhood's end and reminds me so much of myself at his age. He gives me hope for the future. Happy 16th birthday!

Author's Acknowledgments

Thanks to my wife, Rebecca, for working with me to complete this book. I don't know what I would have done without her help in researching and compiling some of the information that appears in this book. She also did a fine job of proofreading my rough draft.

Russ Mullen deserves thanks for his technical edit of this book. He added greatly to the accuracy and depth of the material that you see here. I appreciated the time he devoted to checking my code for accuracy. As I wrote this book, I also spent a good deal of time bouncing ideas off Russ, which was a valuable aid to me.

Matt Wagner, my agent, deserves credit for helping me get the contract in the first place and taking care of all the details that most authors don't consider. I always appreciate his assistance. It's good to know that someone wants to help.

A number of people read all or part of this book to help me refine the approach, test the examples, and generally provide input that all readers wish they could have. These unpaid volunteers helped in ways too numerous to mention here. I especially appreciate the efforts of Eva Beattie and all the others who provided input on Exchange Server. I'd like to thank each person who wrote me with an idea by name, but there are simply too many.

Finally, I would like to thank Katie Feltman, Susan Pink, and the rest of the editorial and production staff for their assistance in bringing this book to print. It's always nice to work with such a great group of professionals.

Publisher's Acknowledgments

We're proud of this book; please send us your comments through our online registration form located at www.dummies.com/register/.

Some of the people who helped bring this book to market include the following:

Acquisition and, Editorial

Project Editor: Susan Pink

Acquisitions Editor: Katie Feltman

Copy Editor: Susan Pink

Technical Editor: Russ Mullen

Editorial Manager: Jodi Jensen

Editorial Assistant: Amanda Foxworth

Sr. Editorial Assistant: Cherie Case

Cartoons: Rich Tennant (www.the5thwave.com)

Composition Services

Project Coordinator: Erin Smith

Layout and Graphics: Reuben W. Davis, Christin Swinford, Ronald Terry, Christine Williams

Proofreaders: John Greenough, Christine Sabooni

Indexer: Ty Koontz

Publishing and Editorial for Technology Dummies

    Richard Swadley, Vice President and Executive Group Publisher

    Andy Cummings, Vice President and Publisher

    Mary Bednarek, Executive Acquisitions Director

    Mary C. Corder, Editorial Director

Publishing for Consumer Dummies

    Diane Graves Steele, Vice President and Publisher

Composition Services

    Gerry Fahey, Vice President of Production Services

    Debbie Stailey, Director of Composition Services

Contents at a Glance

Table of Contents

Introduction

*E*xchange Server is an e-mail server. Some people may stop there. After all, e-mail is a necessary, yet boring, requirement for any organization today. However, Exchange Server is far more than a simple e-mail server, and that's what *Microsoft Exchange Server 2007 For Dummies* is all about. In this book, you discover the amazing capabilities of Exchange Server 2007 SP1 and what it can do for your organization besides serve up e-mail.

About This Book

You may be amazed to know that Exchange Server can help every member of your organization schedule appointments. In addition, it can help them coordinate their appointments so that meetings become easy, rather than too inconvenient to schedule properly. Of course, meetings involve more than people — they also involve resources. Exchange Server helps you create and schedule every resource required for your meeting, and *Microsoft Exchange Server 2007 For Dummies* helps you perform this necessary task.

Exchange Server also provides considerable resources to keep your e-mail experience safe. Microsoft's focus is on using the advanced features of Exchange Server to perform this task. *Microsoft Exchange Server 2007 For Dummies* helps you accomplish this job without investing in multiple servers — a boon for small organizations. Of course, this book also considers the needs of the medium- and large-sized organization as well.

One of the focal points of this book is the Service Pack 1 (SP1) release. Most Exchange Server 2007 books on the market today came out before SP1 was a reality. *Microsoft Exchange Server 2007 For Dummies* provides full SP1 coverage, so you know you're getting the best information possible about Exchange Server 2007.

A second focus of *Microsoft Exchange Server 2007 For Dummies* is performance and the three elements that define it: security, reliability, and speed. Using the techniques in this book will ensure that you obtain maximum Exchange Server performance. In short, rather than simply tell you how Exchange Server works or how to use it, this book goes further and helps you obtain the most out of Exchange Server. Consequently, *Microsoft Exchange Server 2007 For Dummies* is the best book available to get started with your Exchange Server 2007 SP1 experience.

Conventions Used in This Book

I always try to show you the fastest way to accomplish any task. In many cases, this means using a menu command such as File➪New➪Project. When working with Exchange Server, I'll tell you which dialog box tab to access first, and then which feature to use on that tab.

This book also uses special type to emphasize some information. For example, entries that you need to type appear in **bold**. All code, Web site URLs, and on-screen messages appear in `monofont type`. When I define a new word, you'll see that word in *italics*.

Because you use multiple applications when you're working with Exchange Server, I always point out when to move from one application to the next. When a chapter begins, I introduce the main application for that chapter. All the commands in that chapter are for the main application until I specifically tell you to move to another application. I also tell you when it's time to move back to the main application.

What You Should Read

If you haven't worked with Exchange Server before, you should begin with Chapter 1 because this initial chapter contains a lot of information you can use to help define your Exchange Server setup. Planning your Exchange Server configuration is important and this chapter provides the information you need. Anyone, no matter what level of expertise they possess, should read the "Understanding the Service Pack 1 (SP1) Differences" section of Chapter 1. This section of the chapter helps you understand the benefits of installing Exchange Server 2007 SP1 on your server.

Everyone should read Chapters 5 through 8 at some point because these chapters emphasize the SP1 configuration procedures. However, when you read these chapters depends on when you install SP1. If you perform the installation described in this book, you should move on to Chapter 5 immediately after completing the installation. On the other hand, if you install SP1 as an update to your existing Exchange Server installation, you don't need to start reading Chapters 5 through 8 until you complete the upgrade.

Chapters 9 through 13 are essential management chapters. Someone who has never worked with Exchange Server before will probably want to read them from start to finish. After you gain some Exchange Server experience, you use these chapters for reference — picking and choosing just the sections needed to manage your system.

What You Don't Have to Read

Most of the chapters contain some advanced material that will interest only some readers. When you see one of these specialized topics (such as using S/MIME and PGP/MIME encryption in Chapter 1), feel free to skip it. Most of this advanced material appears in sidebars and some of it applies only when you use a specific Exchange Server component. The sidebar title will always indicate the special nature of the advanced material.

You can also skip any material marked with a Technical Stuff icon. This material is helpful, but you don't have to know it to work with Exchange Server. I include this material because I find it helpful in my administration efforts and hope that you will, too.

Foolish Assumptions

You might find it difficult to believe that I've assumed anything about you — after all, I haven't even met you yet! Although most assumptions are indeed foolish, I made these assumptions to provide a starting point for the book.

I'm assuming that you've worked with Windows long enough to know how the keyboard and mouse work. You should also know how to use menus and other basic Windows features.

In all the chapters, I assume you have administrator rights to the machine you use to work with Exchange Server. In addition, this book relies on Windows Server 2008 as the base operating system and Windows XP as the client operating system. You can use any combination of operating systems that Exchange Server and the client application you want to work with support, but the screenshots may differ from those shown in the book. You must know how to work with the advanced features of whatever versions of Windows you choose to use.

Some portions of the book work with Web pages and others use XML; you need to know at least a little about these technologies to use those sections. You don't have to be an expert in these areas, but more knowledge is better. This book doesn't require that you have any developer knowledge of either Web page or XML technology.

I do make an essential assumption in this book in the level of coverage. This book doesn't discuss Edge Transport server, the outside-the-firewall Exchange Server component, in any detail. I did this for an important reason. Many of you will begin using Exchange Server in your organization and will not want to invest a lot of money in multiple servers at the outset. This is the book to get you started. After you acquire the basics found in this book, you can move on to one of those heavy tomes on the market to increase the size of your Exchange Server configuration.

How This Book Is Organized

This book contains several parts. Each part demonstrates a particular Exchange Server concept. In each chapter, I discuss a particular topic and describe how to perform tasks associated with that topic using procedural steps. In some cases, I make recommendations but can't provide a precise procedure because the steps you take vary by organization. This book doesn't require that you download anything unless you plan to use one of the third-party products mentioned in a particular topic. In this case, I provide the URL you use to perform the download.

Part I: An Overview of Exchange Server 2007

The first part of the book is all about discovering (Chapter 1), planning and installing (Chapter 2), considering basic management of (Chapter 3), and configuring (Chapter 4) Exchange Server. These four chapters help you to get to the point of being able to access Exchange Server and perform more advanced management tasks. You'll probably use this part of the book once — during the initial configuration of your server. Of course, you can always return to Part I every time you add another server to your configuration.

Part II: Customizing Exchange Server

Exchange Server requires a lot of configuration before you can use it for anything practical. Just because you can access Exchange Server and send yourself an e-mail doesn't make it useful. Part II describes how to configure mailboxes (Chapter 5), security (Chapter 6), clients (Chapter 7), and forms (Chapter 8). Most of you will follow these chapters in order during the initial configuration of your server, but you'll use this part of the book as a configuration reference as your organization needs change.

Part III: Advanced Techniques

Part III contains a number of advanced techniques that you may not use very often. For example, Chapter 9 tells you how to troubleshoot configuration problems, and I hope you won't need to perform that task every day. The mail recovery techniques in Chapter 10 see the light of day only when something catastrophic happens to your server. The one chapter in this part that you should read end-to-end and use regularly is Chapter 11, which contains maintenance procedures. If you use Chapter 11 regularly, you may find that you need Chapters 9 and 10 seldom or not at all.

Chapters 12 and 13 are special. They show you how to work at the command line using Windows PowerShell (Chapter 12) and the familiar command prompt (Chapter 13). Using the techniques in this chapter can help you perform tasks faster, add automation to your administration tasks, and perform a few tasks that the GUI doesn't support very well.

Part IV: The Part of Tens

Everyone likes helpful tips and resources. The two chapters in Part IV contain descriptions of helpful third-party utilities (Chapter 14) and a list of places where you can obtain additional information (Chapter 15). Although these two chapters don't contain required reading, you'll miss out on an important part of the book if you don't at least scan these two chapters. The tidbits of information you receive may help you work with Exchange Server with considerably less effort. Of course, these are the utilities and online resources that I use. If you find some utilities or online resources that you want to share with me, be sure to write me at JMueller@mwt.net.

Icons Used in This Book

As you read this book, you'll see icons in the margins that indicate material of interest (or not, as the case may be). This section briefly describes each icon in this book.

Tips are nice because they help you save time or perform some task without a lot of extra work. The tips in this book are timesaving techniques or pointers to resources that you should try to get the maximum benefit from Exchange Server.

I don't want to sound like an angry parent or some kind of maniac, but you should avoid doing anything marked with a Warning icon. Otherwise, you could find that Exchange Server melts down and takes your data with it.

Whenever you see this icon, think *advanced* tip or technique. You might find these tidbits of useful information just too boring for words, or they could contain the solution you need to solve an Exchange Server issue. Skip this information whenever you like.

If you don't get anything else out of a particular chapter or section, remember the material marked by this icon. This text usually contains an essential process or bit of information that you must know to use Exchange Server successfully.

Where to Go from Here

It's time to start your Exchange Server adventure! I recommend that anyone who has never worked with Exchange Server go right to Chapter 1. This chapter contains essential, get-started information that you need for getting Exchange Server installed on your system. More importantly, this chapter tells you what you can expect from the SP1 update to Exchange Server.

If you already have Exchange Server installed, but haven't configured it yet, move on to Chapter 4 (for initial configuration) or Chapter 5 (for detailed configuration). Before you can use Exchange Server, you must configure it for use. This means configuring Exchange Server at the organization and server levels, adding mailboxes, setting security, and performing basic tests to ensure you have everything installed correctly.

Those who already have some Exchange Server experience and want to use this book as a reference may want to move directly to Chapter 9 and then review Chapters 5 through 8 as needed for updates. Chapter 9 begins an exciting section of the book where you discover techniques for locating problems on your system and methods you can use to test Exchange Server. In addition, some areas of Part III tell you how to improve Exchange Server reliability, speed, and security — the three cornerstones of good Exchange Server performance.

Part I

An Overview of Exchange of Exchange Server 2007

The 5th Wave   By Rich Tennant

"One of the first things you want to do before installing Exchange Server is fog the users to keep them calm during the procedure."

In this part . . .

What can Exchange Server 2007 SP1 do for you? You may have found some essential tasks that Exchange Server can accomplish, but you may not realize just how powerful this application is and its importance for your organization. Chapter 1 helps you consider all the special features that Exchange Server 2007 SP1 provides, especially those found in SP1 (the features that Microsoft covers least well in their documentation).

The remaining chapters in this part help you install Exchange Server 2007 SP1 for the first time. Chapter 2 helps with the installation process. In Chapter 3, you discover how to work with Exchange Management Console, which is the essential tool for most configuration tasks. By the time you finish with Chapter 4, you have a basic configuration in place that you can test and use to send yourself e-mail.

Chapter 1

Getting to Know Exchange Server 2007

. . . .

In This Chapter

▶ Understanding the new Exchange Server 2007 feature set

▶ Considering what makes Service Pack 1 (SP1) different

▶ Determining which edition you need

▶ Obtaining a trial version of Exchange Server 2007

▶ Using hosted services instead of your own copy

. . . .

*M*ost people know that Microsoft Exchange Server is an application that distributes e-mail and maintains a calendar. It doesn't sound very exciting at the outset. However, Exchange Server 2007 is more than just a simple mail program and calendar organizer. This chapter helps you get to know Exchange Server 2007 a bit better and understand how it can help your organization work more efficiently. A special section on SP1 helps you understand why the SP1 update is so important for your Exchange Server 2007 setup.

Exchange Server 2007 comes in several different editions, and you need to obtain the correct edition to ensure that you get the most out of the product to meet your organization's needs. This chapter also provides you with information on the various Exchange Server 2007 editions and helps you make an informed choice about which edition to get. You'll need to spend time assessing your organization's needs as part of this process. Company size doesn't necessarily dictate the edition you get because different organizations have differing needs.

In some cases, you may not want to buy Exchange Server 2007 today. After all, it's a large investment and you may not know precisely what you want out of Exchange Server 2007 immediately. Fortunately, you have two alternatives to spending big money immediately. First, you can obtain the trial version of Exchange Server 2007 and install it on your own system. Second, you can rely on a hosted version of Exchange Server 2007 loaded on someone else's machine. This chapter examines both options. In either case, you can use the contents of the rest of the book to help make your evaluation more thorough so you can make a better buying decision later.

Considering the Exchange Server 2007 Features

Exchange Server started as a simple mail and calendar program, but over the years it's evolved in a number of ways. First, Exchange Server has become more scalable. You can support more people from a single server, making multiple server setups less necessary. However, when you need to use multiple servers, you can do so with less effort.

Second, as with all Microsoft products, Exchange Server 2007 has more features than previous versions. Microsoft is constantly improving their products by adding features that sound interesting or that their customers request. To some extent, the extra features also increase product complexity, so it's important to choose the right Exchange Server edition and install only the features you need.

Third, as part of an overall effort by Microsoft, you find Exchange Server 2007 features designed to improve reliability, speed, or security. These features may not even be visible and you probably wouldn't know about them unless Microsoft told you they were there. These features are actually the best additions to Exchange because they make everyone more productive and less worried about their data. Table 1-1 provides a description of all three of these feature classes.

Table 1-1		New or Updated Features in Exchange Server 2007		
Feature	*Category*	*Type*	*Chapter in Book*	*Description*
Edge Transport Server Role	Scalability	Antispam and antivirus	4	Helps you support installations at the perimeter (edge) of your network. This server supports Simple Mail Transport Protocol (SMTP) routing. It also provides both antispam and antivirus network for users outside the normal network environment. Unlike most parts of Exchange Server, the Edge Transport server doesn't have direct Active Directory access, but it does support Active Directory access through the Active Directory Application Mode (ADAM). All communication between the Edge Transport server and the rest of the network is encrypted by default.

Feature	Category	Type	Chapter in Book	Description
Connection Filtering	Reliability, speed, or security	Antispam and antivirus	4	Blocks or allows an outside connection based on the IP address of the caller. The server stores the IP addresses of blocked callers based on reputation. The server downloads this list as updates become available. An administrator can also enter additional IP addresses as needed.
Sender and Recipient Filtering	Reliability, speed, or security	Antispam and antivirus	4	Blocks or allows a sender or recipient based on a combination of the Sender ID and the IP address of the SMTP server used to transmit the message. The Edge Transport server can also block a message based on analysis it performs on message transmission trends.
Safe Sender List Aggregation	Reliability, speed, or security	Antispam and antivirus	7	Provides a means for Outlook 2003 and Outlook 2007 users to send their safe senders lists to the server. The server respects these lists when determining whether to accept or reject messages.
Sender ID	Reliability, speed, or security	Antispam and antivirus	6	Supports the industry standard method of verifying users by embedding an identifier within the message. The server can use a combination of the identifier and the IP address of the SMTP server used to transmit the message. This feature reduces the risk of domain spoofing and other message problems.

(continued)

Table 1-1 *(continued)*

Feature	*Category*	*Type*	*Chapter in Book*	*Description*
Content Filtering	Reliability, speed, or security	Antispam and antivirus	6	Analyzes the content of messages using the Intelligent Message Filter (IMF), which is based on Microsoft's SmartScreen content filtering technology. The technology reviews the content of the message and rejects content from fraudulent links and spoofed domains. The technology also provides a certain level of anti-phishing protection.
Outlook E-Mail Postmark	Reliability, speed, or security	Antispam and antivirus	6	Verifies the e-mail postmark attached to a message. Using the postmark feature can help reduce false positives for senders who have little or no reputation on the local system.
Spam Assess-ment	Reliability, speed, or security	Antispam and antivirus	6	Combines the results of the content, connection, sender/recipient, sender reputation, sender ID verification, and Outlook e-mail postmark validation to create an overall spam assessment. The result of this check determines the action Exchange Server takes on the message. The administrator can configure various actions based on any of these criteria.
Service Resilience	Scalability	Antispam and antivirus	4	Controls the rate at which Exchange Server sends and receives messages. The use of message throttling for incoming messages helps prevent Distributed Denial of Service (DDoS) attacks. Checking for message sending patterns helps reduce the probability of a directory harvesting attack.

Feature	Category	Type	Chapter in Book	Description
Anti-Spam Stamp	Reliability, speed, or security	Antispam and antivirus	7	Provides a reason for stamping a message as spam. Administrators can use this information to assess the effectiveness of filtering.
Two-Tiered Spam Quarantine	Reliability, speed, or security	Antispam and antivirus	7	Makes it harder for spam to enter the workplace. At the first level, the administrator checks messages for spam content. If the administrator releases the message, the message is converted into plain text and passed to the junk mail folder in Outlook, where the user can perform a second level of spam checks.
Consolidated Management	Feature	Antispam and antivirus	4	Centralizes the Edge Transport server role and rules management with the rest of Exchange to make it easier to manage the entire Exchange Server setup. This feature also makes it possible to send alerts from Exchange Server to Microsoft Operations Manager (MOM) and produce reports of filter effectiveness.
Attachment Filtering	Reliability, speed, or security	Antispam and antivirus	7	Provides a means of rejecting attachments based on file extension and content, without rejecting the entire message.
Edge Protocol Rules	Reliability, speed, or security	Antispam and antivirus	6	Checks for problematic connections based on rules. This feature makes it possible to reject some connections before an antivirus signature becomes available.
Antivirus Stamp	Reliability, speed, or security	Antispam and antivirus	6	Adds information to the message that defines which engine performed the antivirus scanning, which signature the engine used, and when the engine last scanned the message.

(continued)

Table 1-1 *(continued)*

Feature	Category	Type	Chapter in Book	Description
Deep Integration for Antivirus Scanning	Reliability, speed, or security	Antispam and antivirus	6	Allows better integration between antivirus applications and Exchange Server. This feature lets antivirus programs interact with Exchange Server in a number of new ways, such as locating messages with virus content while they're still in transport so they never appear as part of the message store.
Hosted Filtering Integration	Feature	Antispam and antivirus	1	Provides integration with offsite Hosted Filtering support.
Intra-Org Encryption	Reliability, speed, or security	Confidential messaging	6	Encrypts all messages traveling within an organization by default. Exchange Server uses Transport Layer Security (TLS) for server-to-server traffic, Remote Procedure Call (RPC) for Outlook connections, and Secure Sockets Layer (SSL) for client access traffic (such as Outlook Web Access, Exchange ActiveSync, and Web Services).
SSL certificates automatically installed	Reliability, speed, or security	Confidential messaging	6	Provides Secure Sockets Layer (SSL) functionality automatically.
Opportunistic TLS Encryption	Reliability, speed, or security	Confidential messaging	6	Encrypts messages using Transport Layer Security (TLS) automatically when both the sender and recipient support TLS.
Messaging Records Management	Feature	Compliance	5	Performs automated message management. Depending on the rules that the administrator implements, Exchange Server scans messages in a message folder and retains, expires, or journals messages as needed.

Feature	Category	Type	Chapter in Book	Description
Flexible Journaling	Feature	Compliance	9	Tracks the activities of messages on Exchange Server using rules created by the administrator. You can set rules on a per-database, per-distribution list, or per-user basis.
Multi-Mailbox Search	Scalability	Compliance	7	Allows for searches that span multiple mailboxes. This compliance feature makes it possible to locate all the messages that relate to a particular topic without search each mailbox individually.
Archive Integration	Scalability	Compliance	9	Sends old journal messages to any SMTP address, including an Exchange mailbox or Windows SharePoint Services site, to archive them.
Local Continuous Replication (LCR)	Scalability	Business continuity	10	Provides local replication (backup) of data to ensure that the server can continue to function after a failure.
Cluster Continuous Replication (CCR)	Scalability	Business continuity	10	Provides the same feature as LCR, except at the cluster level. A group of servers replicate each other, making it possible for one server to take over for another after a failure.
Fast and Fewer Backups	Reliability, speed, or security	Business continuity	11	Ensures that the message store is backed up without requiring as much intervention on the part of the administrator.
Database Portability	Scalability	Business continuity	11	Lets you move the message store from one server to another as needed.

Although the list in Table 1-1 is impressive, Exchange Server 2007 provides a number of additional features that aren't discussed in this book. For example, Exchange Server 2007 provides a number of mobile user and Web technologies that you'll normally use for advanced setups. You can find a complete list of Exchange Server features at `http://www.microsoft.com/exchange/evaluation/features/default.mspx`.

Understanding the Service Pack 1 (SP1) Differences

Microsoft seems to provide two kinds of service packs: those that simply fix bugs and those that add a number of new features. Exchange Server 2007 SP1 falls into the second category. Microsoft uses SP1 to roll all the bug fixes it has produced so far into an easy-to-install package. In addition, Microsoft had to provide a way for Exchange Server 2007 to run properly on both Vista and Windows Server 2008 (Exchange Server 2007 requires that you use a 64-bit version of Windows), so SP1 makes installation on these systems easier. Finally, technology has changed since the initial Exchange Server 2007 release, so Microsoft uses SP1 to implement these technology changes as well. Consequently, SP1 is a major update to Exchange Server 2007, and you need to consider whether to install it on your organization's servers.

You may decide that you don't want to obtain and install SP1 immediately. In many cases, organizations need to test service packs for potential problems and want to know that the new features they provide are worth the effort. Fortunately, you can obtain a five-day hosted trial version of SP1 at `https://signmeup.exchange2007demo.com/exchange2007demo/`. This hosted trial relies on the Microsoft servers, so you don't need to upset your current configuration or create a test server for compatibility testing until you know the update is worth the effort. After you decide to test SP1, you can download and install the trial version of Exchange Server 2007 SP1. The "Obtaining a trial version" sidebar of this chapter provides additional details on getting the trial version. The following sections provide an overview of the SP1 features and tell you where to find additional details in the book.

Considering the addition of S/MIME support

The Secure/Multipurpose Internet Mail Extensions (S/MIME) standard provides a means of sending encrypted nontext message content over the Internet. Keeping e-mail content secure is gaining more importance as employees begin sending more sensitive content through e-mail. An alternative to this encryption technique is the Pretty Good Privacy/Multipurpose Internet Mail Extensions (PGP/MIME). You can find a discussion of both encryption technologies and links to their associated standards at `http://www.imc.org/smime-pgpmime.html`.

The addition of support for S/MIME to Exchange server means that you can send encrypted content to anyone who has S/MIME support installed on their system. When working with Exchange Server clients, you can send encrypted content to Outlook, Outlook Web Access, and Windows Mobile 6.0 using Exchange ActiveSync.

Understanding the use of new transport rules

You hear a lot about rules when working with Exchange Server. It seems as if Exchange Server lets you define a rule for any need. The transport rules modify the way Exchange Server sends and receives messages. The transport ensures that Exchange Server follows both corporate and regulatory policies to prevent e-mail from causing legal or other issues.

It's possible to apply transport rules to any e-mail, voice mail, or fax. These rules can fulfill a number of purposes as described in the following list (you can read more about this feature in Chapter 7):

- Add a disclaimer to the message to ensure the recipient knows about any legal requirements in regard to the message.
- Send a copy of the message to the administrator or other individual who manages network legal requirements when the message meets specific requirements.
- Prohibit contact between various sections of your organization.

Relying on standby continuous replication

Standby Continuous Replication (SCR) makes it possible to continuously send backup information for your mail server to other servers. In most cases, these servers appear in other localities, sometimes in different parts of the world. The SCR functionality builds on the LCR and CCR features that already exist in Exchange Server 2007, so this SP1 feature is just an extension of what Microsoft provided in the past.

As the name of this feature implies, the destination server receives continuous updates from the source server. Whenever the source server experiences an error, the administrator can switch to the destination server. As far as the users are concerned, nothing has happened — they continue to send and receive e-mail without interruption. Of course, this feature begs the question of what happens when both the source and destination server fail. This feature lets you work with multiple destination servers, which means that you can provide as many backups as necessary to achieve a particular level of reliability.

It isn't possible to create a system that maintains 100 percent reliability. Given the right event, your server will become unavailable. Using multiple backups does make this event extremely unlikely, but even so, you should always have a plan in place for situations where your mail server becomes inaccessible. You can read more about this in Chapter 10.

Implementing hardware security using device security and management

Most administrators have read about someone losing a device such as a laptop or cellular telephone somewhere and discovering a data breach because of that loss. Fortunately, SP1 provides functionality that lets you set device security. No, the security won't prevent someone from accessing local data, but you can use local encryption to prevent unauthorized local access in many cases. The device security will prevent someone from accessing your Exchange Server without providing a Personal Identification Number (PIN). SP1 provides this functionality by adding 28 new policies you can use to change how Exchange Server interacts with devices. Chapter 7 discusses how to use this feature.

Considering the Web-based messaging additions

Many of the new features found in SP1 make working with mobile devices easier. These Web-based messaging features create a better experience for users and make it less likely that they will experience problems. A detailed description of all these features appears in Chapter 7. The following list provides a quick overview of the features you can expect to see after installing SP1:

- **Outlook 2007 experience:** Microsoft has included a number of new features in Outlook 2007 that provide the user with a better e-mail experience. Exchange Server 2007 now supports these new features fully.

- **Self-service support:** Most users want fast service to fix their problems. After all, they really aren't interested in the technology — they simply want to complete an e-mail. The Outlook Web Access (OWA) 2007 Options menu provides entries that help the user fix the most common causes of support calls. When you install SP1, Exchange Server provides feedback messages when events such as a remote wipe of the data on a mobile device have been completed.

✔ **Outlook Web Access Lite:** Sometimes a user will have to work with a slow or faulty connection. In this case, using the full version of OWA 2007 may not provide satisfactory results. The user now has the option of using a reduced functionality version of OWA. This version provides support for scheduling out-of-office messages (internal and external), Really Simple Syndication (RSS) subscriptions, and Managed E-Mail Folder access.

✔ **WebReady Document Viewing:** This feature is part of the Remote Document Access feature. When using this feature, the user can ask Exchange Server to transform documents from an application-specific format (including Microsoft Word, Microsoft Excel, Microsoft PowerPoint, and PDF files) into HTML. This feature lets the user see the document, even when the device doesn't support the application-specific format. SP1 adds the capability to view Office 2007 document formats.

Understanding the voice features

Exchange Server includes two new voice features. The first is voice mail alerts. Your organization must have Office Communication Server (OCS) 2007 installed to use this feature. Whenever the user receives a new e-mail, they get an alert indicator on their Office Communicator client or they receive a message on their desktop phone.

The second voice feature is the ability to directly dial into Outlook Voice Access. As with the voice mail alerts, you must have Office Communication Server 2007 installed to use this feature. Because the setup for these features is complex and their use somewhat limited, this book doesn't discuss them in any detail.

Other changes in Exchange Server 2007 SP1

Exchange Server 2007 SP1 has a number of other changes in addition to the ones listed in this chapter. Although these changes may seem minor, they do make your computing experience better. The first change is a streamlined setup in Exchange Server 2007 SP1. Chapter 2 shows you how to use the new setup features.

If you're using Windows Server 2008, you need SP1 because Microsoft has made changes to Exchange Server 2007 to let it work with the new features in Windows Server 2008. As an administrator, you won't see any changes with this feature, but you'll know it's there when you begin implementing security or performing other tasks that require Windows Server 2008 functionality.

The final new SP1 feature is the Web Services Application Programming Interface (API). As an administrator, you probably won't interact with this feature. However, the developers creating custom applications for your organization will use it to embed information in Exchange Server messages and interact with Exchange Server in other ways.

Administration tool updates

SP1 includes some additional administration tool features. Microsoft has provided updates for Exchange Management Console (Chapter 3), Exchange Management Shell (Chapter 12), and Public Folder Management Console (Chapter 5). See the appropriate chapter for a full discussion of these changes.

Choosing the Correct Edition for Your Needs

Exchange Server 2007 comes in two editions: Standard and Enterprise. The Standard version is usually more suited to the needs of a small organization, while the Enterprise edition is usually more suited to the needs of a large organization. However, you need to consider how you interact with Exchange Server before you make a buying decision based solely on organization size. A small organization of highly mobile consultants may require the Enterprise edition to obtain the advanced features it provides. Likewise, a middle-sized company of accountants who rarely leave the office may not require the fancy features provided by the Enterprise edition; the Standard edition may work fine in this situation. Table 1-2 provides a list of differences between the two editions.

Table 1-2	Standard and Enterprise Edition Differences		
Feature	*SP1 Required?*	*Standard Edition*	*Enterprise Edition*
Cluster Continuous Replication	No	Not supported	Supported
Database Storage Limit	No	16TB	16TB
Database Support	No	5 databases	50 databases (maximum of 5 databases per storage group)
Local Continuous replication	No	Supported	Supported
Single Copy Clusters	No	Not supported	Supported
Standby Continuous Replication	Yes	Supported	Supported
Storage Group Support	No	5 groups	50 groups

As shown in Table 1-2, the main difference between Standard and Enterprise editions amounts to one of scalability. When deciding how much scalability your organization requires, it's important to ask questions such as, "Will your organization really use more than 80TB of storage space?" The Standard edition supports up to 80TB of storage space, so you may not need anything more than Standard edition in many situations. Of course, if your organization regularly stores huge files, such as videos, you may need the 800TB storage capability of Enterprise edition. The point is to make a decision based on what you actually need.

Choosing an edition isn't quite enough to complete the answer of what to buy for your organization. Exchange Server 2007 also supports two Client Access License (CAL) editions: Standard and Enterprise. Even though the edition determines the scalability of the server, the CAL determines the functionality of the server. You can mix and match the editions and CAL options. Consequently, you may have a Standard edition server with an Enterprise edition CAL. In addition, you can combine both CALs on a single server, so you could have an Enterprise edition server with both the Standard edition and Enterprise edition CALs installed. In short, Microsoft is actually offering six versions of Exchange Server 2007.

To make things more interesting, Microsoft also throws in a requirement for volume licensing for some features. To obtain the target feature, you must buy a volume license. Table 1-3 shows the CAL options.

Table 1-3		**CAL Edition Differences**			
Feature	*SP1 Required?*	*Volume License Required?*	*Standard Edition*	*Enterprise Edition*	*Combined Edition*
Advanced Exchange ActiveSync Policies	Yes	No		X	X
Exchange ActiveSync	No	No	X		X
Exchange Hosted Filtering	No	Yes		X	X
Forefront Security for Exchange Server	No	Yes		X	X
Managed Custom E-Mail Folders	No	No		X	X
Managed Default E-Mail Folders	No	No	X		X

Feature	SP1 Required?	Volume License Required?	Standard Edition	Enterprise Edition	Combined Edition
Outlook Web Access	No	No	X		X
Per-User/Per-Distribution List Journaling	No	No		X	X
Standard features including e-mail, shared calendar, contact management, task management, and administrative tools	No	No	X		X
Unified Messaging	No	No		X	X

Table 1-3 shows that you must have a combined CAL and volume licensing to obtain every feature. Of course, the question is whether you really need every feature for your organization. In most cases, the answer is no, so you need to analyze your requirements carefully before you make a purchase.

You have a final issue to consider before you decide which edition of Exchange Server to obtain. One of the potential hidden problems for administrators is determining how to license Exchange Server. The CAL you obtain will provide either per-device or per-user licensing.

Obtaining a trial version

Choosing e-mail and time management software isn't something you can do quickly or without testing things out. Fortunately, you can obtain a 120-day evaluation copy of Exchange Server 2007 SP1 for your server from http://technet.microsoft.com/en-us/bb736128.aspx. The download doesn't require a lot of time. After you download the trial version, you can install it using the procedures in Chapter 2 and configure it using the resources in the rest of the book, just as you would with a purchased version. The only limitation is that you won't want to configure the server with production data that you intend to keep.

Choosing a licensing option can be tricky. It comes down to one of determining how your users interact with Exchange Server. If the majority of your users rely on a single machine that sits at your office, a per-device license makes sense. However, if your users rely on several machines as they go from one place to another, relying on a per-user license may be a better idea. Choosing the wrong license can cost your organization considerable money, even if you make all the right decisions when it comes to Exchange Server 2007 Edition and CAL Edition.

Considering Microsoft Exchange Hosted Services

Just about everyone in business relies on e-mail today. It's hard to find a business that doesn't make at least part of its sales from e-mail. In addition, e-mail provides a means to communicate with both customers and employees. Even factory jobs often require the use of e-mail to ensure good communication between employees and support staff. Unfortunately, your e-mail is under attack from a number of sources, including:

- ✔ Viruses, worms, and other malware
- ✔ DDoS
- ✔ Phishing
- ✔ Spam
- ✔ Government regulations
- ✔ Legal actions

Microsoft Exchange Hosted Services help you fight these communication problems without making a large investment in Microsoft Exchange Server — you simply rent the services you need from Microsoft. Using Microsoft Exchange Hosted Services isn't the same as obtaining a copy of Microsoft Exchange Server — you don't obtain e-mail, calendaring, and other common features. However, you could use Microsoft Exchange Hosted Services to augment your existing e-mail product without incurring a huge additional cost. The following sections describe Microsoft Exchange Hosted Services in more detail.

Defining the Hosted Services elements

As mentioned, hosted services focus mainly on antivirus and antispam support. An important issue to consider when you review these services is that they all integrate directly into your current Exchange Server solution, so you can view them as an extension to your setup. To obtain the functionality that these services provide, you make a simple Mail eXtension (MX) record change. Theoretically, you should be able to use these services with other e-mail server offerings, although Microsoft is definitely tightlipped about this potential use of Microsoft Exchange Hosted Services. The hosted services that Microsoft provides include four elements:

✔ **Hosted Filtering:** Helps you avoid malware by removing messages that contain content that could compromise your network. You can find a number of alternatives to this feature such as Postini (http://www.postini.com/). Theoretically, Hosted Filtering will provide you with a better experience because you can hook it directly into Outlook for your users. One of the most important considerations for this service is that Microsoft provides policy-based management, which means that you can create business rules for off-site implementation rather than rely on the service provider to maintain rules for you.

✔ **Hosted Archive:** Creates an off-site e-mail archive to help your organization meet government- and client-mandated retention requirements. One of the interesting features of this service is that it provides spam checking before it archives any messages, which ensures that your data store is free of unwanted messages. You can possibly get the same type of archival using other means, such as Amazon's Simple Storage Service (http://www.amazon.com/S3-AWS-home-page-Money/b/ref=sc_fe_1_2?node=16427261), but using this hosted archive is substantially less work.

✔ **Hosted Encryption:** Encrypts e-mail messages to ensure that no one but the intended recipient can read them. Many businesses today require secure e-mail because of the content of e-mail messages. In the past, e-mail didn't contain company secrets, the strategy for your latest acquisition, or other information you don't want others to see. This service makes it possible to create business secrets away from prying eyes. The interesting aspect of this service is that you use policies to determine how and when encryption occurs. In addition, the encrypt takes place without user interaction. As far as the user is concerned, the encryption is invisible.

✔ **Hosted Continuity:** Preserves access to e-mail messages during and after an emergency. This service provides a thirty-day rolling e-mail archive so that you can access existing messages. The service doesn't let you download new e-mail messages, so you can't use it in place of an e-mail server. The message store is fully searchable, so you can find messages of interest quickly.

One of the interesting elements of Microsoft's Hosted Services offering is that you can try out the Hosted Filtering service by itself for 30 days. This offering makes it easy to determine whether you want to use Hosted Filtering in your organization. Sign up for a Hosted Filtering trial at http://www.microsoft.com/exchange/services/trial.mspx.

Buying Hosted Services for your organization

Microsoft offers a number of plans for obtaining Hosted Services for your organization. For example, they have a different plan for schools than they do for enterprises, so you don't have to worry about trying to fit your organization into a plan that doesn't work. You can find out more about the plans and approximate costs for Hosted Services at http://www.microsoft.com/exchange/services/buy.mspx.

The How to Buy Exchange Services Web site includes more than simply prices and plans. It also provides you with the process you use to obtain, install, and implement Hosted Services. Consequently, even if you aren't planning to buy Hosted Services today, you should still go to the Web site to find out more about the current requirements.

Chapter 2

Installing Exchange Server 2007

*I*t's time to install your copy of Exchange Server 2007. The installation process isn't difficult, but you do need to plan. Exchange Server 2007 requires that you have a specific environment in place before you begin the installation. The better you configure this environment, the greater the probability that you'll have the perfect installation when you finish.

After you install the prerequisite software, you need to check your environment to make sure the installation will succeed. The Exchange Server setup program also performs a check, but it does so halfway through the installation, and restarting the installation after you make corrections can be frustrating. Consequently, it's advantageous to check your environment before you begin the installation process to ensure that the Exchange Server setup program check passes.

The actual installation comes next. At this point, all you really need to do is answer a few straightforward questions and watch events play out during the setup process. A few of the steps require extra time, and you'll be able to do something else while you wait. For example, the setup program performs some tasks with Active Directory as part of the installation, and you have to wait for these tasks to complete. When you finish this chapter, you'll have a basic Exchange Server 2007 installation. Of course, you still need to configure your copy of Exchange Server 2007 using the procedures found in Chapters 3 and 4.

Addressing the Installation Prerequisites

Exchange Server requires that you supply a specific environment for it to execute properly. Unlike previous versions of Exchange Server, Exchange Server 2007 comes in only a 64-bit version. Microsoft has this requirement so that Exchange Server 2007 can provide the maximum performance and allow you to create larger databases (see Tables 1-2 and 1-3 in Chapter 1 for Exchange Server 2007 feature listings). With the goal of creating just the right environment in mind, the following sections describe the hardware, configuration, and software you must provide before you begin the Exchange Server 2007 installation.

Understanding the minimum hardware requirements

As mentioned, Exchange Server 2007 requires a 64-bit operating system, which means you must have a 64-bit processor to use it. Consequently, you may not be able to upgrade that old system one more time and instead may need a new system. It's important to keep this requirement in mind because some organizations will certainly try to upgrade an old system, only to find that it doesn't make the grade. Table 2-1 describes the hardware requirements for Exchange Server 2007.

Table 2-1	Exchange Server Hardware Requirements	
Component	**Minimum Requirement**	**Additional Notes**
Processor	You can choose an Intel 64 Architecture such as the Xeon processor or an AMD 64 processor. It's a good idea to use a multicore processor (the test system has a dual physical processor with two cores each for a total of four processors). Microsoft says you can use the Pentium processor, but only for training purposes. In general, you shouldn't use a Pentium processor with Exchange Server 2007.	Exchange Server 2007 doesn't support the Itanium processor. See the "Using the Exchange Server tools on a 32-bit machine" section of the chapter for details on using the Exchange Server tools on your 32-bit machine.

Component	Minimum Requirement	Additional Notes
Memory	2GB RAM for Exchange Server and an additional 5MB for each mailbox when using a single role.	The actual Microsoft specified minimum is 2GB RAM, but most installations will run slowly using this configuration.
	8GB RAM for a multiple role setup that includes the Hub Transport, Client Access, Unified Messaging, and Mailbox server roles. If you plan a complex setup, you may want to use the article at `http://technet.microsoft.com/en-us/library/bb738124(EXCHG.80).aspx` to calculate memory requirements.	The maximum RAM that Exchange Server uses is 32GB when using PC2700 RAM and 16GB when using PC3200 RAM. You can see a discussion of Double Data Rate (DDR) RAM types at `http://en.wikipedia.org/wiki/DDR_SDRAM`.
Paging file size	The amount of memory in the server, plus 10MB. A better planning amount is to double the amount of memory in the server as a page file because doing so can enhance performance. Always try tuning the paging file size to achieve the best performance.	The Microsoft recommended minimum lets Exchange Server record information about server failures. The system sends the content of memory to a DMP file that you can examine later to determine the cause of the failure. The paging file must have enough space to hold all of memory and a little extra for data gathering requirements.
Disk space	A basic system with Windows Server 2008 and Exchange Server 2007 installed on a single drive and 1GB mailboxes for ten users requires approximately 111.8GB (104.8GB for Service Pack 1, abbreviated as SP1).	See the "Detailing hard drive usage" section of the chapter for details on computing this value.
Drive	You must provide a local or network-accessible DVD drive. Using a local drive tends to reduce the risk of installation errors.	When working with an ISO image from a product such as MSDN, you can also theoretically use a virtual DVD drive.

(continued)

Table 2-1 *(continued)*

Component	Minimum Requirement	Additional Notes
Screen resolution	Although you can install Exchange Server using an 800 X 600 display, using most of the utilities requires that you have at least a 1,024 X 768 display.	When working with complex Exchange Server setups, more screen real estate is better.
File format	Microsoft requires that you format all drives using NTFS.	You can use separate partitions for specific tasks. The partitions store system files, Exchange Server binary files, storage group files (including transaction log files), database files, and other Exchange Server files.
Other hardware	Mouse	Theoretically, you can work with Exchange Server using just the keyboard, but having a mouse available makes performing tasks significantly easier.

Many of these requirements are straight from Microsoft, so you need to remember that Microsoft always recommends the absolute minimum. A real system will probably require more than these minimum requirements. Some of these requirements come from my personal testing and from the experiences of other Exchange Server users. The important thing to remember is that Exchange Server 2007 will always accept more capacity but will likely refuse to work at all with less than these minimum requirements.

Using the Exchange Server tools on a 32-bit machine

Just because you can't install Exchange Server on a 32-bit machine doesn't mean you can't use your old 32-bit machine in other ways. You can install the Exchange Server 2007 management tools on a system with a 32-bit processor but should never install any Exchange Server role on such a system. To use the Exchange Server 2007 management tools on a 32-bit processor, you must make a separate download of the 32-bit tools at http://www.microsoft. com/downloads/details.aspx?FamilyId=6BE38633-7248-4532- 929B-76E9C677E802. You can also use a 32-bit system to prepare Active Directory and the domains using the Exchange Server 2007 setup program and the instructions at http://technet.microsoft.com/en-us/library/ bb125224(EXCHG.80).aspx. You can install just the management tools on a 64-bit machine by performing a custom setup and choosing the Management Tools option on the Server Role Selection page, as shown in Figure 2-1.

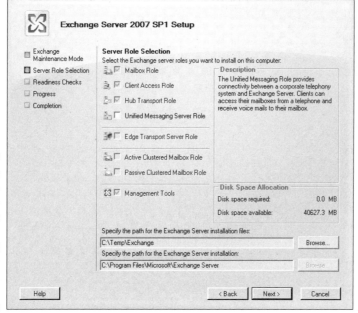

Figure 2-1:
Choose the Management Tools option if you only want the management tools on a system.

Detailing hard drive usage

Microsoft has you perform a complex set of calculations to determine disk space requirements. Unfortunately, you really do need to consider a number of factors when working with Exchange Server 2007. A basic Exchange Server setup that relies on a single drive requires approximately 6.4GB of hard drive space. Remember that 5.9GB is only for Exchange Server — you need additional disk space for Windows and all of the other applications on your system. Here's a list of the drive space requirements you should consider when working with Exchange Server:

- Exchange Server requires 1.2GB on the installation drive.

- Exchange Server requires 200MB on the system drive.

- Each Unified Messaging (UM) language pack requires 500MB

- The message queue database on an Edge Transport server or Hub Transport server requires at least 4GB when working with the RTM.

- The message queue database on an Edge Transport server or Hub Transport server requires at least 500MB when working with SP1.

You also need to add drive space for the Exchange Server database, which includes the size of each mailbox. For example, if you plan to support ten users and give each user 1GB of hard drive space, you'd need a minimum of 10GB for the database.

Microsoft recommends that you provide a minimum of 40GB for Windows Server 2008 (see the Web site at http://www.microsoft.com/ windowsserver2008/en/us/system-requirements.aspx for details). Windows Server 2008 has memory and other requirements that you must consider in addition to the Exchange Server requirements. If you use a different Windows server version, make sure you meet the requirements for that server version.

When you total all of these requirements, the minimum hard drive usage is 5.9GB for Exchange Server (only 2.4GB when using SP1), 10GB for ten users with 1GB mailboxes, and 40GB for Windows Server 2008, for a total of 55.9GB (52.4GB for SP1). After you determine the minimum disk space requirements for everything, double this number (as a minimum) to obtain the minimum drive size. In this case, for a very simple setup, you need 111.8GB (104.8GB for SP1) of drive space.

Verifying your configuration

Exchange Server 2007 requires that you provide a specific configuration. You must provide particular environmental features and an Active Directory setup and meet certain operating system restrictions. The following list describes the environmental features you must provide:

✔ Open the Services console and verify that the Remote Registry service is started — some administrators turn this service off for security reasons.

✔ Remove any existing Network News Transfer Protocol (NNTP) support, including the support provided with IIS or the Exchange Server 2007 installation will complain. In some cases, the installation program won't even complain about the correct problem (as when you have NNTP installed as part of IIS 7).

✔ Remove any existing Simple Mail Transfer Protocol (SMTP) support you have installed. Make sure that you remove the SMTP Server feature. The Exchange Server 2007 installation will complain about this feature but won't offer to remove it for you.

The Active Directory setup comes next. The following list describes the Active Directory requirements your network must meet:

✔ **Schema master:** The schema master normally runs on the first Windows Server in a domain forest. When installing SP1, the schema master can use one of these operating systems:

   • Windows Server 2003 SP1 or later

   • Windows Server 2003 Windows Server 2003 R2

   • Windows Server 2008

✔ **Global catalog server:** Every Exchange Server site must have access to at least one global catalog server running Windows Server 2003 Service SP1 or later. The global catalog server provides support for the following Exchange Server 2007 features:

- Exchange Server 2007 service notifications, so that Exchange Server automatically sees any changes in Active Directory

- User address book browsing in Microsoft Outlook Web Access

- Efficient distribution-list membership lookups

✔ **Domain controller:** The domain controller must meet the following requirements:

- Must be running on Windows Server 2003 SP1 or later

- At least one domain controller must act also as a global catalog server and run Windows Server 2003 SP1 or later

- Must install Exchange Server 2007 SP1 on a server running Windows Server 2008 — the RTM version won't install on Windows Server 2008

✔ **Non-English domain controller:** You must install the hotfix found at `http://support.microsoft.com/?kbid=919166`.

✔ **Read-only domain controller:** Exchange Server 2007 doesn't support read-only domain controllers or read-only global catalog servers. You must provide access to a writeable domain controller and a writeable global catalog server.

✔ **Domain functional level:** The server must support the Windows 2000 Server native functional level. Using a higher functional level is better because you obtain access to additional features.

✔ **Forest functional level:** The server must support the Windows 2000 Server native functional level as a minimum. However, if you want access to features such as checking the availability of other users, you must set the server to use the Windows 2003 Server functional level.

✔ **Multiple forest installations:** Every server must be running on Windows Server 2003 SP1 or later.

✔ **Forest trust relationships:** You must establish trust relationships between forests to use features such as checking the availability of other users.

✔ **Disjoint namespaces:** A disjoint namespace occurs when the primary Domain Name System (DNS) suffix for the server doesn't match the DNS suffix of the domain where the computer resides. For example, the server may have a DNS suffix of `corp.mycompany.com` in a domain with a suffix of `east.corp.mycompany.com`. In general, using a disjoint namespace is a bad idea because you must perform additional configuration for both Exchange Server and Active Directory. If you can't avoid using a disjoint namespace (such as the naming of public facing servers), see the articles at `http://technet.microsoft.com/en-us/library/bb676377(EXCHG.80).aspx` and `http://technet.microsoft.com/en-us/library/aa998420(EXCHG.80).aspx` for additional configuration information.

✔ **DNS:** Make certain that you configure DNS correctly before you begin the Exchange Server installation. Check the DNS event log for a listing of potential problems. In addition, perform communication checks between elements of your network to ensure that local communication works properly and then perform external communication checks as well.

✔ **Single-label DNS names:** A single-label DNS name is one in which you use a single word for the server name such as MyServer. Exchange Server 2007 doesn't support single-label DNS names because they present a number of problems. You can see a complete list of these issues at `http://support.microsoft.com/?kbid=300684`. The bottom line is that your domain name should consist of the usual subdomains that you see on the Internet, such as `www.mycompany.com`.

✔ **Active Directory domain names:** Unlike previous versions of Exchange Server, Exchange Server 2007 doesn't support renaming Active Directory domains. You lose support for a number of Exchange Server 2007 features when you rename the domain. The Knowledge Base article at `http://support.microsoft.com/?kbid=925822` tells you more about this particular issue.

According to the Microsoft documentation, you can theoretically install Exchange Server 2007 on a system running Windows Server 2000 as long as this server can access another server running Windows Server 2003 SP1 or later. However, using this approach is problematic at best. It isn't a good idea to try to install Exchange Server 2007 on a Windows Server 2000 system because you normally encounter installation problems and must also start the setup program from the command line. (Exchange Server 2007 SP1 at least eliminates the requirement to specify the name of a server running Windows Server 2003 SP1 or later.) Windows Server 2000 users will also encounter numerous performance penalties, making tuning Exchange Server 2007 considerably more difficult and time-consuming.

This book assumes that you're using Exchange Server 2007 for all of your servers. You can create a mixed Exchange Server version environment, but the mixed environment will disallow use of some advanced Exchange Server 2007 features. It isn't possible to use Exchange Server 5.5 or older with Exchange Server 2007.

The final configuration verification requirement is the operating system. As mentioned, you must use a 64-bit Windows operating system for an Exchange Server 2007 installation. Exchange Server 2007 SP1 supports the following operating systems:

- Windows Server 2003 Standard x64 Edition operating system with SP2

- Windows Server 2003 Standard x64 Edition with SP2, with Multilingual User Interface Pack (MUI)

- Windows Server 2003 Enterprise x64 Edition operating system with SP2

- Windows Server 2003 Enterprise x64 Edition with SP2, with MUI

- Windows Server 2003 Datacenter x64 Edition operating system with SP2

- Windows Server 2003 Enterprise x64 Edition with SP2, with MUI

- Windows Server 2003 R2 Standard x64 Edition operating system with SP2

- Windows Server 2003 R2 Standard x64 Edition with SP2, with MUI

- Windows Server 2003 R2 Enterprise x64 Edition operating system with SP2

- Windows Server 2003 R2 with SP2, Enterprise x64 Edition with SP2, with MUI

- Windows Server 2003 R2 Datacenter x64 Edition operating system with SP2

- Windows Server 2003 R2 with SP2, Datacenter x64 Edition with SP2, with MUI

- 64-bit edition of the Windows Server 2008 Standard operating system

- 64-bit edition of the Windows Server 2008 Enterprise operating system

- 64-bit edition of the Windows Server 2008 Datacenter operating system

Verify that the system is running the proper 64-bit operating system by right-clicking Computer or My Computer and choosing Properties from the context menu. When working with Windows Server 2008, you see a display similar to the one shown in Figure 2-2. Notice that the display tells you that the target system is running Windows Server Enterprise, that it has SP1 installed, and that the system type is a 64-bit operating system.

If your goal is to install just the Exchange Server 2007 management tools, you have a wider array of choices. The list includes all of the 64-bit operating systems in the list, the 32-bit equivalents, and this list of client operating systems:

- Windows Vista Ultimate

- Windows Vista Home Premium

- Windows Vista Home Basic

- Windows Vista Business

- Windows Vista Enterprise

- Windows XP Professional x64 Edition operating system

- Windows XP with SP2

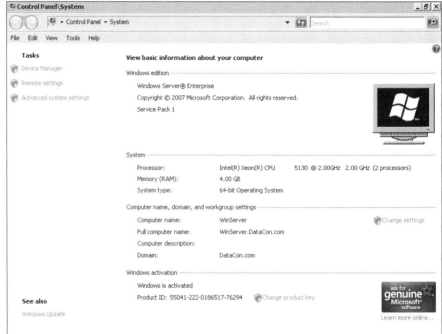

Figure 2-2:
Verify that
your system
is running
the proper
operating
system.

Installing .NET Framework 2.0

Before you can install Exchange Server 2007, you must have a copy of .NET Framework 2.0 available. You can install .NET Framework 2.0 by clicking the Step 1: Install the .NET Framework 2.0 link in the initial Exchange Server setup page, but this option may not provide you with the latest .NET Framework version or all the features you need. Go to `http://msdn.microsoft.com/en-us/netframework/aa731542.aspx` to obtain the latest .NET Framework 2.0 version, language packs, and related distributables. The Web site even includes the option of requesting .NET Framework 2.0 on a DVD so that you don't have to download it. The following steps describe how to install .NET Framework 2.0:

1. **Double-click the DotNetFx.EXE file to start the installation program if necessary.**

   You see the usual Welcome page.

2. **Click Next.**

   The installation program displays the licensing agreement.

3. **Read the licensing agreement and select the I Accept the Terms of the License Agreement check box.**

   The installation program enables the Install button.

4. **Click Install.**

   The installation program initially displays a Setup dialog box that shows you that the system is preparing to perform the installation. Windows installs .NET Framework 2.0 on your system. When the installation is complete, you see a completion dialog box.

5. **Click Finish.**

   .NET Framework 2.0 is ready for use.

Installing Windows PowerShell

Exchange Server 2007 is one of several new Microsoft products that rely on Windows PowerShell to perform tasks. Windows PowerShell is a kind of command prompt, but it's a managed command prompt that relies on .NET Framework 2.0 to run. This new command prompt is less susceptible to viruses, more flexible, and easier to use. The common element between Windows PowerShell and the command prompt you used in the past is that they both require you to input text commands to accomplish tasks.

Windows doesn't install Windows PowerShell by default. Fortunately, the Exchange Server 2007 media comes with a copy of Windows PowerShell. However, if you're using Windows Server 2008, you'll probably want to use the Windows PowerShell that comes with Windows because this version of PowerShell will have all required updates. The following steps describe how to install Windows PowerShell on your system:

1. **Open Server Manager (found in the Administrative Tools folder of the Control Panel).**

2. **Select the Features folder and click Add Features.**

   You see the Select Features window shown in Figure 2-3. Notice that the screen shows the Windows PowerShell feature selected.

3. **Select Windows PowerShell and click Next.**

   Windows displays a Confirm Installation Selections window that shows it will install Windows PowerShell for you.

4. **Click Install.**

   Windows installs Windows PowerShell. When the installation is finished, you see an Installation Results window.

5. **Click Close to complete the installation process.**

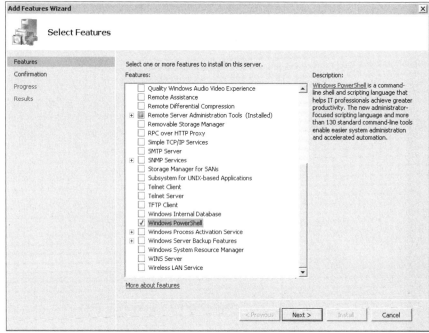

Installing the Internet Information Services role

Exchange Server requires that you provide a copy of Internet Information Services (IIS) for it to use. This book assumes that you use IIS 7 on Windows Server 2008. However, any version of IIS will work. The following steps describe how to install IIS on Windows Server 2008:

1. **Open Server Manager (found in the Administrative Tools folder of the Control Panel).**

2. **Select the Roles folder and click Add Roles.**

   You see the Select Features window shown in Figure 2-4. Notice that the screen shows the Web server (IIS) role selected.

3. **Select Web Server (IIS).**

   You see an Add Roles Wizard dialog box that contains a list of features that you must install for IIS, as shown in Figure 2-5.

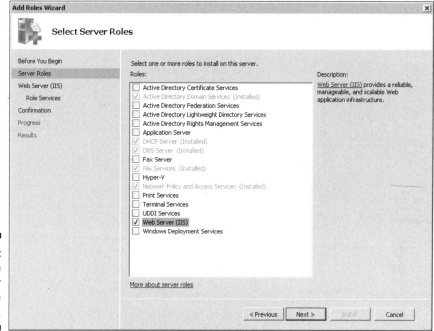

Figure 2-4:
Select the
Web server
(IIS) feature
from the list.

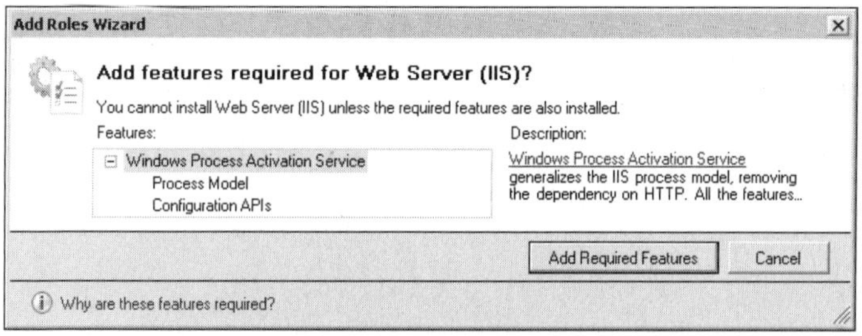

Figure 2-5:
Add any
required
features to
the IIS con-
figuration.

4. **Click Add Required Features.**

   The Add Roles Wizard checks the Web Server (IIS) option.

5. **Click Next two times to accept the default configuration.**

   You see the Select Role Services window shown in Figure 2-6. Exchange
   Server requires that you install some additional IIS features for a complete installation.

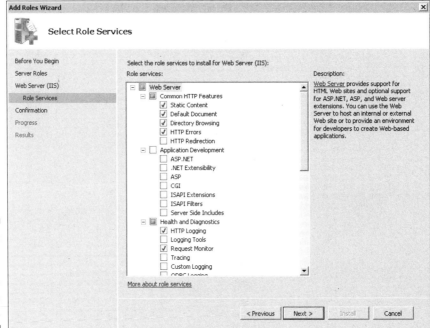

Figure 2-6:
Select the
required
role ser-
vices from
the list.

6. **Select the IIS 6 Management Compatibility, Dynamic Content Compression, Basic Authentication, Windows Authentication, and Digest Authentication options. Click Next.**

7. **Click Install.**

   Windows installs IIS on your system. Eventually, you see the Installation Results window.

8. **Click Close.**

At this point, you need to verify that your copy of IIS is working properly. Open a copy of Internet Explorer, type `http://localhost` in the Address field, and press Enter. You see the Welcome page shown in Figure 2-7. If you don't see this page, make sure that IIS is started and consult the event log for potential problems. Don't go any further until you verify that IIS works properly.

Figure 2-7:
Ensure that IIS works properly before you proceed.

Testing Your Configuration

At this point, you should have a working setup. However, you don't really know that the setup is working and your setup could still fail. Fortunately, Microsoft provides a tool named the Exchange Best Practices Analyzer (ExBPA) to help you get the best results. You find ExBPA in the \setup\serverroles\common folder of the Exchange Server installation media. The following steps show how to test your configuration for potential problems:

1. **Double-click ExBPA.EXE.**

    You see an initial display where ExBPA checks for updates online. The display also lets you choose whether you want to participate in the client experience program and provides a number of other pieces of information.

2. **Click Go to Welcome Screen.**

    ExBPA displays the Welcome screen where you can choose between viewing an existing report or create a new scan of your system. This section shows how to create a new scan to determine whether your system will accept Exchange Server 2007. However, you can use the report link later to view existing system problems while you fix them.

3. Click Select Options for a New Scan.

The Connect to Active Directory page appears. The server name you provide should match the local server name. The only time you need to change this name is if you rely on another server to provide Active Directory support. This book assumes that you use the local server for Active Directory support.

4. In the Active Directory Server field, type the name of the server you want to use.

5. Click Connect to the Active Directory Server.

ExBPA shows you a list of scan options, as shown in Figure 2-8. Notice the list of tests you can run in the Select the Type of Scan to Perform group. These tests help you assess the health of your system as well as determine whether you can use the system to install Exchange Server 2007. Other portions of the book describe how to use the health checks, so you don't need to worry about them now.

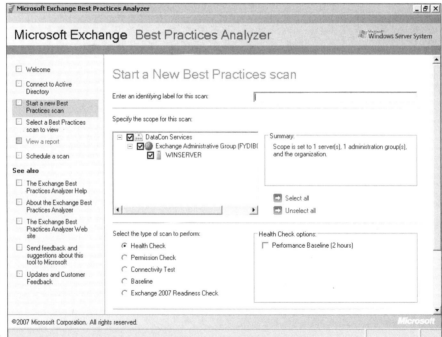

Figure 2-8: Choose one of the tests you want to perform using ExBPA.

6. Select the Exchange 2007 Readiness Check option.

7. In the Enter an Identifying Label for this Scan field, type Readiness Check.

8. Click Start Scanning.

This button isn't shown in Figure 2-8, but it appears at the bottom of the page. You see a Scanning in Progress page. When ExBPA completes the check, it displays a Scanning Completed page. Be patient. The scan can require several minutes, depending on the capabilities of your hardware.

9. **Click View a Report of this Best Practices Scan.**

   ExBPA displays a report page, as shown in Figure 2-9. This page is simply a starting point. You need to drill down into the report to see any errors.

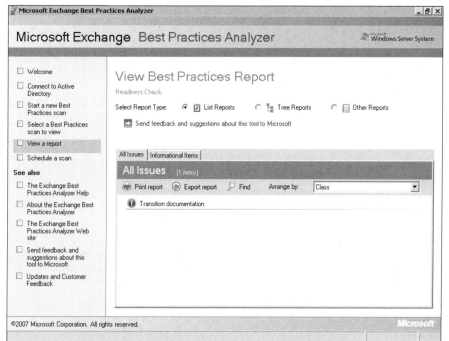

Figure 2-9: Display the report of the scan you completed.

10. **Click Tree Reports.**

    This option provides you with detailed information about the test, as shown in Figure 2-10. Use the output from this report to determine any changes you need to make to your server.

11. **Click Start a New Best Practices Scan in the left pane. Perform Steps 7 through 10 as many times as needed to locate and fix all server problems.**

    When you complete the readiness check without error, you can begin the installation.

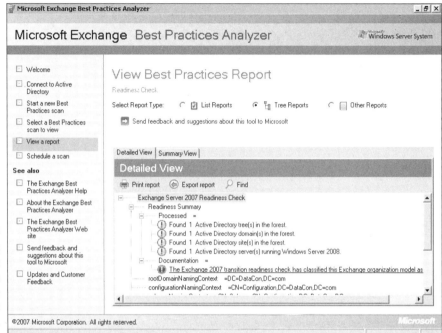

Figure 2-10:
Drill down
into the
report to
locate
errors.

Performing the Installation

After you perform all of the required preinstallation steps and verify that your server is working optimally, it's time to perform the Exchange Server 2007 installation. The following steps get you started.

1. **Place the installation media in the drive.**

   The Autorun feature should display the opening installation dialog box shown in Figure 2-11. If you're using an OEM or MSDN version of the Exchange Server 2007 DVD, you need to navigate to the Exchange2007 folder for your language, such as \English\Exchange2007\SP1\ x64, and double-click the file you find there. After Windows extracts the files, go to the extraction folder and double-click Setup.EXE to start the installation program. You see the opening installation dialog box.

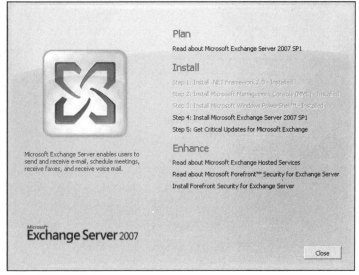

Plan

Read about Microsoft Exchange Server 2007 SP1

Install

Step 1: Install .NET Framework 2.0 - Installed

Step 2: Install Microsoft Management Console (MMC) - Installed

Step 3: Install Microsoft Windows PowerShell™ - Installed

Step 4: Install Microsoft Exchange Server 2007 SP1

Step 5: Get Critical Updates for Microsoft Exchange

Enhance

Read about Microsoft Exchange Hosted Services

Read about Microsoft Forefront™ Security for Exchange Server

Install Forefront Security for Exchange Server

Microsoft Exchange Server enables users to send and receive e-mail, schedule meetings, receive faxes, and receive voice mail.

Microsoft
Exchange Server 2007

Close

Figure 2-11:
The main installation dialog box provides step-by-step tasks.

If you're installing Exchange Server 2007 on Windows Server 2008 (as used for this book), the first two steps are always complete because Windows Server 2008 comes with .NET Framework 2.0 (see the "Installing .NET Framework 2.0" section of this chapter for details) and Microsoft Management Console (MMC) installed. If you're using an older version of Windows, click these two links in turn (starting with Step 1: Install .NET Framework 2.0) and follow the few prompts required to complete these prerequisite installations. In addition, you can use the instructions in the "Installing Windows PowerShell" section of this chapter to install Windows PowerShell.

2. **When you have completed the first three steps, click Step 4: Install Microsoft Exchange Server 2007 SP1.**

   You see an Introduction window that lists some of the new features of Exchange Server 2007.

3. **Click Next.**

   The setup program displays a licensing agreement.

4. **Read the licensing agreement, select I Accept the Terms in the License Agreement, and click next.**

   Microsoft asks whether you want to send error information to them automatically. The Error Reporting window provides you with some details of the process and promises that Microsoft will encrypt your data before sending it over the Internet. Whether you accept or reject this offer depends on your company policy. Make sure you choose the option that your organization allows.

5. **Choose an error reporting option (the default is No) and click Next.**

   You see the Installation Type window shown in Figure 2-12. The Typical Exchange Server Installation option works for most small organizations, many medium-sized organizations, and even a few large organizations. This chapter assumes that you're using the Typical Exchange Server Installation option.

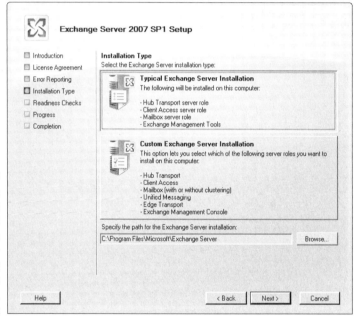

Figure 2-12:
Select the type of Exchange Server installation you want to perform.

6. **Click Browse and choose a location for your Exchange Server installation.**

   In many cases, choosing a location other than your boot drive (the default selection) will improve overall Exchange Server performance. Of course, this option makes a performance difference only when you have multiple physical drives on your system; placing Exchange Server on another partition of the same drive won't provide much of a performance gain because you're still waiting for the same drive to perform tasks.

7. **Select an installation type and click Next.**

   Setup asks you to provide a name for your organization.

8. **In the field provided, type your organization name and click Next.**

   You see a Client Settings folder that might be easy to click past too easily. Make sure you choose the right setting here. If any of your client computers have Outlook 2003 or earlier or Entourage installed, you must select Yes here.

9. **Select a client option and click Next.**

   At this point, the setup program performs a series of readiness tests. These tests determine whether your server will successfully run Exchange Server. It's helpful if you have an Internet connection because the setup program will download the latest version of these tests from the Internet, which tends to reduce the probability of a failed installation.

   If the readiness tests fail, read the reasons carefully and fix each error. Click Retry when you complete the required changes to ensure that the installation will succeed. In some cases, such as changes to IIS, you may have to restart the installation. When the installation fails, perform Steps 1 through 9 again.

10. **Click Install.**

    The setup program shows the progress of the installation. Be patient; some installation steps can take a long time. For example, the time required to import your Active Directory schema depends on the complexity of your Active Directory setup. Even a simple schema on a relatively fast server can require ten or more minutes to complete. Eventually, you see the completed installation screen. Make sure that all completion indicators are green.

11. **Click Finish.**

    You see a reboot notification dialog box.

12. **Click OK.**

    The installation program returns to the initial Exchange Server setup screen shown in Figure 2-5.

13. **Click Step 5: Get Critical Updates for Microsoft Exchange.**

    Windows opens Internet Explorer and takes you to the Microsoft Update Web site. Follow the instructions on this Web page to accept the terms of use and install the Exchange Server update feature in Windows Update. After you follow these steps, you see the Windows Update window. Windows will check for updates to Exchange Server and help you install them.

14. **Reboot your server.**

    The Exchange Server installation is complete. Of course, you still need to configure Exchange Server before you can use it.

Chapter 3

Using Exchange Management Console

*I*nstalling Exchange Server doesn't get you much in the way of useful functionality. You must configure Exchange Server before you can use it. After you install Exchange Server, you see a new Start menu entry for it named Microsoft Exchange Server 2007 that contains three entries: two management tools and a help file. The graphical management tool is Exchange Management Console, which is the focus of this chapter. You can also use a command line tool called Exchange Management Shell (see Chapter 12 for details). In addition to these two management tools, Exchange Server comes with a number of command line tools that appear in Chapter 13.

Exchange Management Console divides the Exchange Server 2007 configuration into five essential areas. The first configuration area you must consider is Exchange Server as a whole, which includes issues such as entering license information and adding a Secure Sockets Layer (SSL) certificate. The next three areas help you configure three progressively limited objects in Exchange Server: organization (which can include multiple servers), server (which contains multiple recipients), and recipient. The fifth area provides access to a number of essential management tools. These tools help you perform configuration management, recover from disasters, manage mail flow, and check performance.

This chapter provides you with information about Exchange Management Console so that you know what it contains and can find what you need to perform Exchange Server management tasks quickly. You won't find actual management tasks discussed in this chapter — these tasks appear in other areas of the book. Use this chapter to locate a particular Exchange Management Console feature quickly.

Getting an Overview of the Configuration

An Exchange Server 2007 configuration consists of roles and hosted services for the most part. These roles and hosted services appear at multiple levels, but it's important to understand that they are essentially divisions of labor within the Exchange Server 2007 setup. Knowing about the functionality that roles and hosted services provide outside the logical levels at which Microsoft places them helps you understand how Exchange Server 2007 is put together and also reduces the complexity of the Exchange Server environment.

When you initially open Exchange Management Console (see Figure 3-1) by choosing Start⇨Programs⇨Microsoft Exchange Server 2007⇨Exchange Management Console, you see what appears as a complex environment. However, notice that some items are repeated. For example, you have a Mailbox role entry at the Organization Configuration, Server Configuration, and Recipient Configuration levels. Yes, the configuration is different at each level, but the essential fact remains that understanding the Mailbox role helps you understand Exchange Server as a whole.

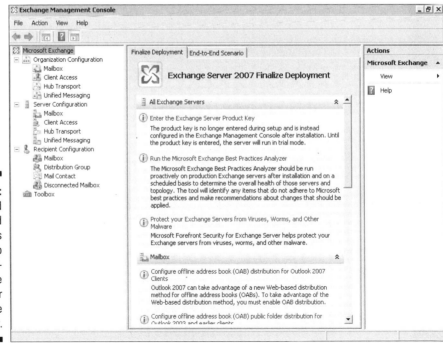

Figure 3-1:
Roles and
hosted
services
make up
the major-
ity of the
details for
Exchange
Server.

Selecting the Microsoft Exchange entry, as shown in Figure 3-1, provides you with a list of help topics based on a specific need. The initial tab, Finalize Deployment, shows you how to finalize your Exchange Server setup, while the End-to-End Scenario tab contains configuration topics. When you click one of these items, you see a help pane that provides you with a list of steps you need to perform to accomplish the specified task. The help topics normally appear in the order in which you need to accomplish them. For example, you usually want to enter the product key before you run Microsoft Exchange Best Practices Analyzer. The help topics are also grouped by functional area, such as All Exchange Servers and Mailbox, to make the topics easier to locate.

The following sections describe the roles and hosted services supported by Exchange Server 2007. You can skip a particular role or hosted service if it isn't installed on your system. These sections act as a reference for the rest of the chapter and for the rest of the book. Use this information to keep focused on the overall goal of a set of configuration steps.

Understanding the roles

A *role* is a task that the server can perform. It consists of the features and components that make accomplishing the task possible. For example, when you install the Mailbox role, Exchange Server adds folders for holding messages of various types. The following sections provide an overview of each of the roles that Exchange Server 2007 supports.

Ensuring you have everything required to implement a role

Microsoft is focusing more on providing administrators with the tools they need to do a good job. In some cases, this means providing something as simple as a checklist. Each Exchange Server role requires some special configuration. In addition, you must perform a few steps to configure Exchange Server for any role. This book provides everything you need to perform basic configuration of any role that Exchange Server supports.

However, you may also want to view the checklist that Microsoft provides at `http://technet.microsoft.com/en-us/library/bb124563.aspx`. This checklist provides a means of verifying your work before you make a particular role active in a production environment. Because of the nature of e-mail today and its importance to your organization, double and even triple checks are necessary to ensure that you have a fully functional setup that's secure, reliable, and fast.

Mailbox role

The Mailbox role provides a number of containers (databases) that let users store e-mail and also provide support for features such as shared folders. The term *e-mail* is a little ambiguous in Exchange Server 2007 because the Mailbox role provides support for address books as well as all the e-mail folders you find in an Outlook 2007 setup:

Calendar	Drafts	Journal
Outbox	Sync Issues	Contacts
Entire Mailbox	Junk E-mail	RSS Feeds
Tasks	Deleted Items	Inbox
Notes	Sent Items	

The Mailbox role also provides support for issues such as meetings, that is, scheduling rooms for conferences between employees. Each of these special issues requires a unique container to avoid contamination between features.

Of course, you must have a database to store all this information. A *database* is a collection of all the information that defines a particular kind of Exchange Server object such as a mailbox. Exchange Server supports a number of database types. You place each database in a storage group. A *storage group* defines the physical location and other hard drive characteristics of the database storage. The default Exchange Server 2007 setup includes two storage groups:

- ✔ **First Storage Group:** Contains the default mailbox database
- ✔ **Second Storage Group:** Contains the default public folder database

Since a mailbox is useless without users, the Mailbox role also provides support for adding and removing users. You can supply a considerable amount of information as part of each user entry. In addition, the user entry determines which Exchange Server features that user can access. Chapter 5 provides more information about the configuration tasks you need to perform for mailboxes. Chapter 7 discusses user client requirements to access the mailboxes you create.

Client Access role

Having a storage location for your e-mail, contacts, calendar, and other Exchange Server items is only the first step. Once you have some type of server configuration in place, you must provide a means for user client applications to access the data. The main client program for users is Outlook. However, you can also use Outlook Express as a desktop application (albeit with far fewer features) and a wealth of third-party clients because Exchange Server provides the required support.

In addition to the standard client application, Exchange server also supports the Microsoft Exchange ActiveSync and Microsoft Office Outlook Web Access (OWA) client applications. The Microsoft Exchange ActiveSync client application provides support for mobile devices.

You access the Microsoft Office OWA application using a special URL such as `https://winserver.datacon.com/owa/`, where `winserver.datacon.com` is the Fully Qualified Domain Name (FQDN) of the server hosting Exchange Server. Figure 3-2 shows a sample of the Microsoft Office OWA application. Note the certificate error shown in the figure. The default Exchange Server setup relies on a self-signed certificate and will display this error when you attempt to create a connection to it.

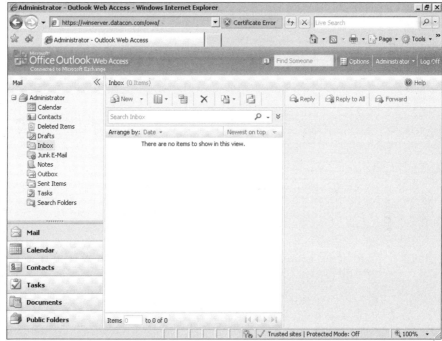

Figure 3-2:
Access your e-mail using a desktop application or the Web application shown here.

Figure 3-2 also shows the display when working with Internet Explorer. You must use Internet Explorer to obtain full access to the mailbox. When working with a third-party product, such as Firefox, you always receive OWA Light access, which provides support for Mail, Calendar, and Contacts. Figure 3-3 shows the Firefox view of OWA Light.

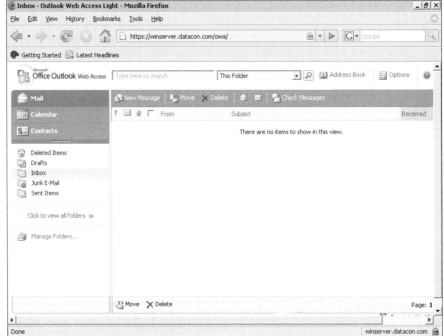

As with many elements of the Internet, Exchange Server relies on protocols to perform communication tasks. A *protocol* is a set of rules that determine how software must act to perform a given task. In this case, Exchange Server supports the Post Office Protocol version 3 (POP3) and Internet Message Access Protocol version 4 rev1 (IMAP4) protocols. The inclusion of POP3 is fortunate because most (if not all) e-mail products support it. Consequently, barring an unforeseen connection problem, you should be able to use any e-mail client with Exchange Server.

Configuring the Client Access role means defining the kind of access: POP3, IMAP4, or OWA. A client setup can also enable Outlook Anywhere, a feature that makes it possible for remote users to access your Exchange Server without relying on a Virtual Private Network (VPN). The Client Access role also determines which devices can use ActiveSync. By default, all standard devices can access ActiveSync, but you may decide to disallow the use of Bluetooth or infrared connections.

Hub Transport role

The Hub Transport role controls local mail flow within your organization. It provides the connection between Exchange Server and the client application within your local network. This role performs the following tasks:

✔ Applies transport rules

✔ Applies journaling policies

✔ Delivers messages

Some administrators confuse the Hub Transport and Edge Transport roles because they perform similar tasks. To keep from confusing the two roles, think of a wagon wheel. The hub is at the center of the wheel, while the rim is at the edge of the wheel. The Hub Transport role always performs tasks on your local network and the Edge Transport role always performs tasks at the edge (extending to the outside) of your network.

Extending the wheel analogy further, you can create subscriptions between the Hub Transport and the Edge Transport. The subscriptions are akin to spokes on the wheel — they make communication between the edge and the hub possible. You can also create send connectors to make transferring messages to an external Simple Mail Transfer Protocol (SMTP) server possible. In some respects, the hub also controls nonuser communication with the outside world. For example, the Hub Transport determines the use of out-of-office messages in your organization.

Edge Transport role

The Edge Transport role is similar to the Hub Transport role, except that it performs tasks for the Internet-facing messages in your organization. The Edge Server appears as part of a separate server, rather than as part of the main Exchange Server setup, to reduce the attack surface of your organization, making your server more secure.

The Edge Transport role is also responsible for providing SMTP relay services and hosted services. The "Understanding hosted services" section of this chapter provides a description of the hosted services that Exchange Server supports.

A significant difference between the Edge Transport and Hub Transport roles is that the Edge Transport role doesn't provide direct Active Directory access. The role relies on Active Directory Application Mode (ADAM) directory service support instead.

A special service called EdgeSync on the Hub Transport server copies data from Active Directory to the Edge Transport server. ADAM acts as a recipient for the data that EdgeSync sends to the Edge Transport server. Consequently, the Edge Transport server has the same configuration information available as the Hub Transport server, but it can't make any changes to that data. Although it's never a good idea to expose Active Directory data to an external source, at least the Edge Transport keeps the external source from making any modifications.

Installing Exchange Server on a Windows Server 2008 system replaces ADAM with Active Directory Lightweight Directory Services (AD LDS). The new service is theoretically more secure than ADAM but performs the same task, so you probably won't even notice any difference as you work with Exchange Server. Microsoft made several other terminology changes when they released Windows Server 2008. You can find a list of these changes at `http://technet.microsoft.com/en-us/library/bb123550(EXCHG.80).aspx`.

Unified Messaging role

Microsoft always seems to be interested in combining things so that you don't have to do as much to access your data. The main use for the Unified Messaging role is to combine voice messaging, fax, and e-mail in a single access component. For example, whenever your inbox receives a message, your telephone rings. When you pick up the receiver, Exchange Server tells you that the message is available. (The chapter uses the term telephone in a generic way — the device you choose to use can include a cellular telephone or other voice device.) Likewise, when you receive a fax, you can have it relayed to your computer rather than rely on a physical device.

Messaging occurs in every direction when using Unified Messaging. For example, you could set up your telephone to send messages to your computer as an e-mail. In this scenario, Unified Messaging interacts with the telephone in the following order:

1. Picks up and establishes contact with the caller

2. Plays your personal greeting

3. Records a message from the caller

4. Packages the message as a voice mail attached to an e-mail

5. Sends the e-mail to the recipient

Unified Messaging configuration requires that you set up connectivity information. For example, you configure access to the telephone using a Dialing Plan. An Auto Attendant provides prompts that the user can use to access the Unified Messaging role on Exchange Server. You create a connection between the user and the various Unified Messaging features using a Mailbox Policy. Exchange Server performs many of the configuration details for you. For example, when you create a Dialing Plan, Exchange Server automatically creates a Mailbox Policy for it. Of course, you can create a custom Mailbox policy whenever needed.

Although the concept of the Unified Messaging role sounds simple, the underlying technology is complex. The amount of interaction you have with the underlying technology depends on the services you decide to make available using this technique, the needs of your users, and the languages you choose to support. You can see an overview of how the underlying technology works at `http://technet.microsoft.com/en-us/library/bb123911(EXCHG.80).aspx`.

Understanding hosted services

A *hosted service* is a method for extending your organization's reach onto the Internet. You use hosted services to reduce administration costs for your Exchange Server and improve overall security by hiding your Exchange Server from view. The following sections provide details on the hosted services that Exchange Server supports.

Filtering hosted service

The Filtering hosted service provides incoming and outgoing message filtering. Configuring this service requires you to make some simple changes to your Domain Name System (DNS) setup and create a new Mail eXtension (MX) record for your Exchange Server. Filtering is a hosted service that you obtain from another vendor. You can discover more about this hosted service at `http://technet.microsoft.com/en-us/exchange/bb676292.aspx`.

Archive hosted service

The Archive hosted service provides a backup of your Exchange Server data, including all Instant Messaging (IM) data. The main purpose of this hosted service is to provide you with off-site backup of data so that a server error won't cause you to lose all your data. For more about this hosted service, go to `http://technet.microsoft.com/en-us/library/cc164320.aspx`.

Continuity hosted service

Your server isn't guaranteed to provide 100 percent uptime. In fact, no server in the world can make this guarantee. However, the Continuity hosted service makes it possible to vastly improve the reliability of your Exchange Server setup by providing additional off-site sources of e-mail. The user won't even notice that your server is offline in many cases. You can find out more about this hosted service at `http://technet.microsoft.com/en-us/library/cc164341.aspx`.

Understanding software as a service

All Exchange Server hosted services rely on the Software as a Service (SaaS) model, which is an industry standard method of sharing software across the Internet. Microsoft makes the software available using the hosted application model approach rather than using software on demand. In general, you don't have to know all the grizzly details of SaaS to use it in Exchange Server, but you can discover more about this technology at `http://searchcrm.tech-target.com/sDefinition/0,,sid11_gci1170781,00.html`, `http://msdn.microsoft.com/en-us/architecture/bb499667.aspx`, and `http://msdn.microsoft.com/en-us/architecture/aa699384.aspx`.

Encryption hosted service

Any data that you don't encrypt, no matter where you store it, is accessible by someone else. Many organizations have found that encryption isn't just a nice feature, it's a must in today's world. Otherwise, you face the prospect of releasing information that you'd rather not have other people see. The Encryption hosted service ensures that all communication outside your network is encrypted so that no one can view the data it contains, even if they do manage to intercept it. Of course, this hosted service applies only to your Exchange Server setup — you still need to encrypt your local data. You can discover more about this hosted service at `http://technet.microsoft.com/en-us/exchange/bb676292.aspx`.

Working with the Organization Configuration

The organization level of configuration affects all Exchange Servers for a particular domain. The servers must be able to see each other in order for the changes you make to take effect on all servers.

When you select Organization Configuration in Exchange Management Console, you see a list of administrators for your copy of Exchange Server. This overview lets you remove and add administrators as needed.

The subfolders provide access to the organization level of the Mailbox, Client Access, Hub Transport, and Unified Massaging roles. The following sections provide an overview of these subfolders.

Considering the organization-level Mailbox

When you select the Mailbox role at the organization level, you can access Mailbox features that affect the organization as a whole, as shown in Figure 3-4. You use these features to modify two basic Mailbox elements, addresses and mail folders. The following list describes the purpose of each of the tabs shown in Figure 3-4 in more detail:

✔ **Address Lists:** Provides a listing of address lists used to send messages. Each of these address lists is a folder containing one or more contacts. When you send a message to the address list, all contacts in the folder receive the message.

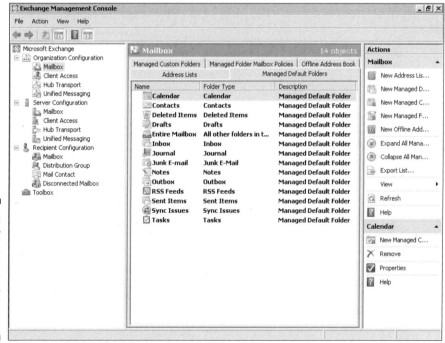

Figure 3-4: Modify addresses and mail folders as needed for your organization.

✔ **Managed Default Folders:** E-mail normally appears in a specific client folder. The application displays these folders so that the user can organize their messages and find them with greater ease. The Managed Default Folders are e-mail folders that the user always sees, such as the Inbox.

✔ **Managed Custom Folders:** In some cases, the user requires specialized folders to hold some types of e-mail. For example, the user may require a special e-mail folder to hold e-mails from a particular project. You could let each user create these custom folders, but each user will probably choose a different name, making cross-mailbox searches impossible. Managed Custom Folders are e-mail folders that the administrator can place in a user's mailbox to hold specific e-mails. A user won't see the folder until it's installed in the e-mail client application. Exchange Server doesn't provide any custom e-mail folders by default. A custom folder offers the additional benefit of specialized management. For example, you can control the size of this folder so that the user can't overload it.

✔ **Managed Folder Mailbox Policies:** A project may require more than one custom folder. You could create the folders one at a time in the user's mailbox, but that process is time-consuming and error-prone. Using a managed folder mailbox policy makes it possible to deploy all custom folders as a group.

✔ **Offline Address Book:** An *Offline Address Book (OAB)* provides a means for clients to view a list of addresses when they aren't connected to Exchange Server. This includes information from the Global Address List (GAL) in Active Directory. The resulting OAB contains both the GAL and any custom address lists that you assign to it. The OAB contains a list of public addresses; users still maintain their own list of personal addresses.

Understanding organization-level Client Access

The Client role settings at the organization level help you configure ActiveSync properties. These settings help determine whether mobile devices that rely on ActiveSync can access Windows file shares and SharePoint services. You use these settings also to configure the password requirements for ActiveSync and any restrictions on mail size and other communications.

The Device tab of the Properties dialog box (double-click the Exchange ActiveSync Mailbox Policy entry) lets you configure the device characteristics. For example, you can determine whether ActiveSync permits synchronization from a desktop. You also have control over the technology used to access ActiveSync, such as Bluetooth and Wireless Fidelity (WiFi).

The Advanced tab of the Properties dialog box helps you configure application accessibility. Microsoft provides you with a number of standard entries such as the browser and consumer mail. You can also create a list of allowed and blocked custom applications.

Working with the organization-level Hub Transport

The Hub Transport role settings at the organization level control the specifics of internal connectivity. As shown in Figure 3-5, the settings determine issues such as the use of out-of-office messages and how Exchange Server handles messages that it accepts. You also control issues such as the formatting of e-mail addresses. The following list describes each of the tabs shown in Figure 3-5.

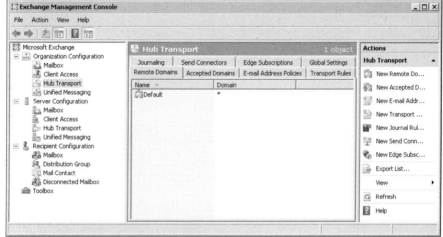

Figure 3-5:
Use these settings to control how Exchange Server interacts with the client.

✔ **Remote Domains:** The remote domain is a server to which you send messages. The settings include the out-of-office message policy, the use of formatting in a message, and the character sets that Exchange Server uses to send messages to the remote domain. For example, you can use the message formatting settings to allow automatic forwarding and automatic replies. It's also possible to change content settings, such as the number of characters used for line wrap in a message. Most of these settings define how to send the message so that the remote server will accept it and the remote client can work with it.

✔ **Accepted Domains:** An *accepted domain* is an external SMTP server used to send and receive messages on behalf of users. The accepted domain is an endpoint for messages that aren't part of this local Exchange Server organization. This tab also lets you configure *relay domains*, which are servers that provide SMTP support for sending messages to another endpoint. For example, you might use an external ISP to send and receive messages on the Internet. The external ISP server is the relay domain.

✔ **E-mail Address Policies:** An *e-mail policy* is a rule for generating e-mail addresses for the recipients in your organization. The e-mail policy makes it possible for users in your organization to send and receive e-mail. In most cases, organizations won't require anything more than the Default Policy that Microsoft provides with Exchange Server.

✔ **Transport Rules:** A *transport rule* is a combination of a condition and an action. You can tell Exchange Server to check each message that it receives for certain conditions, such as messages from specific people or messages marked with a particular importance level. It's possible to combine conditions to reduce the chance of false positives. When the conditions are true, Exchange Server performs a specific task with the message.

✔ **Journaling:** You use *journaling* to send copies of messages to an administrator, a manager, or another responsible party based on specific criteria, such as message sender. Exchange Server makes it possible to track internal, external, or a combination (global) of both message types.

✔ **Send Connectors:** A *send connector* provides the means to deliver messages to an external SMTP server. You use this feature to deliver messages sent by users on the local network to a location outside the local network. It's possible to send messages to another internal Exchange Server, the Internet, or a partner organization, or to create a custom connection with non-Exchange Server setups.

✔ **Edge Subscriptions:** An *edge subscription* associates an Edge Transport server with the Active Directory configuration on another server, which ultimately provides access to the Hub Transport server on that system. You use this association to configure send connectors that enable mail flow between the local system and the Internet.

✔ **Global Settings:** The global settings define connection characteristics for the Hub Transport server, such as the maximum send and receive message size. You also use these settings to define internal SMTP servers so that Exchange Server doesn't apply Sender ID and connection filtering requirements to them. Finally, you can use the global settings to configure Delivery Status Notification (DSN) values for messages so that the sender knows what happened to a particular message, that is, whether the recipient received it.

Defining organization-level Unified Messaging

At the organization level, Unified Messaging (sometimes abbreviated as UM) settings modify the connectivity that Unified Messaging provides. You must define how the various devices connect to transfer data from one device to another. For example, you can't use the telephone to tell the user about a message in the inbox without providing a telephone number. The following list describes the various Unified Messaging organization-level features:

✔ **UM Dial Plans:** The dial plans describe how to contact an external device such as a telephone. You have three options for creating a dial plan: telephone connection, Session Initiation Protocol (SIP) Uniform Resource Identifier (URI), and E.164. The SIP URI option commonly provides access to voicemail or voice-activated systems, while the E.164 option provides access to international telephone connections consisting of a Country/Region Code (CC), a National Destination Code (NDC), and a Subscriber Number (SN). You can read more about SIP URI at `http://community.roxen.com/developers/idocs/rfc/rfc4458.html` and E.164 at `http://en.wikipedia.org/wiki/E.164`. The dial plan includes a provision for securing the communication. You can rely on unsecured, SIP secured, and fully secured communications.

✔ **UM IP Gateways:** The IP gateway creates a connection between a physical gateway or Internet Protocol (IP) Private Branch eXchange (PBX) device and Unified Messaging. This setup associates the physical device and Unified Messaging with a particular dialing plan.

✔ **UM Mailbox Policies:** The mailbox policy creates a connection between the user and Unified Messaging. When the user wants to use Unified Messaging, the mailbox policy creates the required connection and applies any required security restrictions to that connection. You must also associate the mailbox policy with a particular dial plan. Consequently, this entry creates a connection from the user, through Unified Messaging, to a particular external device. A dial plan may have multiple mailbox policies associated with it, but each mailbox policy must have just one dial policy associated with it.

✔ **UM Auto Attendants:** The auto attendant is the only optional part of Unified Messaging. It helps you provide a means for users to transfer data between locations automatically. For example, a receptionist may not know that a particular recipient is away from his or her desk, but the Unified Messaging system does and will send a message to the user wherever that user might be located. The auto attendant associates a dial plan with between 0 and 16 extensions. The auto attendant must provide at least one extension to forward data to another location.

Performing the Server Configuration

Server-level configuration affects just one server. A single server can service your entire organization or just one group in the organization. The point is that the changes you make modify the behavior of just one server.

When you click the Server Configuration entry in Exchange Management Console, you see your server and the connectivity it provides. Click Create Filter to modify the connectivity by reducing the kinds of data flow that it accepts. The filter changes specific server properties: Cluster, Edition, Name, Product ID, Role, Site, and Version. Setting a property value creates a filter that allows only messages with the specified criteria to pass.

You also enter the product key for your server at the Server Configuration folder. If you don't enter the product key within the time that Exchange Server allows, your server will stop working. Exchange Management Console displays a dialog box showing the amount of time you have left every time you start it. The "Entering the Exchange Server product key" section of Chapter 4 discusses how to enter the product key.

The subfolders provide access to the server level of the Mailbox, Client Access, Hub Transport, and Unified Massaging roles. The following sections provide an overview of these subfolders.

Considering the server-level Mailbox

The Mailbox role at the server level provides access to the physical storage location as shown in Figure 3-6. Exchange Server starts with two storage groups: one for the mailbox data and another for public storage folders. Both storage groups start on the installation drive, but you can move them to other locations as needed for better performance, enhanced security, or greater reliability. You also see the status of the databases contained within each storage location. Exchange Server provides access to storage group and database properties, including environmental limits such as the database size.

Selecting the WebDAV tab lets you modify the Web-based Distributed Authoring and Versioning (WebDAV) features of Exchange Server. (You can read more about WebDAV at `http://www.webdav.org/`.) These features provide browser access to e-mail as shown in Figures 3-2 and 3-3.

The four folders you see on the WebDAV tab provide legacy access. Consequently, when you use an URL such as `https://winserver.datacon.com/exadmin`, IIS automatically redirects you to `https://winserver.datacon.com/owa`. The properties you set control WebDAV permissions; you can even set Exchange Server to use .NET Framework forms-based authentication. However, given the status of these folders, you want to make changes to the OWA configuration using the Outlook Web Access tab of the Client Access folder described in the "Understanding server-level Client Access" section of this chapter.

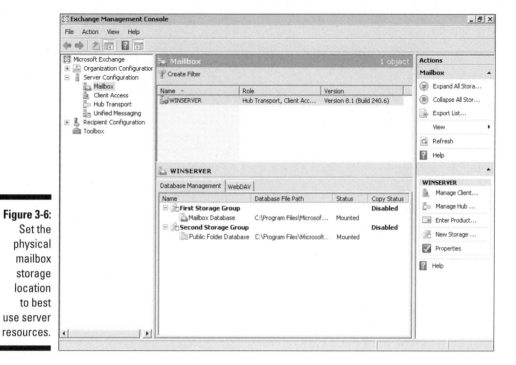

Figure 3-6:
Set the
physical
mailbox
storage
location
to best
use server
resources.

As shown in Figure 3-6, you also have access to the same features you do when you select the Server Configuration folder. This access means that you can enter a product key or add filters to the server at the Mailbox level.

Understanding server-level Client Access

One of the more important folders in Exchange Management Console is server-level Client Access. This folder controls how the user connects to the server to obtain access to e-mail. As shown in Figure 3-7, the user has four main connectivity methods:

- ✔ OWA
- ✔ Exchange ActiveSync
- ✔ OAB Distribution
- ✔ POP3 and IMAP4

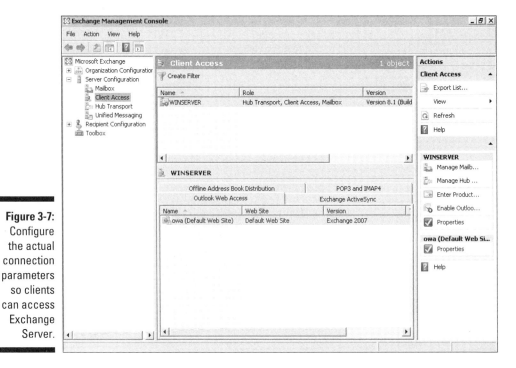

Each of the associated tabs provides connectivity properties for that specific connection type. Chapter 4 describes how to configure each of the connection types in greater detail.

Working with the server-level Hub Transport

The Hub Transport folder at the server level provides connectivity information for the local server. The default Exchange Server setup comes with two connections: Default and Client, as shown in Figure 3-8. The Default connection provides local access to resources; on the other hand, the Client connection provides user access to resources.

When you work with these connections, you define precisely how the connection works. For example, the Client connection relies on port 587, as contrasted to the Default port, which relies on port 25. A connection can use IPv4, IPv6, or both. You also set connection security. For example, you can require that the connection use Transport Layer Security (TLS) and rely on Windows integrated authentication. Finally, you can choose which groups can use the receive connector. The options include

✔ Anonymous users

✔ Exchange users

✔ Exchange servers

✔ Legacy Exchange servers

✔ Partners

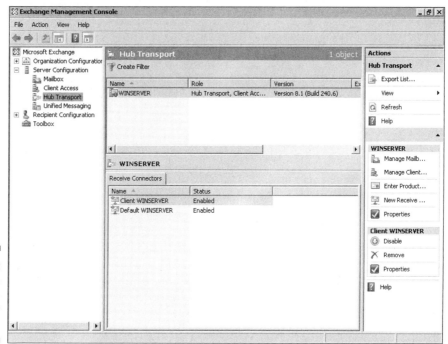

Figure 3-8:
Define the
receive con-
nectors for
your server.

Defining server-level Unified Messaging

Exchange server doesn't install support for Unified Messaging by default —
you must install the server-level support as a separate role. After you install
the required support, you use the Unified Messaging folder to configure the
connections you created at the organization level for the server. In short,
you must define a connection between the device, the user, and Unified
Messaging. Microsoft recommends using a six-step process to accomplish
this task:

1. Verify any existing Unified Messaging components.

2. Create any required new Unified Messaging components.

3. Configure all Unified Messaging components.

4. Associate the Unified Messaging server with a dial plan that you created at the organization level.

5. Configure and deploy an IP gateway.

6. Test the Unified Messaging configuration. Microsoft supplies the Unified Messaging test phone (`ExchangeUMTestPhone.EXE`) for this purpose.

Reviewing the Recipient Configuration

Configuring the organization and the server provides access to Exchange Server features. However, the administrator must create a mailbox account on the server before a user can use these features. In addition, the user needs extras such as distribution lists and access to a standard set of contacts. All of these items appear as part of the Recipient Configuration folder.

When you select the Recipient Configuration folder, you see an overview of objects contained in the subfolders that Recipient Configuration supports. The default objects are the Mailbox, Distribution, and Mail Contacts folder. The Disconnected Mailbox subfolder is special because it doesn't show any standard objects. The following sections describe each of these objects.

Interacting with the recipient Mailbox

The Mailbox folder that appears at the recipient level contains a list of recipients — people who have mailboxes on the server. You control every aspect of the individual user's Exchange Server experience using the Properties dialog box for the individual users in this folder.

The properties include everything you expect, such as the user's name, address, telephone number, and other physical information. The dialog box also contains settings for security, as you might expect. The settings include a few additional items, such as the user's access to Exchange Server features. For example, you can configure a user to Exchange ActiveSync but not to OWA. It's also possible to place restrictions on what the user can send and receive as well as the physical characteristics of the message, such as message size. Chapter 5 discusses mailboxes in more detail.

Defining the recipient Distribution Group

You use distribution groups to simplify e-mail. For example, all members of a particular project might appear as a single distribution group. When you want to address a group concern, you send the message to the distribution group rather than to individuals. Using distribution groups tends to reduce errors because you know that every member of the group will receive the message and those outside the group won't. The Distribution Group folder contains all distribution groups for your Exchange Server setup — the individual objects can include both local recipients and mail contacts.

Working with Mail Contacts

The objects in the Mail Contacts folder work precisely like the contacts in your personal address book. However, the objects in this folder appear to everyone who uses this server. Consequently, the contacts in the Mail Contacts folder are people that the entire organization needs to interact with. For example, you might include a list of common vendors or organizational partners in this folder.

Viewing the Disconnected Mailbox

The Disconnected Mailbox folder is special because you shouldn't see anything in it. You can't create new objects in this folder either. A *disconnected mailbox* occurs when Exchange Server detects a mailbox that doesn't have an Active Directory object associated with it. For example, you see mailboxes in here when a user leaves the company and you remove the user's information from Active Directory. The Exchange Server mailbox is still present, so it appears in the Disconnected Mailbox folder.

Entries in the Disconnected Mailbox folder should serve as a warning. These entries indicate configuration errors on your Exchange Server setup and potential security holes for outsiders. Always fix any configuration errors you see in this folder.

Viewing the Toolbox

The Toolbox folder provides you with access to a number of separate tools, as shown in Figure 3-9. These tools help you configure and manage Exchange Server. You use these tools also to recover from disasters.

You find detailed descriptions of these tools throughout the book. The following list provides a quick overview of the items in the Toolbox:

✔ **Configuration Management Tools:** The configuration management tools help you configure and monitor your Exchange Server setup. You use these tools to establish a workable configuration after you install Exchange Server and then maintain that configuration afterward.

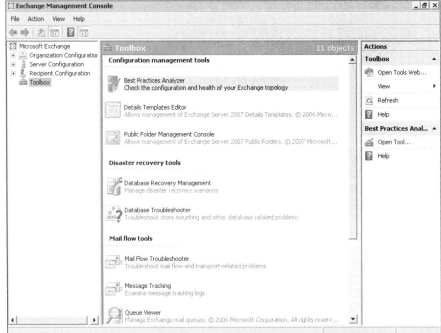

Figure 3-9:
Exchange
Server
provides a
number of
tools you
can use for
configura-
tion and
manage-
ment tasks.

✔ **Disaster Recovery Tools:** Disasters happen to everyone and come in many forms. These tools help you prepare for disasters and then recover from them later. It's important to remember that these tools are Exchange Server-specific. You still need to maintain your server and perform disaster recovery tasks with it.

✔ **Mail Flow Tools:** Exchange Server is all about the e-mail when you get down to it. Yes, the other features are nice, but every organization that installs Exchange Server relies on it for e-mail. Consequently, you find that Microsoft provides an abundance of e-mail tools with Exchange Server. These tools help you do everything from discovering where the e-mail went to why the server won't send e-mail to a particular recipient.

✔ **Performance Tools:** Nothing motivates the user to complain faster than slow e-mail. Users have an expectation of fast e-mail service for their computer, and these tools help you to meet that expectation. However, these tools are Exchange Server-specific, so you should look at them as a starting point. You'll find a number of other interesting tools to improve server performance throughout the book.

Chapter 4

Performing the Initial Configuration

Exchange Server isn't really functional after you install it. Yes, you can open Exchange Management Console to perform tasks, but you can't send an e-mail yet because the required services aren't started. Microsoft makes Exchange Server nonfunctional on purpose to ensure that you aren't instantly exposed to potential problems from the outside world. In addition, there isn't any way that Microsoft can know during installation which people should have e-mail accounts (among other things you must configure for your organization). Consequently, you must perform an initial configuration before you can begin working with Exchange Server even on a test basis.

You can divide configuration into two areas: the tasks you must perform for all servers and the tasks you must perform to configure a specific role. This chapter begins by reviewing the tasks you must perform for all servers, such as entering an Exchange Server product key. Always perform these tasks first to ensure that your server is ready to work with roles. The chapter then takes you through the basic process of setting up a mail server for use with Outlook. To create a mail server, you must configure the Mailbox, Client Access, and Hub Transport roles.

You'll want to test your configuration, so the final section of the chapter explores how you create a connection from Outlook to your Exchange Server. The book will look at other configuration scenarios; this final section is only intended to get you started with a basic check of your Exchange Server setup. Once you finish this final step, you can send e-mail to other people using the same Exchange Server setup, work with calendars, and perform other tasks that you normally associate with group activities on Exchange Server. This chapter doesn't show you how to create a connection to the outside world or how to configure Exchange Server for use with mobile devices.

You perform all configuration steps in this chapter using Exchange Management Console, which you open by choosing Start⇨Programs⇨Microsoft Exchange Server 2007⇨Exchange Management Console. Chapter 3 provides an overview of Exchange Management Console, so this chapter assumes that you're familiar with the location of various elements in Exchange Management Console.

Performing Configuration Required for All Exchange Servers

Before you can do anything with Exchange Server, you must perform some configuration tasks that are common to all server roles. These tasks configure Exchange Server for all roles, so you should perform these tasks first. It's especially important to ensure that you have protection from viruses, worms, and other malware in place before you open your server to e-mail. Running Best Practices Analyzer helps make sure that your configuration is ready for use.

Of the steps listed in the following sections, only the product key installation is optional at the outset. You'll have to live with a constant reminder that the product key isn't in place, as shown in Figure 4-1, but Exchange Server is otherwise fully functional. Make sure you enter the product key before the time shown in Figure 4-1 expires. Otherwise, Exchange Server will become nonfunctional.

Figure 4-1:
Exchange
Server
reminds
you that
you haven't
installed the
product key.

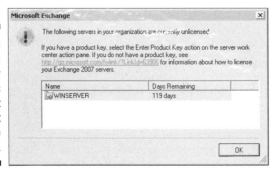

Entering the Exchange Server product key

One of the first steps you should perform with Exchange Server is to enter the product key. Nothing terrible will happen if you put this step off, but the opening nag screen shown in Figure 4-1 is annoying and you don't want to take the chance of forgetting long enough that your copy of Exchange Server becomes nonfunctional. The following steps describe how to enter your Exchange Server product key:

1. **Choose the Server Configuration folder in Exchange Management Console.**

2. **Select the server you want to work with from the list of servers (you may have only one server from which to choose).**

   The bottom half of the Actions pane now includes a number of actions you can perform on the server.

3. **Under the server's entry in the Actions pane, click Enter Product Key.**

   You see the Enter Product Key dialog box, as shown in Figure 4-2. Notice that you type only the characters in the product key — you don't include the dashes.

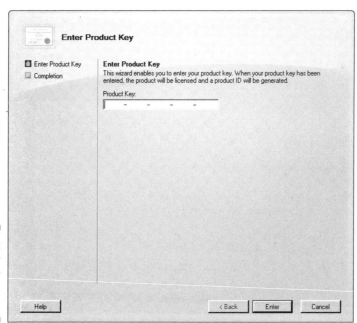

Figure 4-2:
Provide your product key to Exchange Server.

4. **Type your product key in the spaces provided.**

5. **Click Enter.**

   You see the Completion dialog box shown in Figure 4-3. I purposely blocked out the product key for my system. Most Exchange Server configuration tasks follow the pattern shown in this section. The completion dialog box normally shows a process that Exchange Server used to complete a task.

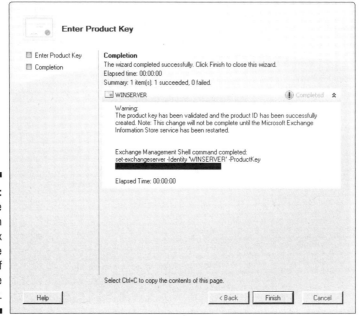

Figure 4-3:
The Completion dialog box shows the result of entering the product key.

6. **Click Finish.**

   The dialog box disappears. Notice that the Enter Product Key option disappears from the Actions pane and the icon for your server changes as well. These visual cues help you determine which servers require product keys when you have multiple servers to manage on your network.

Using Best Practices Analyzer

The "Testing Your Configuration" section of Chapter 2 describes how to use Best Practices Analyzer from the command line to test your server environment before installing Exchange Server. You can also use Best Practices Analyzer to test the setup after you complete the installation. To access Best Practices Analyzer, select the Toolbox folder and double-click the Best Practices Analyzer entry. At this point, you see the Best Practices Analyzer display shown in Figure 4-4. Best Practices Analyzer will update itself, and you're ready to go.

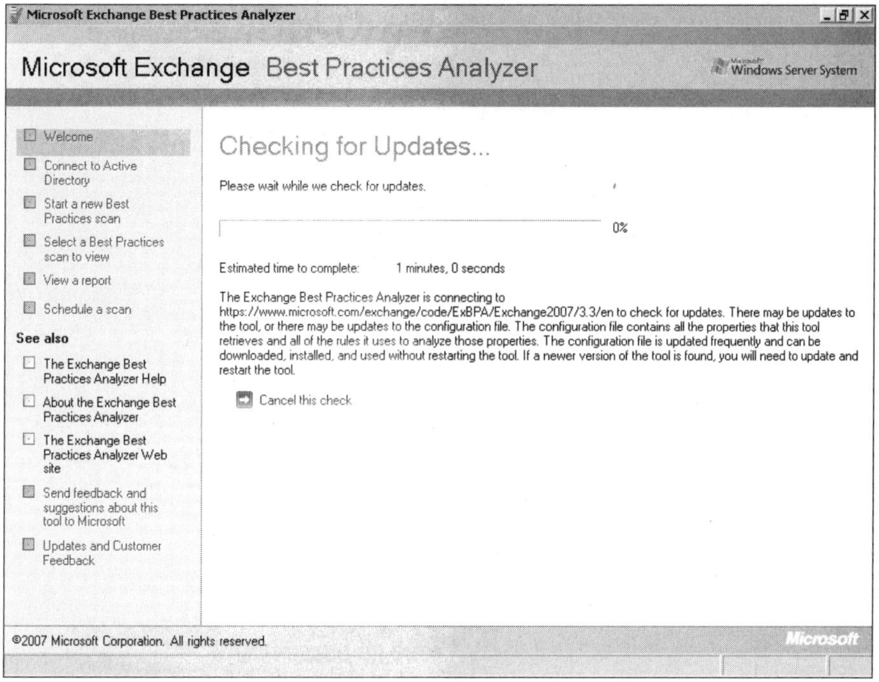

Figure 4-4:
Use Best
Practices
Analyzer to
check your
server con-
figuration.

Chapter 2 shows you how to perform an Exchange 2007 Readiness Check. You can perform that test again to make sure the installation hasn't created any new problems for your server. After you check your server for readiness, it's important to perform a Health Check immediately and at regular intervals to ensure that your Exchange Server runs as anticipated. The Permission Check, Connectivity Test, and Baseline scans occur after you complete the server configuration and whenever you make a configuration change. You see all these tests on the Start a New Best Practices Scan page, as shown in Figure 4-5. The following sections describe these tests.

Performing a Health Check

You use the Health Check to proactively verify that your Exchange Server is in good health — that Active Directory is set up properly, the connections work, the server is performing well (that it performs tasks without undo loss of time), and that none of the data stores are misconfigured or damaged. That's a lot for a single test to do, and you can count on the test taking a while, especially when you decide to use the performance test. The following steps describe how to perform a Health Check on your server (see the "Creating Performance Baseline Health Check" section of Chapter 11 for a description of the Performance Baseline option).

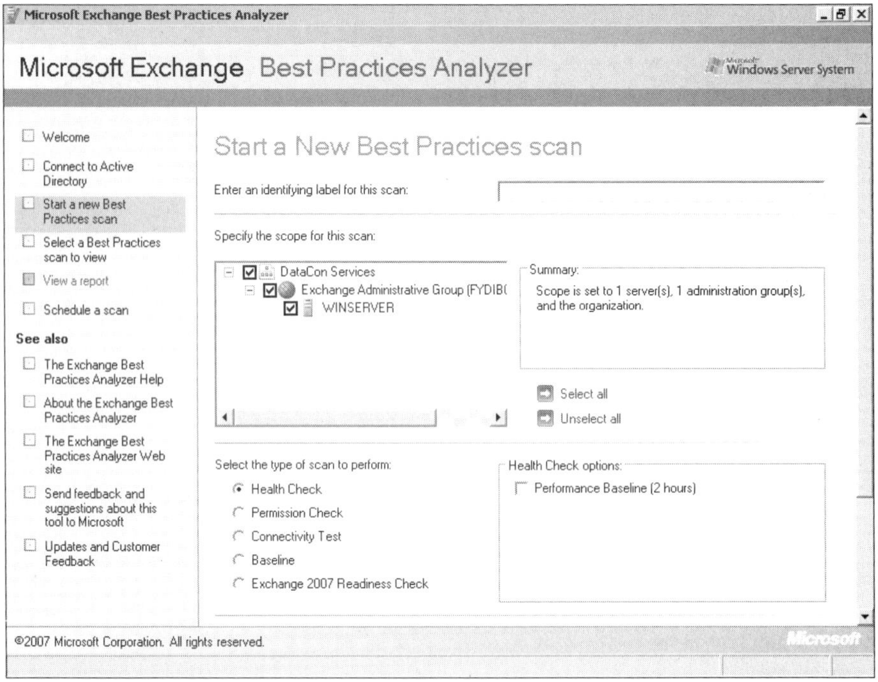

Figure 4-5:
Select the
test that
you want to
perform.

1. **In the Enter an Identifying Label for This Scan field, type a name for the scan.**

   Best Practices Analyzer will use the current date and time as a label if you don't supply one. However, using the current date and time isn't helpful because Best Practices Analyzer supports a number of scan types. Use a label that identifies the scan type as well as the current date and time as necessary.

2. **In the Select the Type of Scan to Perform list, select Health Check.**

   You see an option for adding a Performance Baseline check in the Health Check Options list (refer to Figure 4-5). This check requires a minimum of two hours, and you use it after you configure your system as part of a maintenance check. Chapter 11 describes this process in detail. For now, you won't need to worry about the Performance Baseline option.

3. **In the Select the Speed of the Network to Adjust Estimated Time Estimate field, choose the network speed.**

   Best Practices Analyzer tells you the approximate amount of time the Health Check requires. The values range from about 2 minutes for a high-speed network connection to 12 minutes for a Wide Area Network (WAN) connection. In most cases, you want to give Best Practices Analyzer plenty of time to complete the check.

4. Click Start Scanning.

You see a Scanning in Process display similar to the one in Figure 4-6. This display gives you an idea of how the Health Check is progressing. However, the progress indicator provides only an estimate — the actual test may take more or less time than shown.

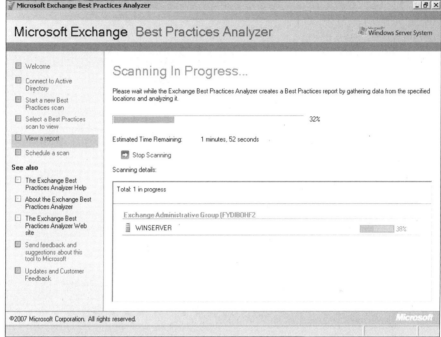

Figure 4-6:
The Scanning in Process display provides an estimate of the test's progress.

5. Click View a Report of This Best Practices Scan.

You see a list of items you must address. The Critical Issues tab shows the need to create an Offline Address Book (OAB) during the initial configuration, as shown in Figure 4-7. The "Associating an OAB with a mailbox" section of this chapter tells how to resolve this issue.

As shown in Figure 4-7, the report contains items you address as part of your Exchange Server configuration and health maintenance. If you want to see only errors that will stop your Exchange Server from working, select the Critical Issues tab. However, you also want to address warnings and view unfamiliar informational messages as well. In this case, select the All Issues tab to see summaries of every issue that Best Practices Analyzer found.

When you want to address an issue, click that issue's entry in the report. The report now provides you with a more detailed description of the error, as shown in Figure 4-8. In addition, you see three options for addressing the issue.

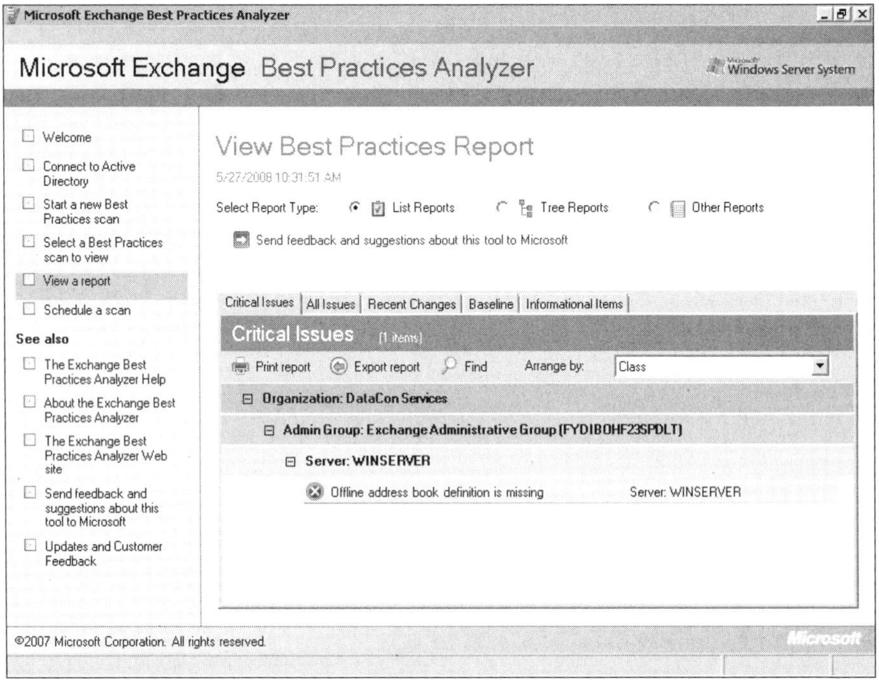

Figure 4-7:
The report
tells you
about issues
regard-
ing your
Exchange
Server
setup.

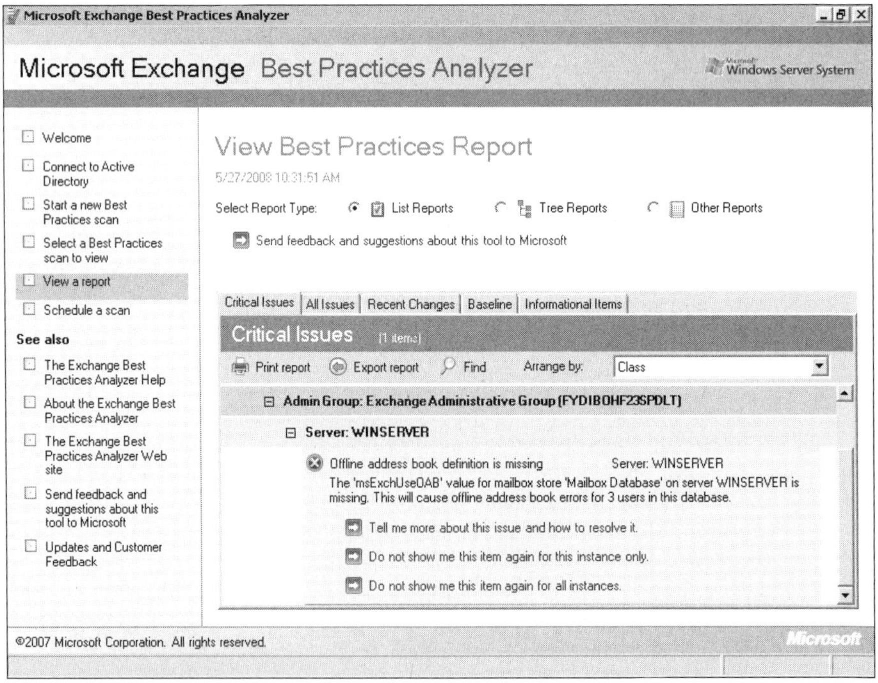

Figure 4-8:
Best
Practices
Analyzer
provides a
number of
methods for
dealing with
problems.

Deciding when to act on warnings

Microsoft provides you with a relatively complete list of warnings and information entries as part of the output of Health Check. However, you may not need to act on all of these entries and may even choose to ignore one or two of them. For example, Microsoft marks your desire to keep Exchange Server failures private with a warning. They place a strong emphasis on reporting errors to them. If you disagree, you can chose to either ignore the warning or tell Best Practices Analyzer not to present it again.

Depending on your setup, you may also see a number of configuration warnings. Best Practices Analyzer will tell you that a particular configuration is supported but not recommended. You don't want to tell Best Practices Analyzer not to present these issues in the future because your configuration may change and you want to know about any problems that these changes present. However, you may choose not to act on them. For example, if you have two Network Interface Cards (NICs) installed on your system and one of them is connected to the Internet, you may see warnings that Best Practices Analyzer has detected multiple default gateways. Whenever you see a warning of this type, investigate it fully but feel safe to ignore it if the warning doesn't apply to your configuration.

Click Tell Me More About This Issue and How to Resolve It to open a Web page containing detailed information about the issue. In many cases, the detailed information includes a procedure for fixing the problem (the procedure works in most cases).

When viewing an error or warning message, never click the Do Not Show Me This Item Again for This Instance Only option or the Do Not Show Me This Item Again for All Instance option. Hiding these messages won't resolve the problem and will make it more difficult to find the message in the future. You can choose these options for informational messages that appear consistently and don't affect the performance of your system. When in doubt, keep the message in view rather than hiding it.

Testing security with Permission Check

The Permission Check provides one method you can use to verify that the security for Exchange Server is configured correctly. Of course, it's important to remember that a single tool can't do everything. You should use other tools to check server security and to verify the security of other applications. In addition, nefarious outsiders are always finding new ways to make your life difficult, so the ultimate security tool is the time you spend monitoring your server for unusual activity.

The steps for performing a Permission Check are the same as those for the Health Check (see Steps 1 through 5 in the "Performing a Health Check" section of the chapter). All you need to do is select the Permission Check option instead of the Health Check option in Step 2. This scan doesn't provide any special options. Figure 4-9 shows the output from this scan.

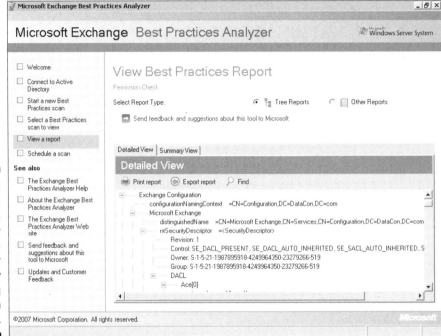

The report can be difficult to use because it requires that you work with low-level security details. For example, the report displays the Security Identifier (SID) of an object rather than a friendly name. Unfortunately, Microsoft doesn't provide a method to convert a SID to a username, so you need to speak SID or you need a third-party utility to perform the conversion for you. The "Converting a SID to a Username with User Info" section of Chapter 14 tells you how to overcome this issue.

The security information is complete. You can view the Discretionary Access Control List (DACL) information in detail, including each Access Control Entry (ACE). The ACE information shows the ACE type, the right bestowed, any special flags, and the associated SID. In short, you can discover every detail about your security configuration, but you need to understand Windows security to do it.

Ensuring communication with Connectivity Test

Exchanging e-mail is all about connectivity. If you don't have a connection, the e-mail collects in the local database and doesn't go anywhere. The Connectivity Test option helps you determine whether your server connects properly to both network resources and the outside world. Just how the server connects depends on you. The basic Exchange Server setup provides internal connectivity — you add the Edge Transport role to provide external connectivity.

The steps for performing a Connectivity Test are the same as those for the Health Check (see Steps 1 through 5 in the "Performing a Health Check" section of the chapter). All you need to do is select the Connectivity Test option instead of the Health Check option in Step 2. This scan doesn't provide any special options. Figure 4-10 shows the output from this scan.

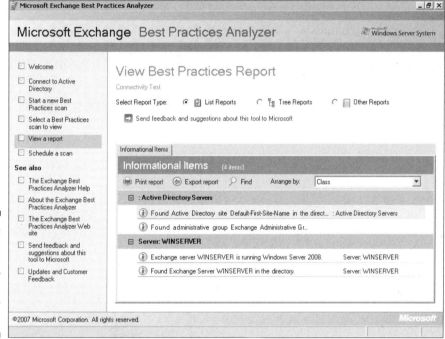

Figure 4-10:
Determine server con-nectivity using the Connectivity Test.

As shown in Figure 4-10, the list tells you where Exchange Server can con-nect. If you don't see a destination that you expect to see, you need to check the configuration of your server.

Of course, the server configuration is only the first step. Connectivity is a flow of data that moves through many levels. A broken cable can ruin your day just as effectively as a configuration error will. Consequently, you can't look at Exchange Server configuration issues, decide that none of them fix the prob-lem, and then just throw your hands in the air. Begin with Exchange Server, but then move on to Windows, other applications installed on the server, the physical connections, routers and other external devices, and continue with external sources such as your Internet Service Provider (ISP). The point is that connectivity is a continuum, and you need to explore it thoroughly when something doesn't work.

Performing a Baseline test

The Baseline test performs an analysis of your server configuration. You use it to discover the details of your configuration, save those details for later comparisons, and then use the information to make repairs. The Baseline test is more than a simple scan. It's also possible to specify source values as part of the test, making it possible to test limits on your server. The following steps help you perform the Baseline test:

1. **In the Enter an Identifying Label for This Scan field, type a name for the scan.**

   Best Practices Analyzer uses the current date and time as a label if you don't supply one.

2. **In the Select Type of Scan to Perform list, select Baseline.**

   The Baseline test doesn't provide any special options in the Baseline Options field.

3. **In the Select the Speed of the Network to Adjust Estimated Time Estimate field, choose the network speed.**

   Best Practices Analyzer tells you the approximate amount of time the Baseline test requires. Supposedly, this is a very fast test, so you may see a value of 0 for the test time. However, the test time varies by the number of Baseline test features you request.

4. **Click Baseline Options.**

   Best Practices Analyzer presents a list of Baseline options, as shown in Figure 4-11. In most cases, you run the Baseline test using the standard options on the first pass. Later, if you decide that you want to test specific values after viewing the preliminary results, run the Baseline test again and choose source values for specific test parameters.

5. **In the Enter a Label for This Compare or Enter a New One field, choose an existing comparison or type a label for a new comparison.**

   When you select an existing compare, Best Practices Analyzer configures the setup to match that compare. The default compare, Baseline Options, performs a simple informational scan of your system. To truly use this feature for comparison, you must enter a new label and configure the source values. Clear the check mark next to the Baseline Options entry if you want to perform a quick check that doesn't rely on any source values.

6. **(Optional) Select Source Values to enable all source value items. Select each of the properties you want to configure and then type a value for that property.**

   You have the option of testing all source values or only some of them. The test value is also optional. If you don't supply a test value, Best Practices Analyzer shows all objects of that type. For example, you can select ActiveSync Tracing Enabled to check for any value of that item. If you type True in the field next to this item, Best Practices Analyzer displays only test objects that have this value set to False.

7. **Select each of the items in the Test Objects tree that you want to test.**

   Even if you have a source item configured, Best Practices Analyzer checks it only if you have the correct test objects selected.

8. **Click Start Scanning.**

   You see a Scanning in Process display similar to the one shown in Figure 4-6. This display gives you an idea of how the Baseline test is progressing. However, the progress indicator provides an estimate only — the actual test may take more or less time than shown.

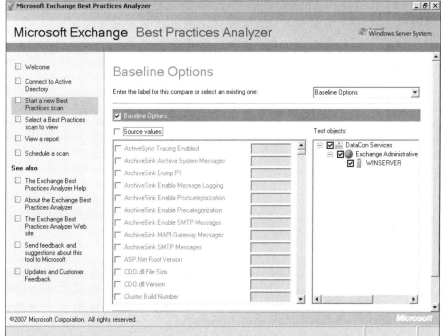

Figure 4-11:
The Baseline test provides a number of complex options for tuning the results.

9. **Click View a Report of This Best Practices Scan.**

   This report is a little different from other reports that Best Practices Analyzer produces. In this case, you see a list of items that differ from the configured values you provide. For example, as shown in Figure 4-12, the ASP.Net Root Version number differs from the value I provided. In this case, the ASP.Net Root Version number is correct — the value I provided is incorrect. Consequently, this report tells you how the system varies from the ideal values you provide, rather than providing a measure of correct or incorrect values.

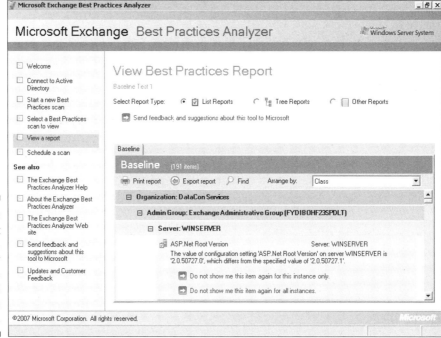

Figure 4-12:
The output shows when the server fails to match ideal values you provide.

Protecting Exchange Server from spam, viruses, worms, and other malware

The presence of spam, viruses, worms, and other malware on the Internet is well documented. These blights might also exist on your own network due to the careless nature of some user activities. All users need to do is load unauthorized software on a system or visit a Web site you'd rather not have them view. It would require an entire book to discuss the topic of protecting your system from attack. The following sections provide information about some Exchange Server-specific topics. Even after you address these items, you still need to perform general tasks for your system and network as a whole.

Addressing common configuration items

One of the advantages of using Windows Server 2008 as your host for Exchange Server is that it comes with some of the common items you need to shield your server from unwanted outside sources. For example, you can configure the firewall to provide only the access needed to perform the tasks required for the server and reduce your attack surface. The *attack surface* of your server is the area that an individual can use to overcome the security measures you have in place. A smaller attack surface is better because someone can gain access in fewer ways. However, they can still gain access, so monitoring is essential.

Make sure you lock down Exchange Server. Chapter 6 provides you with the information you need to make Exchange Server as secure as possible. Of course, you also want to configure security on Windows Server to provide the minimum access that users require. Administrators are users. Always configure a user account for the administrators on the network for their non-administrative activities.

Microsoft also encourages you to install Forefront Security for Exchange Server. This is a standalone product that you obtain separately from Exchange Server. The "Using Microsoft Forefront Security for Exchange Server" section of Chapter 14 provides an overview of Forefront Security for Exchange Server and provides you with a few usage tips.

Setting a Spam Confidence Level (SCL) threshold

One of the better ways to keep malware out of your Exchange Server setup is to keep it away from the user. Setting an SCL threshold helps Exchange Server move less friendly messages from the user's Inbox folder to the Junk E-Mail folder. The default level of 8 is normally too high for effectively keeping spam and other unwanted messages at bay. Consequently, Best Practices Analyzer will normally flag this value for you as a warning. Use the following steps to modify the SCL threshold to a more useful value. (Microsoft recommends a level no higher than 4.)

1. **Choose Start⇨Programs⇨Microsoft Exchange Server 2007⇨Exchange Management Shell.**

   You see what looks like a standard command prompt. However, this is a special PowerShell command prompt for Exchange Server. In most cases, you won't need to use this command prompt to manage Exchange Server, but this is one case where you do need it.

2. **Type** Set-OrganizationConfig -SCLJunkThreshold 4 **and press Enter.**

   Nothing appears to happen, but Exchange Server has modified the SCL threshold. Fortunately, you can use another command to verify the change.

3. **Type** Get-OrganizationConfig **and press Enter.**

   The Get-OrganizationConfig command displays a list of configuration values, including the SCLJunkThreshold value shown in Figure 4-13.

4. **Type** Exit.

   Windows PowerShell closes the window.

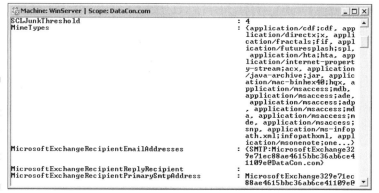

Figure 4-13:
Verify that
the SCLJunk
Threshold
value is set
correctly.

Setting the Application log size

Exchange Server makes a number of entries in the Application log. If Best Practices Analyzer finds that this log is too small, it displays an informational message. Nothing terrible happens, but the messages that Exchange Server creates might expire before you see them. Consequently, you can miss important information. Microsoft recommends a minimum Application log size of 40MB when using Exchange Server. The default size is 20MB, so you normally need to configure the Application log as part of your Exchange Server setup. Follow these steps:

1. **Open the Event Viewer console, which is in the Administrative Tools folder of Control Panel.**

2. **Right-click the Windows Logs\Application folder and choose Properties from the context menu.**

   You see the Log Properties – Application dialog box shown in Figure 4-14.

3. **In the Maximum Log Size (KB) field, type** 40960, **as a minimum.**

   Windows sets the new Application log size.

4. **Click OK and close the Event Viewer console.**

   Monitor the Application event log to ensure that you don't miss any critical Exchange Server messages.

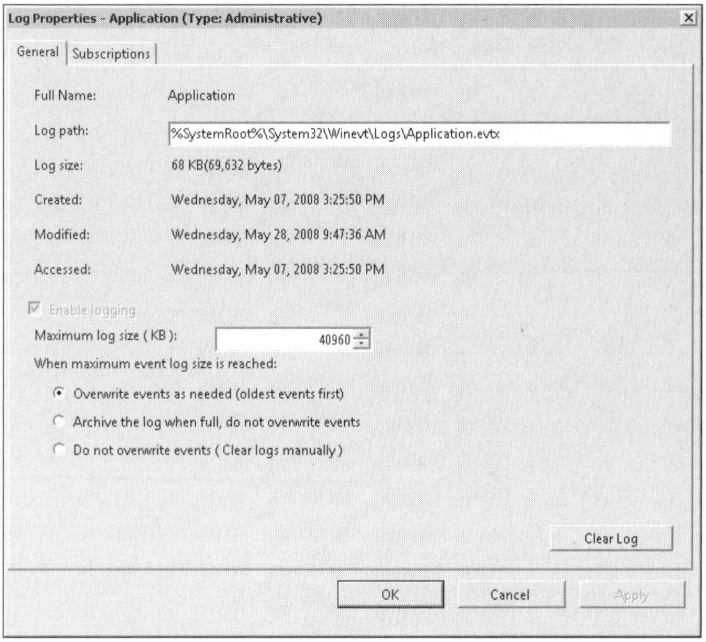

Log Properties – Application (Type: Administrative) ✕

General | Subscriptions |

Full Name: Application

Log path: %SystemRoot%\System32\Winevt\Logs\Application.evtx

Log size: 68 KB(69,632 bytes)

Created: Wednesday, May 07, 2008 3:25:50 PM

Modified: Wednesday, May 28, 2008 9:47:36 AM

Accessed: Wednesday, May 07, 2008 3:25:50 PM

☑ Enable logging

Maximum log size (KB):   40960

When maximum event log size is reached:

⊙ Overwrite events as needed (oldest events first)

○ Archive the log when full, do not overwrite events

○ Do not overwrite events (Clear logs manually)

Clear Log

OK   Cancel   Apply

Figure 4-14:
Set the
Application
log size
for at least
40MB
when using
Exchange
Server.

Configuring the Basic Mailbox

The basic mailbox includes some essential components for sending and receiving mail. The following sections view mail from the administrator perspective. Chapter 5 takes what you create here and views it from the user perspective. The question that the following sections answer is how you as an administrator provide basic services to a user.

Adding a user

Before you can do anything with Exchange Server, you must have an account. In fact, every user has to have an account before he or she can even connect to Exchange Server. Exchange Server comes with one built-in account that you should never remove — the Administrator account. However, a single account won't accomplish much, so one of your first tasks is to add other users. Even though this section shows how to add just one user, you can use the techniques to add any number of users necessary for your organization. The following steps show how to add a user:

1. **Choose the Recipient Configuration\Mailbox folder in Exchange Management Console.**

   You see a list of users who have mailbox accounts.

2. **In the Actions pane, click New Mailbox.**

   Exchange Management Console displays the New Mailbox wizard shown in Figure 4-15. This wizard helps you create four kinds of mailboxes. This section describes the user mailbox. You find the other mailbox types described in the "Working with the alternative mailboxes" section of Chapter 5.

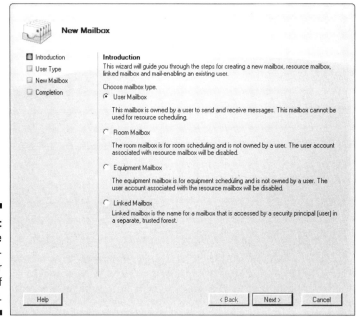

Figure 4-15:
Exchange
Server sup-
ports four
types of
mailboxes.

3. **Choose the User Mailbox option and click Next.**

   Exchange Server asks you to provide a user type. The user type specifies whether you want to create a new user or use an existing user. In many cases, you create a new user that has a new mailbox. Creating a new user here also creates a new user account in Active Directory. Consequently, you don't create a new user when you want to define a mailbox for a user that already exists on the system.

   You always select the Existing Users option when an existing Active Directory user requires a mailbox. You can also create an additional mailbox for an existing user so that user has multiple mailboxes. For example, an administrator might have an administrative mailbox and a separate personal mailbox that contains nonadministrative e-mail. It's also possible to add multiple users to a single mailbox. A group may require a mailbox for a project.

4. **If you want to create a new user, select New User and click Next.**

   You see the User Information dialog box shown in Figure 4-16. The values you enter here depend on company policy. For example, the user's mailbox may use the same password as his or her login (to make the password easy to remember) or you might assign a completely different password for security features. Proceed to Step 8.

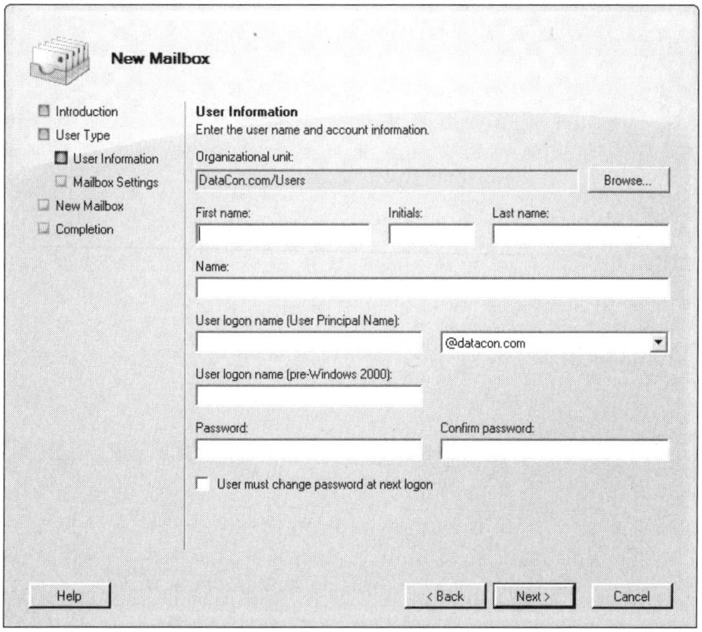

Figure 4-16:
Provide the required user information as part of creating a new mailbox.

5. **If you want to use an existing user account, select Existing User.**

6. **Click Add, choose a User from the Select User dialog box, and click OK.**

   The wizard adds the existing user to the list. Perform this step as often as needed to add the full list of users for the mailbox.

7. **Click Next.**

   You see the New Mailbox dialog box. This dialog box contains the alias for the mailbox, the database used to store it, and security policies for both the managed folder and Exchange ActiveSync. You must provide the mailbox alias and the name of the database to use. Proceed to Step 9.

8. **Type the required user information and click Next.**

9. **Type an alias for the mailbox or use the name provided by the wizard.**

10. **Click Browse next to the Mailbox Database field. Select one of the mailboxes listed in the Select Mailbox Database dialog box and click OK.**

11. **(Optional) Select Managed Folder Mailbox Policy. Click Browse next to the Managed Folder Mailbox Policy field. Select one of the policies listed in the Select Managed Folder Mailbox Policy dialog box and click OK.**

12. **(Optional) Select Exchange ActiveSync Mailbox Policy. Click Browse next to the Exchange ActiveSync Mailbox Policy field. Select one of the policies listed in the Select Exchange ActiveSync Mailbox Policy dialog box and click OK.**

13. **Click Next.**

    You see a configuration summary. Verify the information in the summary. Even if you make a mistake in the original configuration, you can modify the values later.

14. **Click New.**

    The wizard creates the new mailbox for you.

15. **Click Finish.**

    You see the new mailbox listed in the Recipient Configuration\Mailbox folder.

Providing an Offline Address Book (OAB)

Whenever a user connects to the server, they download the OAB. The OAB lets the user continue working with a client application such as Outlook. The process for configuring an OAB for Outlook 2007 is different from the process for Outlook 2003 and earlier. The following sections describe how to configure both e-mail client types.

Working with Outlook 2007

Exchange Server provides a comprehensive level of interaction with Outlook 2007, so you can configure Outlook 2007 to connect directly. The following steps describe how to make Exchange Server accessible to Outlook 2007:

1. **Select the Organization Configuration\Mailbox folder. Click the Offline Address Book tab.**

   You see one or more OAB entries. The setup program creates one OAB entry for you. However, you can add as many OAB entries as needed to support your organization.

2. **Right-click the OAB entry you want to configure and choose Properties from the context menu.**

   Exchange Management Console displays the OAB Properties dialog box.

3. **Click the Distribution tab.**

You see the distribution options shown in Figure 4-17. Exercise care in how you configure these options because some options work with Outlook 2007 and others work with Outlook 2003 and earlier.

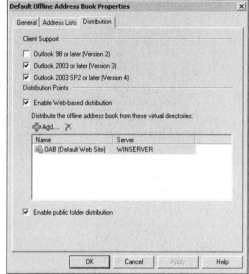

Figure 4-17:
Define the distribution options for Exchange Server.

4. **Select the Enable Web-based Distribution option.**

5. **Click Add.**

   Exchange Management Console displays the Select OAB Virtual Directory dialog box.

6. **Locate a virtual directory location and click OK. Click OK to close the OAB Properties dialog box.**

   At this point, you have configured OAB for local network use. If you need support only for the local network and don't expect to work with a remote network (including the Internet), you can exit the procedure now. However, if you need remote network connectivity, continue with Step 7.

7. **Select the Server Configuration\Client Access folder.**

   The upper half of the Results pane shows one or more servers.

8. **Select the server you want to interact with and then click the Offline Address Book Distribution tab.**

   You see one or more OAB entries. The setup program creates one OAB entry for you.

9. **Right-click the OAB entry you want to configure and choose Properties from the context menu.**

Exchange Management Console displays the OAB (mailbox name) Properties dialog box.

10. Click the URLs tab.

You see a list of URLs associated with this OAB, as shown in Figure 4-18. It's essential to provide the correct URL in the proper location. The Internal URL field shows the URL used on your local network, and the External URL field shows the URL used by a remote network. You must have a registered domain name and the proper Internet setup to use a remote network. Consequently, you can't simply provide an External URL value and expect it to work. In most cases, you use the same domain as you do for your Web site and the OAB folder.

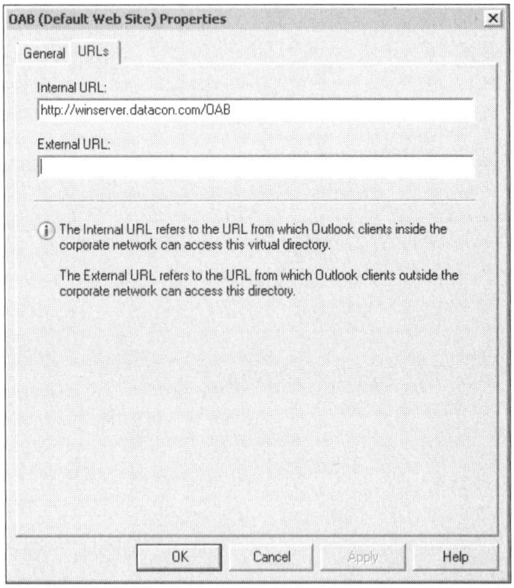

Figure 4-18: Provide internal and external URLs as needed.

OAB (Default Web Site) Properties

General | URLs

Internal URL:

http://winserver.datacon.com/OAB

External URL:

ⓘ The Internal URL refers to the URL from which Outlook clients inside the corporate network can access this virtual directory.

The External URL refers to the URL from which Outlook clients outside the corporate network can access this directory.

OK | Cancel | Apply | Help

---

11. In the External URL field, type the URL for your external connection and click OK.

A remote network copy of Outlook 2007 can now access the mailbox.

Working with Outlook 2003 and earlier

An Outlook 2003 or earlier client requires a public folder database to access Exchange Server. The client doesn't access Exchange Server in the same way that Outlook 2007 does. Consequently, your first step in configuring Exchange Server to work with Outlook 2003 and earlier is to create the required public folder database. Each server can be associated with only one public folder database. The following steps describe how to create the public folder database:

1. **Select the Server Configuration\Mailbox folder.**

   The upper half of the Results pane shows one or more servers.

2. **Select the server you want to interact with and then click the Database Management tab.**

   You see one or more storage group entries, which are storage folders for related databases. Each storage group can contain zero or more database entries. Exchange Server supports two kinds of databases: mailbox databases and public folder databases. The mailbox database is the one that Outlook 2007 can access directly, and the public folder database is the one that Outlook 2003 and earlier can access.

3. **Right-click the storage group entry you want to use to store the public folder database and choose New Public Folder Database from the context menu.**

   Exchange Management Console starts the New Public Folder Database wizard shown in Figure 4-19. Note that you can't change the storage group in this wizard, so choosing the correct storage group at the outset is essential.

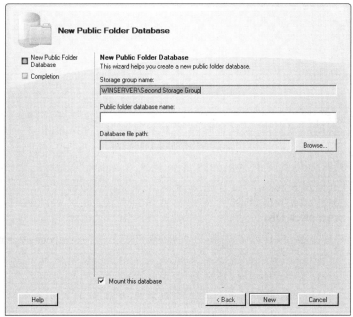

Figure 4-19:
Use the New Public Folder Database wizard to create a database for Outlook 2003 and earlier.

4. **In the Public Folder Database Name field, type a name for the public folder database.**

5. **Click Browse.**

   An Exchange Database dialog box appears.

6. **In the File Name field, type a name for the new database file and click Save.**

   The wizard adds the new file to the New Public Folder Database dialog box shown in Figure 4-19.

7. **Click New.**

   The wizard creates the new public folder database, configures it, and mounts it. Mounting the database makes it accessible for use. Certain maintenance tasks require that you dismount the database. The procedure for dismounting the database appears later in the book — you don't need to worry about it now.

Now you have a shiny new public folder database to use with Outlook 2003 and earlier clients. It's time to configure Exchange Server to provide access to that database. The following steps describe how to perform this task:

1. **Select the Organization Configuration\Mailbox folder. Click the Offline Address Book tab.**

   You see one or more OAB entries. The setup program creates one OAB entry for you. However, you can add as many OAB entries as needed to support your organization.

2. **Right-click the OAB entry you want to configure and choose Properties from the context menu.**

   Exchange Management Console displays the OAB Properties dialog box.

3. **Click the Distribution tab.**

   You see the distribution options shown in Figure 4-17. Exercise care in how you configure these options because some options work with Outlook 2007 and others work with Outlook 2003 and earlier.

4. **Select the Client Support options you require for your users.**

   Exchange Server 2007 SP1 provides support for Outlook 98, Outlook 2003, and Outlook 2003 SP2. Use only the options you actually require because selecting more options could open potential security holes.

5. **Select the Enable Public Folder Distribution option and click OK.**

   Exchange Server makes the mailbox accessible to the Outlook 2003 and earlier clients that you selected.

Associating an OAB with a mailbox

Every mailbox needs an OAB. However, when you initially configure Exchange Server 2007 and subsequently create additional mailboxes, the mailbox doesn't have an OAB and your Health Check will display an error message. The following steps describe how to fix this problem:

1. **Choose the Server Configuration\Mailbox folder in Exchange Management Console.**

   You see a number of storage groups, including First Storage Group and its associated mailbox, Mailbox Database.

2. **Right-click the mailbox entry you want to change (Mailbox Database in an initial configuration) and choose Properties from the context menu.**

   Exchange Management Console displays the mailbox Database Properties dialog box as shown in Figure 4-20. (Exchange replaces *mailbox* with the specific name of the mailbox.)

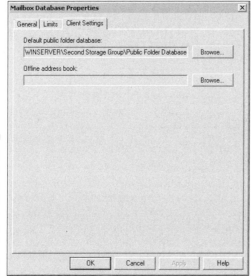

Figure 4-20: The mailbox Properties dialog box shows configuration settings for the client.

3. **Click the Client Settings tab.**

4. **Click Browse next to the Offline Address Book field.**

   Exchange Management Console displays the Select Offline Address Book window shown in Figure 4-21. This figure shows just the default OAB, but you can see any number of OABs in the list. The OAB you select should match the requirements of the users of the associated mailbox.

5. **Highlight the OAB you want to use and click OK.**

   The mailbox Properties dialog box now includes an entry for the OAB you selected.

6. **Click OK to close the mailbox Properties dialog box.**

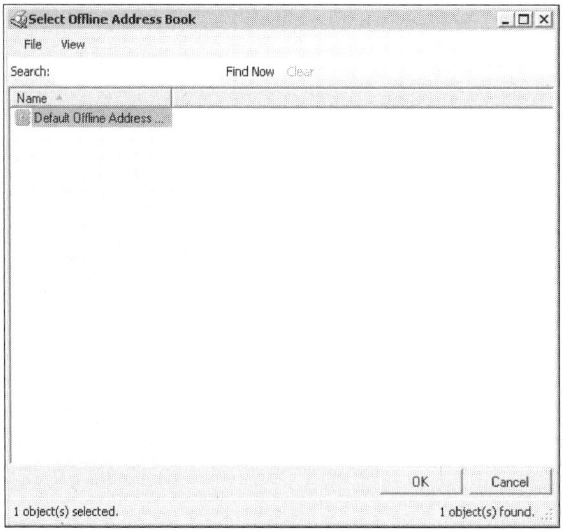

Figure 4-21:
Choose the required OAB for your mailbox.

Providing Client Access

Users will want e-mail access that is reliable, fast, and secure. This section of the chapter discusses the bare minimum you need to create a connection that is both reliable and secure. It may not be as fast you would like, but it won't be incredibly slow either. Consider this chapter the starting point in a longer process designed to tune Exchange Server for your organizational needs.

Chapter 6 fills in details of the security part of the question, and Chapter 7 discusses more about reliability. You find the added performance tricks you can use with Exchange Server in Chapters 9 and 11. For now, what you really want is just a connection so you can send and receive e-mail, manage your calendar, and interact with other Exchange Server users. The following sections help you get started.

Defining the Secure Sockets Layer (SSL) configuration

Exchange Server normally creates a self-signed SSL certificate for you during installation. The certificate uses the server name, rather than the Fully Qualified Domain Name (FQDN), so you'll probably see a warning when viewing your Health Check report. Resolving this warning means creating a new SSL certificate with the FQDN. If you have a certificate from a trusted third party, you should use that certificate, rather than creating a new self-signed certificate as described in this section.

Using the Internet Information Services (IIS) Manager console

One method of defining a new Exchange Server certificate is to use IIS. This technique is easy and error free but lacks the flexibility of the Windows PowerShell method described in the "Using Windows PowerShell" section of the chapter. The following steps describe how to create a new self-signed SSL certificate when needed for your private Exchange Server setup:

1. **Open the Internet Information Services (IIS) Manager console, which is in the Administrative Tools folder of Control Panel.**

2. **Highlight the server entry in the hierarchy.**

    You see a number of configuration icons, as shown in Figure 4-22. Note the Server Certificates icon that is highlighted in the screenshot.

Figure 4-22: Modify the SSL certificate for IIS to provide the correct FQDN.

3. **Double-click Server Certificates.**

    You see one or more certificates. One of these certificates is named Microsoft Exchange, as shown in Figure 4-23. This is the certificate that has the incorrect FQDN. Don't modify any other certificate in the list because your server could stop working.

Figure 4-23:
Locate the
certificate
that has the
incorrect
FQDN.

4. **Highlight the incorrect certificate and click Remove.**

   IIS removes the errant certificate from the list.

5. **In the Actions pane, click Create Self-Signed Certificate.**

   You see the Create Self-Signed Certificate wizard.

6. **In the Specify a Friendly Name for the Certificate field, type Microsoft Exchange. Click OK.**

   IIS creates the new certificate and displays it in the list. At this point, you must bind the certificate to the Web site that hosts the Outlook Web Access (OWA) application. Otherwise, no one will be able to access the Web site, even though the Best Practices Analyzer check will succeed. Exchange relies on the Default Web Site for support unless you specify another location as part of a custom setup.

7. **Select the Sites\Default Web Site folder.**

   You see configuration icons for the Default Web Site in the center pane and actions for the Default Web Site in the right pane.

8. **In the Actions pane, click Bindings.**

   IIS displays the bindings for the Default Web Site, as shown in Figure 4-24.

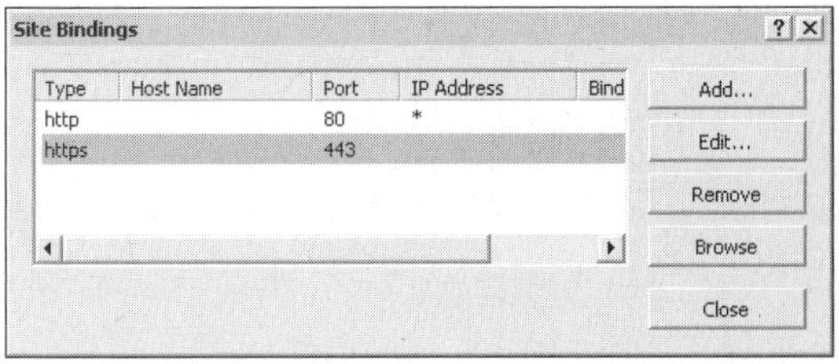

Figure 4-24: Display the list of bindings for the Default Web Site.

9. **Highlight the https entry and click Edit.**

   IIS displays the Edit Site Binding dialog box shown in Figure 4-25. This entry is probably blank. You must supply a certificate; otherwise IIS can't provide access to the Web site.

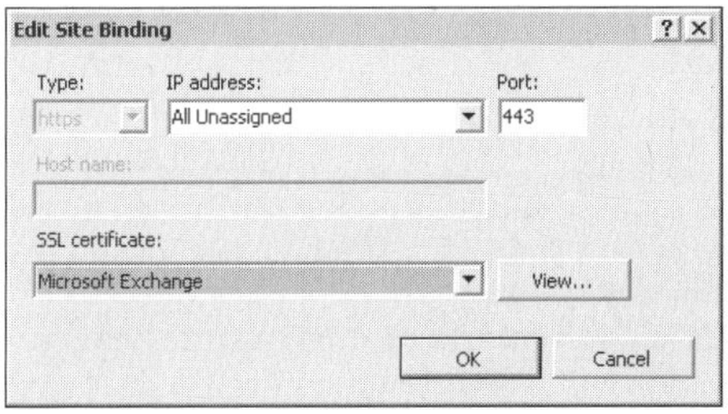

Figure 4-25: Add the correct SSL certificate to the binding.

10. **In the SSL Certificate field, choose Microsoft Exchange, as shown in Figure 4-25. Click OK.**

    The binding now points to a correctly formatted self-signed certificate. In most cases, you should be able to restart IIS to use the new certificate. However, you may have to restart the server in some cases.

11. **In the Actions pane, click Restart.**

    IIS restarts. Test the connection using a browser to open an OWA session.

12. **If the OWA connection fails, restart the server to ensure that the new certificate works as needed.**

Using Windows PowerShell

Some administrators will find that Windows PowerShell is significantly faster than working with the Internet Information Services (IIS) Manager console. In addition, Windows PowerShell provides additional flexibility because you can provide arguments that affect how the system interacts with the certificate. Chapter 12 provides a full discussion of how to work with the Exchange Server version of Windows PowerShell. To open a copy of Windows PowerShell for Exchange Server, choose Start⇨Programs⇨Microsoft Exchange Server 2007⇨Exchange Management Shell.

Many of the certificate-related commands require that you provide something called a certificate thumbprint. The thumbprint is a series of hexadecimal numbers that uniquely identify the certificate, much as your thumbprint uniquely identifies you. Type **Get-ExchangeCertificate** and press Enter to see the certificates installed on your system and their associated thumbprint, as shown in Figure 4-26.

Figure 4-26: Many commands require that you provide a thumbprint for certificate identification.

There are six certificate-specific commands for Exchange Server. You use each command to perform a specific task, such as creating a new certificate (New-ExchangeCertificate) or exporting the certificate for installation on a user machine (Export-ExchangeCertificate). The following list shows these commands and provides a URL where you can obtain additional help using them. Chapter 12 also provides additional help that you'll want to review:

- **Get-ExchangeCertificate:** http://technet.microsoft.com/en-us/library/bb124950(EXCHG.80).aspx

- **New-ExchangeCertificate:** http://technet.microsoft.com/en-us/library/aa998327(EXCHG.80).aspx

- **Export-ExchangeCertificate:** http://technet.microsoft.com/en-us/library/aa996305(EXCHG.80).aspx

- **Import-ExchangeCertificate:** http://technet.microsoft.com/en-us/library/bb124424(EXCHG.80).aspx

- **Remove-ExchangeCertificate:** http://technet.microsoft.com/en-us/library/aa997569(EXCHG.80).aspx

- **Enable-ExchangeCertificate:** http://technet.microsoft.com/en-us/library/aa997231(EXCHG.80).aspx

Adding the certificate to the client machine

To allow client access to your server without the certificate warning messages that browsers present about the certificate not being signed by a trusted authority, you must provide a means for installing that certificate on the client machine. The first part of this process is to export the certificate from your server store to a file. The following steps tell how to perform this task:

1. **Open the Internet Information Services (IIS) Manager console, which is in the Administrative Tools folder of Control Panel.**

2. **Highlight the server entry in the hierarchy.**

   You see a number of configuration icons (refer to Figure 4-22). Note the Server Certificates icon highlighted in the screenshot.

3. **Double-click Server Certificates.**

   You see one or more certificates, as shown in Figure 4-23, any of which you can export. One of these certificates is named Microsoft Exchange as shown in the figure. This is the certificate that you want to export in all cases. However, make sure you export all the certificates that the client will require.

4. **Double-click the certificate and click the Details tab.**

   You see the certificate information shown in Figure 4-27.

Figure 4-27: The certificate information tells you about the certificate you want to export.

5. **Click Copy to File.**

Windows displays the Certificate Export Wizard welcome dialog box.

6. **Click Next.**

You see the Export Private Key dialog box. This dialog box gives you the option of exporting the private key. Never export the private key to a client machine because then the client machine can use the private key to sign objects and the entire purpose behind using a certificate is lost.

7. **Select the No, Do Not Export the Private Key option and click Next.**

The wizard asks which file format you want to use to export the certificate.

8. **Choose an export file format and click Next.**

The technique you use depends on the security needs of your organization. However, the DER Encoded Binary X.509 (.CER) option works fine for most organizations and tends to produce the fewest number of compatibility concerns.

9. **In the File Name field, type a path and filename for the certificate.**

Use a name that is easy to remember and identify. Remember to use the file extension that is appropriate for the certificate you're creating. For example, you might type C:\MyCerts\MyCert.CER as a destination.

10. **Click Next, and then click Finish.**

The wizard presents a summary of the export process. Then the wizard creates the output file for you and displays a success dialog box.

11. **Click OK to close the success dialog box.**

You now have a new certificate that you can install on the user machine. In most cases, the administrator performs this task on each user machine as part of the setup. Some organizations also request that the user download the certificate and install it since the installation process is relatively easy. The following steps describe how to install a certificate on the client machine:

1. **Double-click the certificate.**

You see the Certificate dialog box shown in Figure 4-28. The dialog box provides full identification information for the certificate.

2. **Click Install Certificate.**

Windows displays the Certificate Import Wizard dialog box.

3. **Click Next.**

The Certificate Import Wizard asks where you want to store the certificate. In most cases, you want to use the default location because the wizard usually knows the best place to store it. The only time you use a specific store is when a developer writes an application to use a special store or when you need specialized access to the Web site. In this case, you need specialized access because you're using a self-signed certificate.

Figure 4-28:
Use the
Certificate
dialog box
to verify
certificate
authenticity.

4. **Choose the Place All Certificates in the Following Store option. Click Browse and choose the Trusted Root Certification Authorities option. Click OK.**

    The Trusted Root Certification Authorities store appears in the Certificate Store field.

5. **Click Next.**

    The wizard displays a summary of the import process.

6. **Click Finish.**

    The wizard installs the certificate for you and displays a success dialog box.

7. **Click OK to close the success dialog box.**

Setting SSL at the correct level

Exchange Server assumes that you want to secure your entire Web site with SSL, so it sets the SSL security at the Web site level. However, you may find that you don't want to secure the entire Web site. Fortunately, you can modify this configuration to secure just the Exchange Server site. Use the following steps:

1. **Open Internet Information Services (IIS) Manager.**

2. **Choose the Sites\Default Web Site folder.**

    You see a number of icons associated with the Default Web Site.

3. **Double-click the SSL Settings icon.**

   IIS displays the SSL Settings page.

4. **Deselect the Require SSL option and click Apply in the Actions pane.**

   The Default Web Site is now accessible without using SSL encryption. However, you still want to secure the Exchange Server access.

5. **Choose the Sites\Default Web Site\OWA folder.**

   You see a number of icons associated with the OWA application.

6. **Double-click the SSL Settings icon.**

   IIS displays the SSL Settings page.

7. **Select both the Require SSL option and the Require 128-bit SSL option. Click Apply in the Actions pane.**

   The OWA application is secured, so no one can access Exchange Server without using the proper SSL encryption.

Configuring a connection

It's time to create the connection that the client will use to access your server. All of these settings appear in the Server Configuration\Client Access folder. You choose the connection type from the tabs supplied in the lower half of the display. The following sections discuss the four kinds of connection that you can create using Exchange Server.

Outlook Web Access

The OWA connection is the only one that works completely when you install Exchange Server. You can access it as soon as you finish installing the product. Of course, the only e-mail account you can access at first is the Administrator account. Adding the user accounts you need is one of the first steps to making this connection work.

The basic connection requires two additional configuration setups: the connection URL and the authentication type. Exchange Server comes with an internal connection configured. If you want to provide external access to the OWA application, you must configure it as part of your Exchange Server setup using the following steps:

1. **Select the Server Configuration\Client Access folder.**

   The upper half of the Results pane shows one or more servers.

2. **Select the server you want to interact with and then click the Outlook Web Access tab.**

   You see one or more OWA entries. The setup program creates one OWA entry for you.

3. **Right-click the OWA entry you want to configure and choose Properties from the context menu.**

   Exchange Management Console displays the OWA (Web site) Properties dialog box.

4. **Click the General tab.**

   You see a list of URLs associated with this OWA, as shown in Figure 4-29.

   It's essential to provide the correct URL in the proper location. The Internal URL field shows the URL used on your local network, and the External URL field shows the URL used by a remote network. You must have a registered domain name and the proper Internet setup to use a remote network. Consequently, you can't simply provide an External URL value and expect it to work. In most cases, you use the same domain as you do for your Web site and the OWA folder.

Figure 4-29:
Provide internal and external OWA URLs as needed.

5. **In the External URL field, type the URL for your external connection.**

6. **Click OK.**

   An external user can now use a Web browser to access his or her e-mail.

The other potential configuration change is how the user authenticates. Exchange Server defaults to using forms-based authentication. Using forms-based authentication requires that the user log onto the system by supplying a username and password. If this is an internal network or you simply want to make logging into the system easier, you could modify the login to rely on integrated Windows authentication. In this case, you use the options found on the Authentication tab of the OWA (Web site) Properties dialog box shown in Figure 4-30.

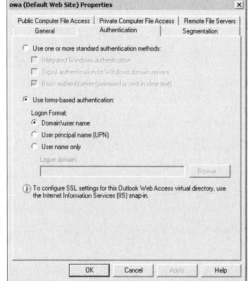

Figure 4-30:
Modify the
authenti-
cation to
meet spe-
cific user
require-
ments.

Note from the figure that you have multiple methods of authenticating the user. The digest and basic authentication methods are nearly worthless from a security perspective and you shouldn't use them under any circumstance. Basic authentication is the worst choice because it transmits the username and password in clear text, making it incredibly easy for anyone to steal the credentials required to access your network. The integrated Windows authentication method is a good choice for local networks because it reduces user confusion in many cases.

When you use forms-based authentication (recommended), you should tailor the form to match your organization's needs. Large organizations need both domain and username to perform proper authentication, but smaller organizations normally need just the username because they have only a single domain.

Exchange ActiveSync

Exchange ActiveSync is the technology you use to connect a mobile device to your Exchange Server. Once the mobile device requests information about your e-mail account, Exchange Server automatically broadcasts changes to the status of your mailbox to the mobile device. The technology that makes this all possible is Direct Push. You can read more about Direct Push at http://technet.microsoft.com/en-us/library/ aa997252(EXCHG.80).aspx.

Note that the firewall used in the Direct Push article is ISA Server 2006 — not the Windows Firewall that you probably use with Windows Server 2008. Consequently, you don't need to worry about the ISA Server-specific configuration changes mentioned in the article. However, you still need to think about the timeout value, which means opening a command prompt in administrator mode (right-click the Command Prompt entry in the Start menu and choose Run As Administrator from the context menu). At the command prompt, type **NetSH HTTP Show Timeout** and press Enter. You see the current timeout value for the `IdleConnectionTimeout` property. If this value isn't at least 120, type **NetSH HTTP Add Timeout TimeoutType=IdleConnectionTimeout Value=120** and press Enter.

Exchange Server should have configured an Exchange ActiveSync mailbox policy for you during installation. To verify that the policy exists, choose the Organization Configuration\Client Access folder. You should see a Default mailbox policy. If you do not, create a policy using the following steps:

1. **Click New Exchange ActiveSync Mailbox Policy in the Actions pane.**

   You see the New Exchange ActiveSync Mailbox Policy dialog box shown in Figure 4-31. The default that Exchange Server creates doesn't require a password but does allow attachments and nonprovisionable devices. You should configure this dialog box to match your organization's policies.

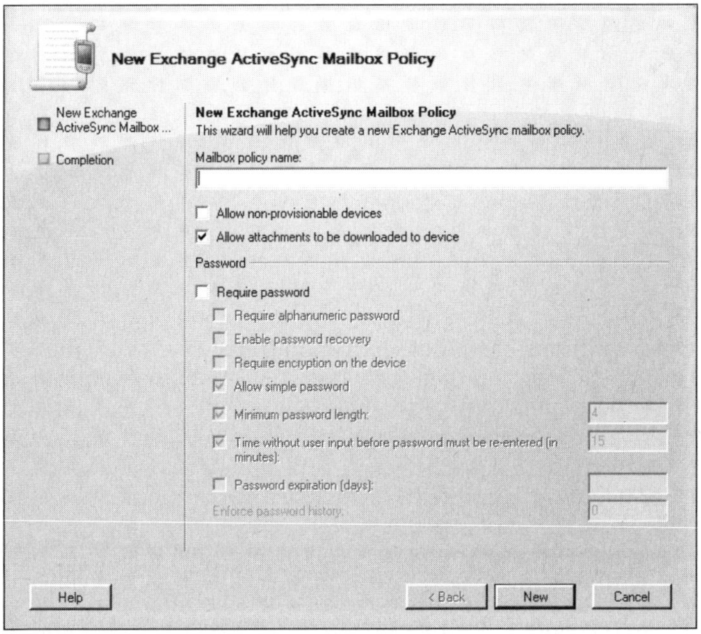

Figure 4-31:
Create a policy that reflects your organization's policies.

2. **In the Mailbox Policy Name field, type a name for the policy.**

   The first mailbox policy should use the name Default, but this is only a convention and you don't have to follow it.

3. **Choose whether you want to allow nonprovisionable devices.**

   A nonprovisionable device is an older product that may not support all the policies you configure for the Exchange ActiveSync mailbox policy. This device represents a potential security hole because it doesn't honor all the policies you put in place. Of course, if you don't allow nonprovisionable devices, some users are almost certainly going to complain.

4. **Choose whether you want to allow attachment download.**

   Mobile devices don't commonly provide a firewall and full virus scanning. Consequently, a user who downloads an attachment won't have the same protection as someone who relies on a desktop or laptop computer. Allowing attachments presents another security hole for your organization.

5. **(Optional) Select Require Password, and then select the password options you want to use.**

   Passwords protect your network from inadvertent or undesired access by third parties, so using password protection is another requirement for good security. Of course, you must balance the need for passwords with the user's ability to input passwords using a mobile device. If you select a password policy that proves difficult for the mobile user, you'll definitely receive complaints and many mobile users won't use Exchange ActiveSync at all (causing all kinds of other woe for the administrator when management figures out they can't reach someone on the road).

6. **Click New.**

   The New Exchange ActiveSync Mailbox Policy dialog box shows the result of adding the new policy to Exchange Server.

7. **Click Finish.**

   At this point, you see a new mailbox policy added to the list. Double-click the new policy to configure additional settings, such as the devices allowed to connect to the mailbox through Exchange ActiveSync.

Exchange Server 2007 SP1 adds a new feature to the Exchange ActiveSync mailbox policy. The first mailbox policy you create is the default for all new users you add to Exchange Server. If you create a second mailbox policy, you can make it the new default policy by right-clicking the mailbox policy and choosing Set as Default from the context menu. Every new user you create will receive this new Exchange ActiveSync mailbox policy. See the "Adding a user" section of the chapter for details on adding a new user to Exchange Server.

You may need to configure existing users to rely on the new Exchange ActiveSync mailbox policy. Use the following steps to reconfigure users as needed:

1. **Choose the Recipient Configuration\Mailbox folder.**

   You see a list of mailbox users.

2. **Double-click the user entry you want to modify.**

   Exchange Management Console displays a user Properties dialog box.

3. **Select the Mailbox Features tab.**

   The dialog box presents you with a list of mailbox features, including Exchange ActiveSync.

4. **Highlight Exchange ActiveSync and click Properties.**

   Exchange Management Console displays an Exchange ActiveSync Properties dialog box, where you can choose the policy for Exchange ActiveSync.

5. **Click Browse.**

   You see the Select ActiveSync Mailbox Policy dialog box.

6. **Highlight the mailbox policy you want to use and click OK. Click OK twice more to close the Exchange ActiveSync Properties and User Properties dialog boxes.**

   Exchange Server makes the changes you requested to the user account.

POP3 and IMAP4

You use the POP3 and IMAP4 connections mainly for external applications. These are the same protocols that your ISP uses to provide connectivity for your e-mail. The most popular connection today is Point-of-Presence version 3 (POP3), and this is the option you should select when providing connectivity for external clients where you won't know the client capabilities in advance. Use Internet Messaging Access Protocol version 4 (IMAP4) when you have better control over which clients connect to your system. IMAP4 provides two special features that make it worthwhile to implement in an enterprise environment (discover additional details at `http://www.pocketpcfaq.com/pocketpc.com/pop3imap4.htm`):

- ✔ IMAP4 provides an online mode to allow reading e-mail directly on the server, rather than downloading it first.

- ✔ POP3 transmits your password in plain text, but IMAP4 provides security features that make the password and your e-mail content less accessible.

Exchange Server configured both POP3 and IMAP4 for you during the setup process. You can find these entries in the POP3 and IMAP4 tab of the Server Configuration\Client Access tab of Exchange Management Console. The only setting you should need to change in most cases appears on the Authentication tab. Double-click the protocol you want to modify and choose the Authentication tab in the protocol's Properties dialog box. Choose a logon method from the list. If you choose a secure logon, make sure that the X.509 Certificate Name field contains the name you assigned to your SSL certificate.

Microsoft doesn't enable POP3 or IMAP4 by default. You must start the services. Open the Services console found in the Administrative Tools folder of Control Panel. If you want to enable POP3, locate the Microsoft Exchange POP3 service. If you want to enable IMAP4, locate the Microsoft Exchange IMAP4 service. Right-click the service entry and choose Properties from the context menu. In the service Properties dialog box, choose Automatic in the Startup Type field and click Start. You're ready to go with the protocol you chose.

Setting Up the Hub Transport

The Hub Transport server is the part of your Exchange Server setup that interfaces with the outside world. If your only goal is to provide internal mail routing on your own network, you don't have to perform any of the configuration tasks in this section. You already have everything needed for an internal network.

The Hub Transport server provides a number of flexibility options that you need to consider. The most important decision is how to configure Internet access. You have two main configuration options:

✔ **Edge Transport server:** Use the Edge Transport server when most of your communication occurs through online connections. Microsoft has created this option for larger organizations. It provides numerous, flexible, configuration options. However, this option has the disadvantage of requiring more resources, adding complexity, and needing a second server. A complete discussion of the Edge Transport server is outside the scope of this book, but the book does provide insights as to how you'd implement an Edge Transport server as part of your Exchange Server setup.

✔ **Internet Mail Flow:** This is the traditional option for smaller organizations. The advantage of using this approach is simplicity, which also implies reliability. Internet Mail Flow relies on the Hub Transport server to transfer data to and from the Internet, which means that this option isn't as secure as using the Edge Transport server.

As an alternative to configuring an Edge Transport server, you can also use Microsoft's hosted services (described in the "Considering Microsoft Exchange Hosted Services" section of Chapter 1). Using the hosted services option means that you obtain the benefit of the Edge Transport server without incurring the added expense and management requirements.

Defining the e-mail domains

An *accepted domain* is a domain with which you intend to send and receive e-mail. It's a kind of permission. If you intend to send e-mail to an external Simple Mail Transfer Protocol (SMTP) server, you must create an accepted domain for it. You use an accepted domain entry for situations in which Exchange Server is authoritative — it delivers e-mail on behalf of the SMTP server. An accepted domain is also the correct option when Exchange Server relays e-mail for another SMTP server. This isn't the correct option to use when you want to create a connection to the outside world using the Hub Transport server.

Every Exchange Server configuration includes one accepted (authoritative) domain by default — the host domain for the Exchange Server. Consequently, when you view the Organization Configuration\Hub Transport folder in Exchange Management Console, you should see an entry for your domain. If you don't see your domain in the list, then Exchange Server won't provide local communication. You add other domains to this local domain list when you want to communicate with other domains.

E-mail domains also let you communicate with other Exchange Servers in your organization. Consequently, if your organization has multiple domains, you see an entry for each domain with which you want to interact. In fact, you can use accepted domain entries to create three types of connection:

- ✔ **Authoritative domain:** Exchange Server hosts mailboxes for a particular SMTP domain in most cases. The SMTP domain is the authoritative domain for Exchange Server — the one over which it has authority to deliver e-mail. In some cases, an organization has more than one SMTP domain. You must create authoritative domain entries for every domain that the Exchange Server hosts. For example, if your company has e-mail for both MyCompany.com and MyCompany.org, you need authoritative domain entries for each domain as long as Exchange Server hosts mailboxes for both domains.

- ✔ **Internal relay domain:** In some cases, you need to relay information from one SMTP server to another. For example, you may have an Exchange Server that connects to the Internet through an Edge Transport server. The Exchange Server may receive e-mail for a domain that is internal to your organization and doesn't have an Internet connection. In this case, you configure an internal relay domain for Exchange Server that has the Internet connection. This relay sends the e-mail from the Internet to the internal Exchange Server (the one without the Internet connection).

Setting up a relay of any kind uses resources on the server that hosts the relay. In some cases, the resource usage can become extreme and cause poor performance on the host server. Make sure any relays you configure are necessary and won't slow the host server excessively. You can read more about potential hazards of configuring a relay domain at http://technet.microsoft.com/en-us/library/bb124423(EXCHG.80).aspx.

✔ **External relay domain:** An external relay domain is much like an internal relay domain, except it handles e-mail that is external (and usually unrelated) to your organization. You might set up such a relay for a partner organization or to connect external parts of your organization. For example, you might use an external relay domain to connect the London office with the New York office.

Use external relay domains with extreme caution. The load on your server becomes onerous when you set up an external relay domain incorrectly. In addition, your server can become a tool for nefarious individuals for e-mail spoofing and other illegal activities.

Now that you have a better idea of what e-mail domains provide, it's time to look at how you create one. The following steps help you create an e-mail domain:

1. **Choose the Organization Configuration\Hub Transport folder.**

2. **In the Actions pane, click New Accepted Domain.**

   Exchange Management Console displays the New Accepted Domain dialog box shown in Figure 4-32. Note that you must define the kind of connection as part of creating the accepted domain entry.

3. **In the Name field, type a human-friendly name for the accepted domain.**

4. **In the Accepted Domain field, type the actual domain name.**

   Make sure you type the domain name precisely as it is used by the other domain. For example, if you want to communicate with the server at MyServer.MyDomain.com, you type MyDomain.com here and don't include the server name.

5. **Choose one of the connection types and click New.**

   Exchange Server creates the new entry and displays the results.

6. **Click Finish.**

   The accepted domain is ready for use.

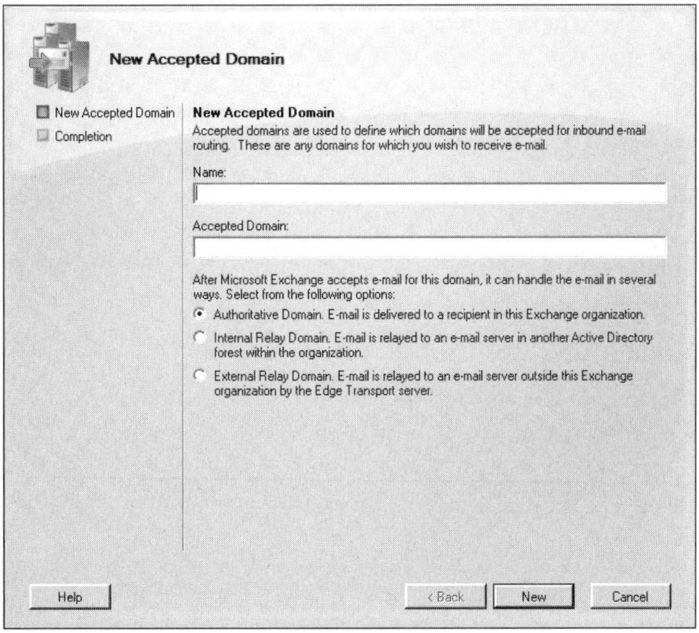

Figure 4-32:
Define
a new
accepted
domain for
your server.

Modifying Internet mail flow

A *mail flow* is a description of how e-mail leaves a sender, moves between servers through some type of media, and arrives at the recipient. Exchange Server supports three kinds of mail flow: Edge Transport server, Hub Transport server, and hosted services. In all three situations, you must configure a send connector and a receive connector. The send connector tells where to send e-mail, and the receive connector defines which e-mail you want to receive.

The difference in the three kinds of mail flow is the configuration of the send and receive connectors. When you configure the Hub Transport server to interact directly with the Internet, you provide a send and receive connector that provides a broad range of potential addresses. On the other hand, when working with the Edge Transport server, you configure a send and receive connector that only works with the Edge Transport server. The same configuration requirement holds true for a hosted service — you interact with only that server. The following sections provide details on creating send and receive connectors.

Creating the send connector

You may have received a warning message during the Exchange Server SP1 installation that says, "Setup cannot detect an SMTP or Send connector with an address space of '*'." This message is normal and you don't have to worry about it during the installation process. However, you do need to provide a fix for it during the initial configuration process. The following steps describe what you need to do to fix this problem:

1. **Choose the Organization Configuration\Hub Transport folder.**

2. **Click the Send Connectors tab.**

   You normally won't see any connectors listed.

3. **In the Actions pane, click New Send Connector.**

   Exchange Server displays the New SMTP Send Connector dialog box shown in Figure 4-33. You use this dialog box to configure send connectors of different types: Custom, Internal, Internet, and Partner.

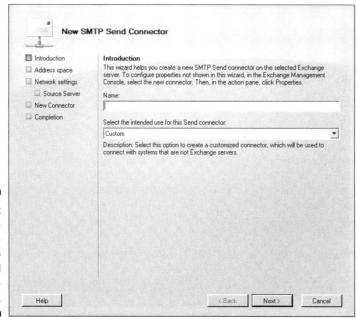

Figure 4-33:
Create a send connector to send e-mail to an external server.

4. **Type a name for the send connector.**

5. **In the Select the Intended Use for This Send Connector field, choose a send connector type. Click Next.**

The wizard asks you to provide one or more address spaces. When working with a direct Internet connection, you create an SMTP address space of * (asterisk), which is all Internet addresses except the local address. When working with the Edge Transport server or a hosted service, you provide the specific address space for that server.

6. **Click Add.**

   You see the SMTP Address Space dialog box.

7. **Type the address space you want to use. Select Include All Subdomains when the address space contains more subdomains you want to access. Type a value that represents the cost of using this address space (always a value of 1 for Internet connections). Click OK.**

   The wizard displays the address space in the list. The *cost* of an address space is a value you assign to the address space that helps Exchange Server know when to use a particular route. A connection across a slow router will have a higher cost than a connection across a fast router. The cost may also reflect personal preference. You may prefer to load one server more than another server to preserve a company mandated Quality of Service (QoS) level. Since Exchange Server has no method of determining the cost of a connection, it relies on you to provide this value.

8. **Repeat Steps 6 and 7 for each address space you want to add.**

9. **Click Next.**

   You see the Network Options page of the wizard. This page asks you to define whether you want to use the Domain Name System (DNS) or smart hosts to route the e-mail. In most cases, you rely on DNS to perform the task. In fact, when in doubt, use DNS because using smart hosts requires a special setup that you would know about if you adopt this approach.

10. **Choose a network routing option. When you choose the Route Mail Through the Following Smart Hosts option, you must also click Add to add smart hosts to the list.**

11. **Select Use the External DNS Lookup Settings on the Transport Server when configuring an Internet connection.**

    Using the external DNS server makes it possible to send e-mail to any location. If you don't select this option, Exchange Server won't be able to forward the e-mail to the external servers.

    12. Click Next.

    You see a list of source servers. Normally, Exchange Server provides the local host as the default source server. The only time you need to change this entry is when you want to allow use of multiple source servers.

    13. Click Add, if necessary, and choose additional source servers. Click Next.

    The wizard displays a summary of the new send connector.

    14. Click New.

    Exchange Server creates the new send connector and displays the results.

    15. Click Finish.

    The send connector is ready to use.

Configuring the receive connector

To receive e-mail from another location, you must create a receive connector. Exchange Server creates two such connectors for you. The first is for Exchange Server users, and the second receives e-mail from everyone else. The receive connector of interest in this section is the general, or default, receive connector — not the one used for Exchange Server users. The following steps tell you how to modify the receive connector for use with Internet connections:

    1. Choose the Server\Hub Transport folder.

    You see a list of receive connectors in the lower half of the display.

    2. Double-click the Default receive connector.

    Exchange Server displays the default receive connector properties.

    3. Click the Permission Groups tab.

    The list shows the groups that can access Exchange Server for the purpose of sending e-mail (the e-mail that Exchange Server receives using this connector). The default setting doesn't allow anonymous users, which cuts out any Internet activity as shown in Figure 4-34.

    4. Select Anonymous Users. Click OK.

    The receive connector is now configured for use with anonymous users.

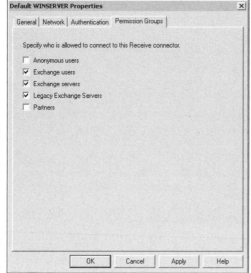

Figure 4-34:
Allow
anonymous
access so
that you
can receive
Internet
e-mail.

Connecting to Exchange Server with a Client

After all the configuration you've performed in this chapter, it's important to discuss one additional need. The purpose of placing Exchange Server on your system is to provide e-mail and other support to one or more clients. Precisely how you use this support depends on your organization, but Chapter 5 provides you with a wealth of ideas.

Simply because you use Exchange Server doesn't mean that you must use it as your only provider. A small to medium-sized organization could rely on Exchange Server for internal e-mail and requirements and rely on an external ISP to connect to the Internet. Outlook and many other e-mail client applications support this approach. Using this dual-provider approach might seem like it would be problematic, but it works incredibly well and most users don't even realize that they have two providers.

You have already seen how you can use the OWA approach to connecting to Exchange Server. It's also possible to create a POP3 or IMAP4 account with Exchange Server, just as you do with your ISP. The POP3 or IMAP4 approach works well when you need to access Exchange Server across an Internet connection and want a standards-based approach. These are all standard connection options.

Microsoft also provides a special Exchange Server connection for Outlook. This section provides a view of the connection procedure for Outlook 2003, but the process is the same for Outlook 2007 — a few of the screenshots may look a little different, but that's about it. The following steps get you connected to Exchange Server using Outlook:

1. **Close Outlook.**

   You can't add an Exchange Server account in Outlook with Outlook running.

2. **Open the Mail applet in Control Panel.**

   Windows displays the Mail Setup – Outlook dialog box.

3. **Click E-mail Accounts.**

   You see the E-mail Accounts wizard.

4. **Select Add a New E-mail Account and click Next.**

   The wizard presents you with a list of e-mail account types, as shown in Figure 4-35.

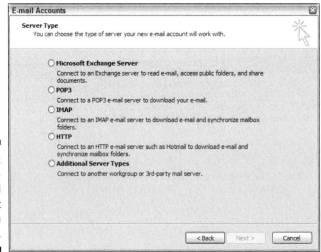

Figure 4-35:
Choose the e-mail account type you want to use.

5. **Select Microsoft Exchange Server and click Next.**

   The wizard displays the Exchange Server Settings page where you provide the name of the Microsoft Exchange Server and your username.

6. **In the Microsoft Exchange Server field, type the FQDN of the server.**

7. **In the User Name field, type your username.**

8. **Click Check Name.**

   An error here means that you don't have one of the configuration settings correct. In many cases, you should check the server name, especially if Outlook tells you that it needs a connection before it can interact with Exchange server. After a successful check, Outlook simply underlines both the server and the username.

9. **Click Next.**

   The wizard tells you that the Exchange Server e-mail will appear in your regular inbox.

10. **Click Yes.**

    You see a success message.

11. **Click Finish.**

    The Exchange Server-specific account is ready for use.

Part II
Customizing Exchange Server

The 5th Wave   By Rich Tennant

"You the guy having trouble staying connected to the server?"

In this part . . .

After you have an initial installation in place, you must customize it to meet your organization's needs. For example, everyone in your organization must have a mailbox to send and receive e-mail. You also need mailboxes for various resources in your organization so that you can schedule their use. Chapter 5 gets you started performing this essential task.

Before you open your Exchange Server configuration to outsiders, you want to configure security. Chapter 6 helps you understand the security requirements for Exchange Server and customize them to meet your organization's requirements.

Chapter 7 opens your server to outsiders. Now that everyone has secure access to a mailbox, they can begin sending e-mail, scheduling meetings, and working with company resources.

In Chapter 8, you discover how to interact with forms and customize them. You may not want all users to have access to every Exchange Server feature, so this chapter provides important configuration information. Of course, you'll need to work with Exchange Server for a while before you discover all the changes you want to make to forms, so you'll probably visit this chapter often.

Chapter 5

Working with Mailboxes

*T*he previous four chapters of the book helped you set up, install, and configure Exchange Server for initial use. The only problem with the setup is that it's functional without providing for the specific needs of your organization. Exchange Server can supply a connection, serve up e-mail, and that's about it. You want to customize Exchange Server further to ensure that the users in your organization can make full use of the product. Now that you can create a connection and test things, it's time to take a step back and discover what else you can do. This chapter helps you perform that task. It helps you customize Exchange Server.

One of the first tasks is understanding how to manage messaging records. Users will have a lot of questions for you about the messages they receive, and you need to know how to handle them. Of course, once you begin talking about users, you also need to consider how those users will interact with their mailboxes. Many users don't want to understand e-mail — they want to communicate with other people. The communication could easily take the form of a letter, a telephone call, or a meeting at a restaurant. E-mail is simply a conduit for the user, so you need to think about it as something the user doesn't want to understand — any more than the user wants to understand the inner workings of a telephone.

Once you understand user needs in your organization, you can begin creating the user experience. This means setting up calendars, working with resources such as meeting rooms, and handling scheduling requirements. These special needs are where some of the real work with Exchange Server begins because there aren't any hard rules for how a user will interact with Exchange Server. Yes, you can make a good guess at what the user wants, but you also need to listen to user complaints and act on them to refine the Exchange Server setup.

The final part of the configuration process is more mechanical, in that you can follow some best practices and get a good result. You must finish configuring the mailbox database, public folder database, and distribution groups that the user requires. The following sections address all of these requirements.

Considering How Users Work with Mailboxes

Most users today don't simply use their mailboxes for e-mail. An Exchange Server mailbox serves a number of purposes for the user, most of which are critical to the business. These purposes consist of the following general tasks:

- E-mail
- Task list
- Calendar
- Contact list
- Notes
- Journal
- Shared folders

All of these features are business critical. For example, if you remove a user's contact list, you may as well send them home for the day because that contact list provides them with access to other people with whom they interact. A journal may almost seem like a vanity item, until you consider that users rely on it to fill out business reports and tell about the latest conference they attended. A journal can also help an organization put the user's thoughts back together again should the user become unavailable.

Exchange Server also makes it possible to perform specialized tasks. These specialized tasks take the focus off the individual user and place it on the group. A group can be anything from the entire organization to the set of users who work on a particular project. These specialized tasks include:

- Conference room reservations
- Shared resource usage such as company cars
- Meeting requirements such as agendas
- Collaborative work, including work on documents

In addition to common and specialized tasks, you must also consider user needs. For example, nothing terrible will happen if the user doesn't provide an out-of-office message. However, leaving this feature out can prove inconvenient. Other users may spend time needlessly trying to determine the status of a user on vacation. Of course, the out-of-office message may eventually become a thing of the past — some people remain connected all the time (see the interesting article on this topic at `http://www.eweek.com/c/a/Careers/Has-the-Disconnected-Vacation-Become-Extinct/`).

These concerns affect every user in your organization. However, some users may have special requirements, which means you must interview them in some way. For example, a user may have a special physical need, such as poor eyesight or hearing loss, which you must consider as part of their mailbox setup. A salesperson may not actually spend any time at her desk, so configuring a setup that follows her to different locations is a must. On the other hand, a user that normally spends all his time at his desk may become annoyed by a setup that follows him to the bathroom, among other places. Keeping special user needs in mind doesn't require a lot of time and it makes users more likely to follow the policies your company has in place.

Understanding Messaging Records Management

Messaging records management describes the use of managed folders to hold certain information in a user's mailbox. For example, the user relies on the Inbox folder to hold new e-mail. The Inbox is an example of a default managed folder. Exchange Server also supports custom managed folders, which are folders that you define for organization-specific purposes, such as e-mail from a particular project.

The feature that makes a particular managed folder a messaging records management folder is the addition of a special configuration. You then assign a mailbox policy to the managed folder and add the policy to the user's mailbox. The result is that the user sees the managed folder as he or she would any other folder in Outlook (or another e-mail client). The following sections take you through the process of creating a managed folder, configuring it, assigning it a mailbox policy, and applying that policy to a user mailbox. You also see how to use Managed Folder Assistant to make working with managed folders easier.

The managed folder feature doesn't work with every version of Outlook. You receive full support when using Outlook 2007. Use Outlook 2003 SP3 and newer to receive support for most managed folder features. Microsoft recommends using version blocking with Outlook 2003 SP2 and older. Use the Set-CASMailbox command to block older versions to avoid potential problems. Chapter 12 shows how to use the Exchange Management Shell to perform this task.

Creating a managed custom folder

The first step in adding a new folder to the user's e-mail client is to create the required managed folder. This folder will hold the messaging records associated with the content that the user places in the folder. The following steps show how to perform this task:

1. **Choose the Organization Configuration\Mailbox folder. Click the Managed Custom Folders tab.**

   You see an area that can hold managed folders. However, Exchange Server doesn't provide any folders by default in this area, so the first time you view the list, it is blank.

2. **Click New Managed Custom Folder in the Actions pane.**

   Exchange Management Console displays the New Managed Custom Folder dialog box shown in Figure 5-1.

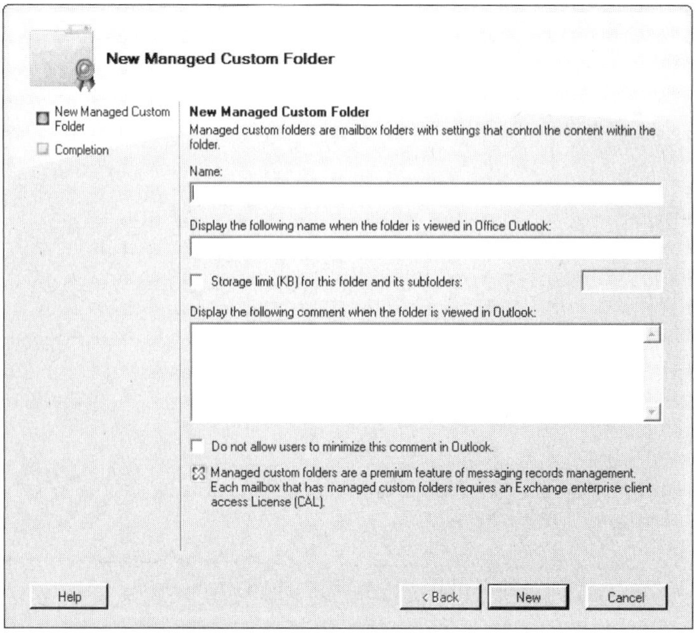

Figure 5-1:
Provide some basic input for a custom folder the users will see in their e-mail client.

New Managed Custom Folder	

New Managed Custom Folder
Completion

New Managed Custom Folder
Managed custom folders are mailbox folders with settings that control the content within the folder.

Name:

Display the following name when the folder is viewed in Office Outlook:

☐ Storage limit (KB) for this folder and its subfolders:

Display the following comment when the folder is viewed in Outlook:

☐ Do not allow users to minimize this comment in Outlook.

⚠ Managed custom folders are a premium feature of messaging records management. Each mailbox that has managed custom folders requires an Exchange enterprise client access License (CAL).

Help   < Back   New   Cancel

3. **Type a name for the managed folder in the Name field.**

   This first field contains the name you use to work with the managed folder. You can provide a different display name that the user will recognize. The two names should reflect the contrast between how you interact with the folder and the kind of information the user stores in it.

4. **Type the display name for the managed folder in the next field.**

5. **(Optional) Select Storage Limit (KB) for This Folder and Its Subfolders. Type a value for the size limit in KB.**

   Selecting this option reduces the chance that the user will continue to fill the mailbox well beyond the capacity of your server to store information. You should set an ample size for the folder to ensure that the user doesn't complain about not being able to store enough information. Both you and the user receive a message when the folder becomes too full.

6. **Type a comment that reflects the use of the folder.**

   A good comment can help the user make the best use of the storage space provided by the folder.

7. **(Optional) Select Do Not Allow Users to Minimize This Comment in Outlook.**

   In most cases, you won't select this option because comments can consume a lot of space in Outlook. Considering the amount of space that Outlook already consumes with various gizmos, some users rightfully complain that they have a hard time seeing their messages. However, you might keep the comment displayed when the folder contains sensitive information or the user must follow a specific procedure when using it.

8. **Click New and then Finish.**

   Outlook creates the new folder for you.

Creating a managed default folder

In a very few cases, you may find that you want to modify some aspect of a default folder. Perhaps you need to add a subfolder to hold special information. Microsoft suggests using multiple copies of standard folders for special reasons — three copies of the Inbox could hold mail that is 30, 60, and 90 days old. The following steps describe how to create a managed default folder:

1. **Choose the Organization Configuration\Mailbox folder. Click the Managed Default Folders tab.**

   You see a list of default folders that Exchange Server provides. Always review this list to ensure that you really do need a new default folder for a particular task.

2. **Click New Managed Default Folder in the Actions pane.**

   Exchange Management Console displays the New Managed Custom Folder dialog box shown in Figure 5-2.

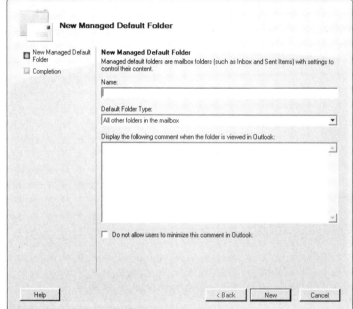

Figure 5-2:
Create new
default
folders as
needed
for special
tasks.

3. **Type a name for the managed folder in the Name field.**

   This field contains the name that you use to manage the field. You can't modify the name the user sees, which makes comments especially important in this case.

4. **Choose a default folder type to copy in the Default Folder Type field.**

   The option you choose determines the kind of folder the user sees.

5. **Type a comment that reflects the use of the folder.**

   A good comment can help the user make the best use of the storage space provided by the folder. In this case, the comment also helps the user understand why you have two versions of the same folder in the e-mail application.

6. **(Optional) Select Do Not Allow Users to Minimize This Comment in Outlook.**

   Unlike custom managed folders, you may have a good reason to keep the comment displayed. Otherwise, users will become confused as to why you have multiple copies of the same folder in their e-mail application. It's essential to keep the comments short but informative.

7. **Click New and then Finish.**

   Outlook creates the new folder for you.

Configuring a managed folder

The managed folder can have a number of settings that control how it interacts with the messages that it contains. For example, you can choose to limit
the lifespan of messages or journal (copy) the message to another location.
These settings help you control how users work with messages and also help
you monitor potentially hazardous problems such as an increase in spam.
Exchange Server lets you add as many settings as needed to control the message content of a managed folder completely. The following steps describe
how to add configuration settings to a managed folder.

1. **Choose the Organization Configuration\Mailbox folder. Click the
   Managed Default Folders or the Managed Custom Folders tab.**

   You see a list of managed folders.

2. **Right-click the folder you want to manage and choose New Managed
   Content Settings from the context menu.**

   Exchange Management Console displays the New Managed Content
   Settings dialog box shown in Figure 5-3. This first page contains the
   settings name, the type of content it affects, and the length of time
   Exchange Server retains the message.

3. **Type a name for the settings in the first field.**

4. **Choose the kind of message that this setting affects in the Message
   Type drop-down list.**

   You can choose between all message content and a particular kind of
   message, such as a calendar entry. The RSS Items entry applies only to
   Outlook 2007 because you must use a third-party RSS reader when using
   Outlook 2003. The setting applies only when the user actually uses the
   specified message type.

5. **(Optional) Select Length of Retention Period (Days). Type the number
   of days you want to keep the message. Choose a start time and action.
   Some actions also require that you choose a destination folder.**

   These options let you choose how long to keep the message in a particular folder. The action can permanently delete the item or delete it and
   allow the user to recover it later. You can also move items to a folder or
   simply mark the item as old.

6. **Click Next.**

   You see the Journaling page shown in Figure 5-4. Journaling sends a copy
   of the message to another location. You may have an interest in particular
   messages or need to archive the messages for legal or other reasons.

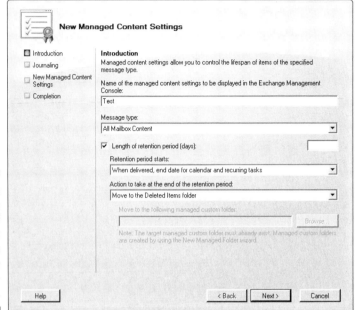

Figure 5-3:
Define the
length of
time that a
message
remains in
the man-
aged folder.

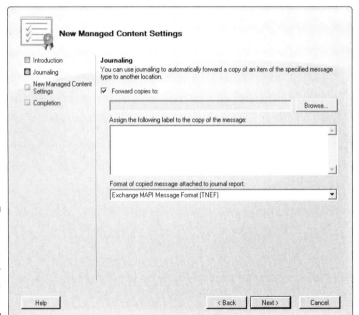

Figure 5-4:
Send mes-
sages to
another
location as
needed.

7. **(Optional) Select Forward Copies To. Click Browse to display the Select Recipient dialog box, select a user from the list, and click OK. Type an explanatory label for the forwarded copy. Choose a format for the journal message.**

   These settings determine how you receive journal messages. You can only select one recipient. If multiple people need to receive a journal copy, you must configure multiple settings — one for each person. The explanatory label you provide should describe in detail why you're receiving the journal copy. Otherwise, it's too easy to receive a journal message and not be able to figure out why you need it.

8. **Click Next.**

   The wizard presents a summary of the settings you provide.

9. **Click New and then click Finish.**

   Exchange Management Console adds the new setting. However, you won't see the new setting immediately. Click the plus sign (+) next to the managed folder and you see the setting as a child of the managed folder, as shown in Figure 5-5.

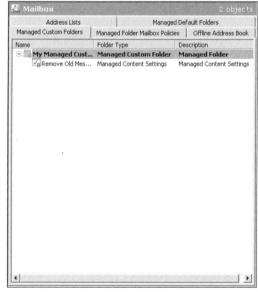

Figure 5-5:
Managed folders can have as many settings entries as needed.

Setting the managed folder mailbox policies

Your company and its users probably have use for more than one managed folder. Of course, you can always assign the managed folders that users require one at a time, but doing so is time consuming and error prone. A better way to handle the assignment of multiple managed folders to a user or group is to assign them at one time using a mailbox policy. Creating a mailbox policy groups the managed folders and makes it easier to assign them. The following steps describe how to create a mailbox policy:

1. **Choose the Organization Configuration\Mailbox folder. Click the Managed Folder Mailbox Policies tab.**

   You won't see any entries in the Results pane until you add some. Afterward, the Results pane displays all the managed folder mailbox policies for your system.

2. **Click New Managed Folder Mailbox Policy in the Actions pane.**

   Exchange Management Console displays the New Managed Folder Mailbox Policy dialog box shown in Figure 5-6.

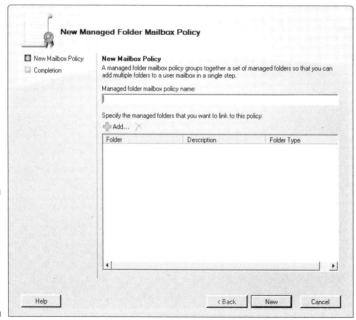

Figure 5-6:
Group managed folders using a managed folder mailbox policy.

3. **Type a name for the policy in the Managed Folder Mailbox Policy Name field.**

4. **Click Add. Highlight the managed folder you want to add from the list in the Select Managed Folder dialog box. Click OK.**

   The list contains all the default managed folders and any custom managed folders you create. You can use Ctrl+click to select multiple files in the list. After you click OK, managed folders you select are displayed in the folder list of the New Managed Folder Mailbox Policy dialog box.

5. **Repeat Step 4 as needed to add all required folders to the managed folder mailbox policy.**

6. **Click New and then click Finish.**

   The new policy is added to the Managed Folder Mailbox Policies tab.

Applying a managed folder policy to a user mailbox

By the time you reach this section, you have a managed folder and have added one or more settings to it. If you don't have all the settings in place, you can always add them later. However, mailboxes work best when you have the required settings in place at the outset. You must also create a policy for the managed folders, even if the user has only one managed folder added to his or her client. This section assigns the managed folder to a particular user. Exchange Server doesn't provide the capability to assign a managed folder to a group. The following steps show how to add the managed folder to the user's client application:

1. **Choose the Recipient Configuration/Mailbox folder.**

   You see a list of users for the Exchange Server setup.

2. **Right-click the user you want to modify and choose Properties from the context menu.**

   Exchange Management Console displays the user's Properties dialog box.

3. **Click the Mailbox Settings tab. Highlight the Messaging Records Management entry and click Properties.**

   The Messaging Management Records dialog box appears, as shown in Figure 5-7. Note that there is a single space for the policy you want to use. You must provide a single policy for each user that requires managed folders as part of his or her Exchange Server experience. However, the user policy need not be unique. If a group of users all have the same entries required for their mailbox, you can use the same policy for each user.

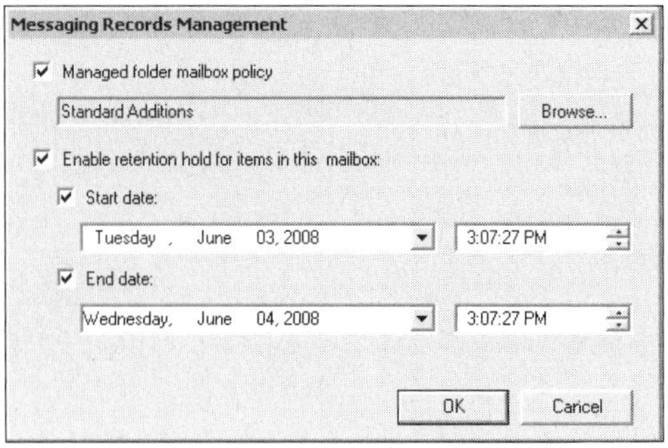

Figure 5-7:
Configure
a messag-
ing records
manage-
ment entry
for users
who access
managed
folders.

Messaging Records Management   ☒

☑ Managed folder mailbox policy

Standard Additions   Browse...

☑ Enable retention hold for items in this mailbox:

  ☑ Start date:

    Tuesday ,   June   03, 2008   ▼   3:07:27 PM   ⬍

  ☑ End date:

    Wednesday,   June   04, 2008   ▼   3:07:27 PM   ⬍

                                    OK   Cancel

4. **Select Managed Folder Mailbox Policy. Click Browse, highlight an entry in the Select Managed Folder Mailbox Policy dialog box, and click OK.**

    The policy appears in the Messaging Management Records dialog box (refer to Figure 5-7).

5. **(Optional) Select Retention Hold for Items in This Mailbox.**

    This feature holds items in the mailbox even if the managed folder settings would normally delete them or interact with them in some other way.

    a. **(Optional) Select Start Date. Choose a starting date and a starting time.**

    b. **(Optional) Select End Date. Choose an ending data and an ending time.**

6. **Click OK twice.**

    Exchange Management Console assigns the managed folders to the user. You may see a warning dialog box at this point. Outlook 2003 SP2 and older can't use managed folders. Make sure you block these older versions using the Set-CASMailbox command.

Scheduling Managed Folder Assistant

The policies you apply to a user's account don't take effect immediately. You must run Managed Folder Assistant to apply the changes you've made to the user's account. Microsoft doesn't enable Managed Folder Assistant by default to give you time to complete a setup before the first changes appear as part of the user's account. If you have multiple Exchange Servers, you must enable Managed Folder Assistant on each server. The following steps tell how to enable Managed Folder Assistant:

1. **Choose the Server Configuration\Mailbox folder.**

The upper half of the Results pane shows a list of servers that you can manage.

2. **Right-click the server you want to manage and choose Properties from the context menu.**

3. **Click the Messaging Records Management tab.**

4. **Click Customize.**

   You see a Schedule dialog box where you can set a time for Managed Folder Assistant to run.

5. **Schedule times for the Managed Folder Assistant to run (grayed squares show run times).**

   It's important that you choose a time when the user is unlikely to have his or her mailbox open to ensure that the user sees the changes as soon as possible. Running Managed Folder Assistant also slows server performance, so you want to choose a time when the server is least loaded.

6. **Click OK.**

   Notice that the Schedule the Managed Folder Assistant field automatically changes to Use Custom Schedule. If you don't see this change, select Use Custom Schedule from the drop-down list box.

7. **Click OK.**

   The changes you make to the managed folder setup appear only after Managed Folder Assistant runs. Consequently, you won't see changes you make immediately in most cases unless you run Managed Folder Assistant by scheduling it to run at the current time.

Working with Users

Users have a number of special needs. For example, they need help managing calendars, booking resources such as conference rooms, and adding out-of-office times using a number of special Exchange Server features. Exchange Server 2007 adds a considerable number of changes to the user experience that become available only after the user connects to Exchange Server. As an administrator, you can help the user become aware of these changes and possibly provide some training on using them. A complete discussion of these features is outside the scope of this book (we're focusing on Exchange Server 2007 specifically). However, it's also important to know where to find additional information about these new client features. The best place to review the features is at `http://technet.microsoft.com/en-us/library/aa998820(EXCHG.80).aspx`.

These features rely on Exchange Server, so you also need to interact with them to an extent. A few of these features, such as Calendar Attendant and Resource Booking Attendant, require use of Exchange Management Shell; these are discussed in Chapter 12. The new calendar features, such as Scheduling Assistant, require use of the Availability and Autodiscover services. You may find that you have to troubleshoot these services; troubleshooting techniques for them are discussed in Chapter 9. The following sections provide information about the few configuration tasks you must perform to work with the new user features.

Configuring Message Folders

The default Exchange Server configuration for message folders comes with a standard set of settings that meet most needs. However, most organizations have at least a few special needs, such as tracking who has access to the company car at a given time or which piece of equipment is checked out at the moment. In addition, users have special needs, such as a requirement to access their e-mail using a mobile device. Fortunately, message folders come in a variety of forms and provide a myriad of adjustments. The following sections describe how you can use these alternatives to your benefit.

Modifying the calendar retrieval options for IMAP4 and POP3

Exchange Server provides a number of methods for retrieving calendars using either IMAP4 or POP3. The following steps describe how to access and modify these settings:

1. **Choose the Server Configuration\Client Access folder. Click the POP3 and IMAP4 tab.**

   You see the POP3 and IMAP4 entries in the lower half of the Results pane.

2. **Select the Server you want to modify in the upper half of the Results pane.**

3. **Double-click the POP3 or IMAP4 icon.**

   Exchange Management Console displays the protocol's Properties dialog box.

4. **Click the Retrieval Settings tab.**

   You see a list of calendar retrieval options, as shown in Figure 5-8.

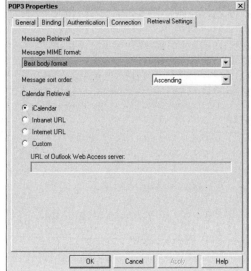

Figure 5-8:
The calen-
dar retrieval
options pro-
vide some
flexibility in
obtaining
calendar
information.

5. **Select one of the calendar retrieval options. If you select the Custom option, you must also provide the URL of the Outlook Web Access server.**

6. **Click OK.**

Exchange Server makes the requested retrieval change.

Both POP3 and IMAP4 support four retrieval options, including the Custom option:

- ✔ **iCalendar:** Relies on the iCalendar standard for exchanging calendar information. You can discover more about iCalendar at `http://www.ietf.org/rfc/rfc2445.txt`. The article at `http://www.w3.org/2000/01/foo.html` is also helpful because it provides an explanation of the standard.

- ✔ **Intranet URL:** Lets you specify an internal URL for retrieving calendar information.

- ✔ **Internet URL:** Lets you specify an external URL for retrieving calendar information.

- ✔ **Custom:** Uses the OWA URL to retrieve calendar information.

Working with the alternative mailboxes

Microsoft supplies three alternative mailboxes for Exchange Server. These alternative mailboxes help you manage rooms and equipment. In addition, you can create links between mailboxes. The following sections describe how to uses these alternative mailboxes.

Creating a room mailbox

The room mailbox doesn't belong to a user; it belongs to a room. As such, you really don't expect the room to receive e-mail. Microsoft disables the e-mail address associated with this mailbox. Instead, a room relies on a calendar for scheduling. The following steps describe how to create a room mailbox:

1. **Choose the Recipient Configuration\Mailbox folder.**

2. **Click New Mailbox in the Actions pane.**

   You see the New Mailbox dialog box shown in Figure 5-9.

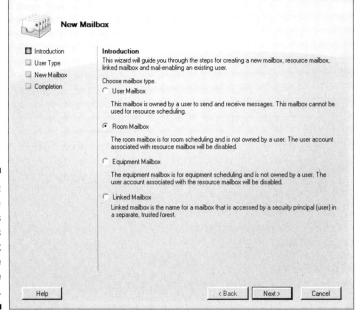

Figure 5-9:
Use the options in this dialog box to create alternative mailboxes.

3. **Select Room Mailbox and click Next.**

4. **Select New User.**

The wizard asks whether you want to create a new user or use an existing user. Unless you have room information already entered into Active Directory, you select New User. The wizard isn't really asking you about a new user, it needs to know about the room.

5. **Click Next.**

The wizard displays a User Information dialog box. You won't use all the fields in this dialog box. The room doesn't have a first or last name, for example, so you simply provide an entry in the Name field.

6. **Type a room number or other name in the Name field.**

7. **Type the content that you provided in the Name field earlier in the User Logon Name field.**

Make certain that the Name and User Logon Name fields provide unique values.

8. **Type a password in both the Password and Confirm Password fields.**

9. **Click Next.**

You see a mailbox settings dialog box. It doesn't pay to fill out any of this information because the room mailbox can't access the e-mail account.

10. **Click Browse, select a mailbox database entry in the Select Mailbox Database dialog box, and click OK.**

11. **Click Next.**

The wizard presents a summary of the new mailbox.

12. **Click New and then Finish.**

Exchange Management Console creates the mailbox. Note that a room mailbox uses a different icon than a user mailbox. The icon and name difference from a normal user should make it easy to spot a room mailbox in the list. At this point, you might think you're finished, but a room mailbox provides an additional feature that you should configure.

13. **Double-click the new room mailbox entry. Click the Resource Information tab.**

You see the resource information shown in Figure 5-10. It's essential to fill out this tab; otherwise people won't know anything about the room unless they physically inspect it. At a minimum, provide the room capacity and a listing of its features, such as a network connection or whiteboard.

14. **Type the number of people that the room holds in the Resource Capacity field.**

15. **Click Add, select a resource in the Select Resource Custom Property dialog box, and click OK.**

    You should see one or more custom resources that you can define for this room. If you don't see any entries, create entries using the Set-ResourceConfig command described in Chapter 12. The Select Resource Custom Property dialog box displays only room-specific property values, so you won't see any equipment values in this case.

16. **Click OK.**

    The room mailbox is now configured. You can add other properties using the techniques described in the "Setting the user mailbox properties" section of the chapter.

Creating an equipment mailbox

The equipment mailbox helps you schedule equipment of any type in your organization — everything from a heavy-duty truck to a screen projector. In fact, you should consider creating an equipment mailbox for every piece of equipment in your organization that has multiple users. As with the room mailbox, the e-mail address for this mailbox type is disabled.

You use the same process to create an equipment mailbox that you do to create a room mailbox. Simply perform the steps in the preceding section, but choose Equipment Mailbox instead of Room Mailbox in Step 3. When you finish the procedure, you see an equipment mailbox whose icon differs from the user mailbox and room mailbox icons. The name should also tell you that this is an equipment mailbox.

Defining a linked mailbox

You use a linked mailbox to access e-mail found in another trusted, forest. An enterprise administrator could use a linked mailbox to access e-mail from every forest of responsibility. This feature makes sense only in very large organizations with a number of Active Directory forests. The following steps describe how to create a linked mailbox:

1. **Choose the Recipient Configuration\Mailbox folder.**

2. **Click New Mailbox in the Actions pane.**

   You see the New Mailbox dialog box (refer to Figure 5-9).

3. **Select Linked Mailbox and click Next.**

   The wizard asks whether you want to create a new user or use an existing user. The account you choose can't have a mailbox already associated with it. In most cases, this means you must create a new account for the link.

4. **Select New User and click Next.**

   The wizard displays a User Information dialog box. As when you create any other new user account, you use all of the fields in the dialog box.

5. **Click Browse, choose an organizational unit from the Select an Organization Unit dialog box, and click OK.**

6. **Type first name, initials, and last name in the appropriate fields.**

   The wizard automatically enters a name in the Name field for you.

7. **In the User Logon Name field, type the user's logon name.**

8. **In both the Password and Confirm Password fields, type a password.**

9. **Click Next.**

   You see a mailbox settings dialog box. As with any user account, you choose the options for this user. However, you must also remember that this is a linked account, so you may not need all the local special additions. Choose a policy that works with the remote account, rather than based on local requirements.

10. **Click Browse next to the Mailbox Database field, choose an option in the Select Mailbox Database dialog box, and click OK.**

11. **(Optional) Select Managed Folder Mailbox Policy. Click Browse next to the Managed Folder Mailbox Policy field, choose a policy in the Select Managed Folder Mailbox Policy dialog box, and click OK.**

12. **(Optional) Select Exchange ActiveSync Mailbox Policy. Click Browse next to the Exchange ActiveSync Mailbox Policy field, choose a policy in the Select Exchange ActiveSync Mailbox Policy dialog box, and click OK.**

13. **Click Next.**

    The wizard displays the Master Account dialog box shown in Figure 5-11. This dialog box lets you enter all the information required to create a link between the local mailbox and the mailbox on the remote system.

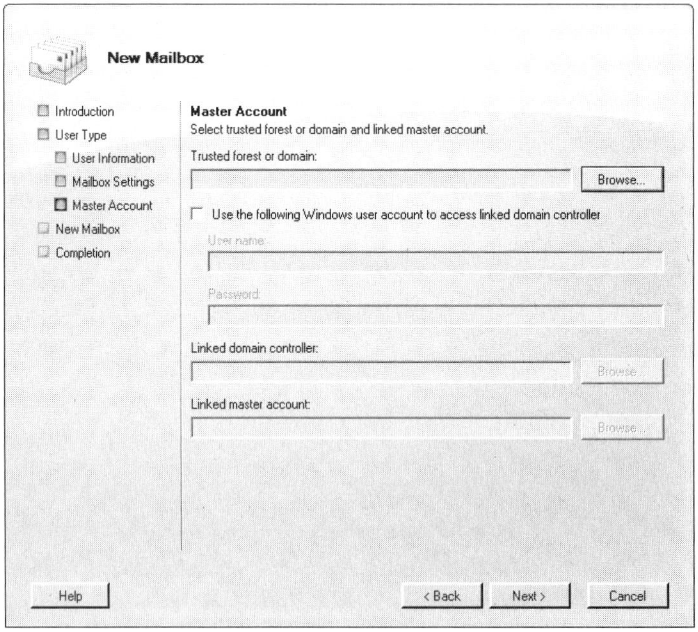

Figure 5-11:
Provide the required remote link information.

14. **Click Browse next to the Trusted Forest or Domain field, choose an entry in the Select Trusted Forest or Domain dialog box, and click OK.**

15. **(Optional) Select the Use the Following Windows User Account to Access the Linked Domain Controller. Type the appropriate values in the User Name and Password fields.**

16. **Click Browse next to the Linked Domain Controller field, choose an entry in the Select Linked Domain Controller dialog box, and click OK.**

17. **Click Browse next to the Linked Master Account field, choose an entry in the Select Linked Master Account dialog box, and click OK.**

18. **Click Next.**

    The wizard presents a summary of the new mailbox.

19. **Click New and then click Finish.**

    Exchange Management Console creates the mailbox. Note that a room mailbox uses a different icon than a user mailbox. The icon and name difference from a standard user mailbox should make it easy to spot a room mailbox in the list. At this point, you might think you're finished, but a room mailbox provides an additional feature that you should configure.

Setting the user mailbox properties

Every user mailbox contains a number of settings you can use to make that user's Exchange Server experience better. Whenever you double-click a user entry, you see a Properties dialog box like the one shown in Figure 5-12. The tabs on this dialog box provide configuration settings in three essential areas as described in the following sections.

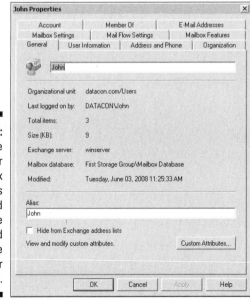

Figure 5-12: Configure the user mailbox properties as needed to provide a good Exchange Server experience.

Defining general and user information

The General, User Information, Address and Phone, and Organization tabs provide essential information about the user. This information tells you who the user is, where the user works within the organization, and the user's manager name. The following list describes each of these tabs:

- ✔ **General:** Contains information about the user's physical mailbox. For example, this is the tab where you find the user's mailbox size and the number of items it contains. This tab also contains an interesting setting, Hide from Exchange Address Lists. Select this option and no one can see this mailbox. This is an exceptionally useful feature for accounts that you'd rather remain out of sight. Click Custom Attributes and you can enter custom attributes — items that the other tabs don't cover — for this particular user.

- ✔ **User Information:** Contains basic information about the user including name, display name, Web page URL, and any notes you have about the user.

- ✔ **Address and Phone:** Provides contact information for the user. This tab provides places for more than one telephone number, including the user's cellular (mobile) phone number.

- ✔ **Organization:** Details the user's organizational information such as company, title, department, and manager. A Direct Reports field shows any users that this user manages.

Configuring the mailbox-specific settings

The mailbox-specific settings appear on the Mailbox Settings, Mail Flow Settings, and Mailbox Features tabs. These tabs are probably the most important tabs when it comes to user mailbox configuration. In fact, entries from these tabs appear in a number of places in the book (including this chapter). The following list provides a brief overview of these tabs:

- ✔ **Mailbox Settings:** Defines physical aspects of the mailbox database. The two entries used in this book are Messaging Records Management and Storage Quotas.

- ✔ **Mail Flow Settings:** Shows how messages flow from this mailbox to other mailboxes. The three entries control delivery options, message size restrictions, and message delivery restrictions.

- ✔ **Mailbox Features:** Contains a list of features the user can access, such as Outlook Web Express, Exchange ActiveSync, Unified Messaging, MAPI, POP3, and IMAP4. You see these options described in a number of places in the book. If a feature is enabled, the user can interact with it.

Understanding the account and security settings

Security is an important part of any configuration. Chapter 6 provides a full discussion of security features that Exchange Server provides. The user mailbox security and account settings appear on the Account, Member Of, and E-mail Addresses tabs. The following list provides an overview of each of these tabs:

- ✔ **Account:** Defines the user's logon name.
- ✔ **Member Of:** Provides a list of groups to which the user belongs. The group affiliation determines rights that the user has on the system and presents one of the ways to control user access.
- ✔ **E-mail Addresses:** Contains a list of one or more e-mail addresses that the user can employ to access the mailbox.

Using Public Folder Management Console

Public Folder Management Console helps you manage folders that are accessible to Exchange Server users. The user sees these folders in a number of ways, but not always directly. For example, when a user clicks his or her address book, the user actually sees the content of the Offline Address Book folder, but not directly — the user sees it as an address book. Exchange Server provides access to a number of default (custom) and system public folders. In most cases, you won't need to interact with the system public folders — Exchange Server maintains them for you. However, you may want to create and use default public folders to store special information for the user.

You access Public Folder Management Console by double-clicking its entry in the Toolbox folder of Exchange Management Console. Public Folder Management Console doesn't provide any default public folders as part of the initial installation, but it does provide a wealth of system public folders. Figure 5-13 shows the collection of folders you can expect to see after installation.

As shown in Figure 5-13, the number of public system folders is extensive. The following sections describe how to create and interact with public default folders. The same techniques work with the public system folders. However, you want to modify the public system folders with care because incorrect modifications can prevent some client application folder features from working properly.

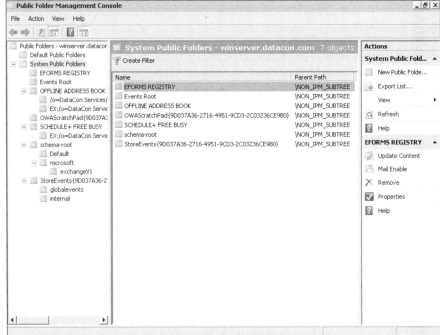

Figure 5-13:
Use Public
Folder
Manage-
ment
Console
to access
public
Exchange
Server
folders.

Creating new folders

Using the Default Public Folders folder as a starting point, you can create individual public folders and hierarchies of folders. These folders can store everything from shared user data to reports on the status of a project. You use these folders as you would any other folder. The difference is that these folders appear in the user's e-mail client and the user can access these folders wherever they might be without using anything more than the e-mail client application. The following steps describe how to create a new public folder:

1. **Highlight the parent folder you want to use to hold the public folder.**

   The uppermost folders that you can select are Default Public Folders and System Public Folders.

2. **Click New Public Folder in the Actions pane.**

   You see the New Public Folder dialog box.

3. **Type a name for the folder in the Name field.**

4. **Click New and then click Finish.**

   The wizard adds the new folder under the parent folder you selected.

Modifying existing folders

It isn't possible to modify the properties of the Default Public Folders folder and System Public Folders folder. However, you can modify the properties of any folder that these two parent folders contain. To modify a child folder, select the parent folder in the left pane, highlight its entry in the Results pane, and choose an activity from the Actions pane. The following sections describe the tasks you can perform with the child folders.

Viewing folder properties

The major difference between a mail-enabled folder and a default folder is the properties you can change. A mail-enabled folder provides access to all the tabs described in the following list. However, a default folder provides access to only the General, Replication, and Limits tabs:

- ✔ **General:** Displays the name of the folder, along with the number of items the folder contains, the folder space usage on disk, its last modification date, and the database in which the folder appears. The one setting that this tab contains is important. Exchange Server maintains information about whether each user has read the content of the folder. If you deselect this option, only one person has to read a particular item to mark it as read.

- ✔ **Replication:** Determines how Exchange Server replicates (copies) the content of the folder for backup purposes. The default setting uses the public folder database replication schedule, which is normally all you need to protect the data. Using a custom schedule tends to affect Exchange Server performance negatively.

- ✔ **Limits:** Defines the quota, retention, and age limits for the items in the folder. The quota limits define the size of the folder. Retention limits affect how long Exchange Server retains deleted items so that you can recover them. The age limits define how long Exchange Server maintains replicas.

- ✔ **Exchange General:** Shows the alias, display name, and simple display name of the folder. You can also choose to hide the folder from Exchange address lists and set custom attributes for the folder.

- ✔ **E-mail Addresses:** Contains a list of one or more e-mail addresses that the user can employ to access the folder.

- ✔ **Member Of:** Provides a list of groups to which the folder belongs.

- ✔ **Mail Flow Settings:** Shows how messages flow from this mailbox to other mailboxes. The three entries control delivery options, message size restrictions, and message delivery restrictions.

Mail-enabling a folder

Mail-enabling a folder makes it accessible in the client e-mail application. Simply click Mail Enable in the Actions pane to make the folder accessible.

After you mail enable a folder, you see a new entry in the Actions pane, Manage Send As. When you click this option, you see the Manage Send As Permission dialog box. Every name that appears in this list can send messages using this public folder. Consequently, you can use the public folder for communication between members of a project if desired.

Removing unneeded folders

At some point, you won't need a particular folder any longer. When you want to remove a folder, highlight its entry in the Results pane and click Remove in the Actions pane. Microsoft Exchange will ask whether you're sure you want to remove the folder. Click Yes to complete the action.

Configuring Distribution Groups

Distribution groups make working with other users considerably easier because you can address a single group rather than each user individually. Chapter 3 discusses distribution groups as part of the recipient configuration. You find a discussion of dynamic distribution groups, which are a helpful performance aid in some situations, in the "Considering the use of dynamic distribution groups" section of Chapter 11. The following sections discuss how to create and configure standard distribution groups.

Creating a distribution group

As mentioned, a distribution group provides a method for addressing a group of users using a single name. Consequently, the first task in creating a distribution group is to create the list of names that will appear as part of the distribution group. For example, you might create a list of all managers in an organization for a manager distribution group or a list of all members of a particular project. You must also exercise care in creating groups — too many groups can prove confusing to users, making them almost worse than not creating enough of the right groups. The following steps describe how to create a group:

1. **Choose the Recipient Configuration\Distribution Group folder.**

   You see zero or more groups listed in the Results pane. Exchange Server doesn't provide any default groups.

2. **Click New Distribution Group in the Actions pane.**

   Exchange Management Console displays the New Distribution Group dialog box.

3. **Choose New Group and click Next.**

   The wizard asks you to provide some distribution group information.

4. **(Optional) Click Browse, choose an organizational unit in the Select Organizational Unit dialog box, and click OK.**

   You need to select a new organizational unit only when the default organizational unit places the group in the wrong place in the Active Directory hierarchy. Exchange Server normally provides the correct location when working with a smaller Active Directory hierarchy.

5. **Type a group name in the Name field.**

   The wizard automatically fills out the content of the Name (Pre-Windows 2000) and Alias fields. However, you can type new values in these fields if desired.

6. **Click Next.**

   The wizard presents a summary of the new group.

7. **Click New and then Finish.**

   The new group is ready for use.

Defining distribution group properties

Creating a new group doesn't make it useful. The new group doesn't have any members, so e-mailing the group doesn't send the message anywhere. You must also provide security settings for the new group so it has the right to perform certain tasks. To modify an existing group, double-click its entry in the Recipient Configuration\Distribution Group folder. The following list describes the purpose of each tab in the resulting Properties dialog box:

- **General:** Displays the group name and alias. Click Custom Attributes to assign custom values, such as group purpose, to the group.

- **Group Information:** Displays the group name, pre-Windows 2000 name, manager name, and notes about the group.

- **Members:** Presents a list of group members. New groups don't have any members. To add new members, click Add, highlight names in the Select Recipient dialog box, and click OK. Delete members by highlighting their names in the list and clicking Delete. You can use Ctrl+click to select multiple names in a list.

- **Member Of:** Provides a list of groups to which the group belongs.

✔ **E-mail Addresses:** Contains a list of one or more e-mail addresses that the group can employ to access the mailbox.

✔ **Advanced:** Configures special group features. The Simple Display Name field contains a short non-Unicode version of the group name that the user can see in older e-mail clients. The Expansion Server defines which server to use to expand the group membership to send out messages to individual members. You can also use this tab to configure the group so no one can see it in the Exchange address list and so the group sends an out-of-office message when appropriate. Finally, this tab lets you tell Exchange Server where to send delivery reports (a message saying who received the group message) or whether to send the delivery report at all.

✔ **Mail Flow Settings:** Shows how messages flow from this group to system mailboxes. The two entries control message size restrictions and message delivery restrictions.

Chapter 6

Configuring Security

. . . .

In This Chapter

▶ Configuring user security

▶ Configuring mailbox security

▶ Tracking user activities

▶ Providing antispam support

▶ Keeping viruses and other malware at bay

▶ Encrypting your data

. . . .

Security is a hot word today. Depending on whom you talk to, security can be drudgery, the most important part of the configuration, or something in-between. Every administrator is aware of security today because of the problems that have occurred at every level — everything from e-mail used in court situations to lost customer data. The most important concept you can take from this chapter is that you must address security because you simply can't ignore it and keep your data safe any longer.

It would be nice to say that this single chapter has everything you need to secure Exchange Server. Unfortunately, an entire book can't discuss the topic in adequate detail to ensure success. This chapter does provide the essentials of security Exchange Server. When you combine the information in this chapter with proper operating system security, network security, and user security training, you have a good chance of keeping your setup moderately secure.

Fortunately, Microsoft does give you a hand with security in Exchange Server 2007. As with many Microsoft products today, Exchange Server is shipped to present a low security risk. You must actually open security holes to use the product successfully. In fact, adding users, creating groups, starting services (such as POP3 and IMAP4), and all of the other configuration tasks in previous chapters have opened security holes that let Exchange Server work for you. The essential role of this chapter is to help you close unnecessary security holes you created during the configuration process.

To secure your system, this chapter helps you configure user and mailbox security, track user activities, and provide both antispam and antivirus support. In addition, the chapter shows what you need to do to encrypt your data so that no one can read it (at least, not immediately) should it get into the wrong hands.

Shorter URLs headed your way

This chapter contains a new experiment, and I'd appreciate hearing your comments on it. Microsoft has a habit of providing extremely long, nearly impossible to type URLs. The TinyURL Web site (`http://tinyurl.com/`) can take these long URLs and make them considerably shorter in most cases (I won't use a TinyURL when it doesn't save space). This chapter contains both the standard URL and the TinyURL for every Web site. I need to know whether you find the TinyURL easier to use and whether you're confident that the TinyURL will lead you to the right place. My goal in using TinyURL is to make your life easier. Of course, I also want you to feel secure in using the URLs presented in my books. Future offerings will contain either the original URL or the TinyURL, but not both. Please let me know what you think of TinyURL by writing me at `JMueller@mwt.net`.

Setting User Security

Exchange Server security and Windows security are tied together when it comes to the user. Select the Recipient Configuration/Mailbox folder in Exchange Management console. Double-click a user and click the Member Of tab. What you see is a list of groups to which the user belongs, as shown in Figure 6-1. Note that many of these groups are the same groups that you use with Windows to provide user security.

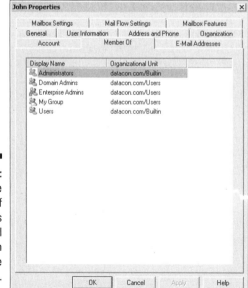

Figure 6-1:
The Member Of tab shows user-level security in Exchange Server.

The exception in the list shown in Figure 6-1 is the My Group entry. The My Group entry provides access to a distribution group in Exchange Server. It's possible to create both distribution and security groups in Exchange Server. A *distribution* group controls e-mail flow, and a *security* group controls both e-mail flow and access to mailboxes. When you view the Member Of tab, you must consider that some entries come from Exchange Server and others come from Windows.

Figure 6-1 also shows the most important security risk that you should overcome in your organization. Anyone who has administrator privileges should use a separate account when working with e-mail. Even administrators receive e-mail that contains malware. In many instances, all it takes is a single click for that malware to use the administrator privileges to do some nasty things to the local machine and then follow them up on the network.

You use the same practices you always have for modifying the user's Windows security and the Windows group security. Nothing changes with Exchange Server. However, you also need to configure both user and group message restrictions and the Active Directory portion of a distribution group's security. The message restrictions appear on the Mail Flow Settings tab of the user or group Properties dialog box. You use the Active Directory Users and Computers console to modify the distribution group security settings. The following sections describe these tasks.

Understanding message delivery options

Exchange Server doesn't enable the message delivery options contained in the Delivery Options dialog box shown in Figure 6-2 by default. There isn't any need to enable the Send On Behalf feature unless you want to allow someone to send e-mail on someone else's behalf. This feature is used when someone is acting on behalf of someone else, such as an assistant who takes reservations for conference rooms.

It's important to understand precisely what the Send On Behalf feature does — the recipient of the message will see the e-mail address of the room or other object, not the e-mail address of the assistant. Consequently, someone with ill intent could use this feature for spoofing. The e-mail the person sends would appear to come from someone else's e-mail address. It's important not to enable this feature unless you really need to do so. Consider not using the feature and simply telling others to contact the alternate e-mail address directly.

The Forwarding Address field isn't as big a concern. This option sends e-mail from a particular address to the address you specify. You could use this option to allow someone to answer business e-mail for someone else while that person is on vacation. Of course, the vacationing employee won't want their personal e-mail read, so you still need to use this option with extreme care.

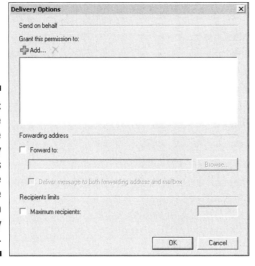

Figure 6-2:
Use the
message
delivery
options
with care
because
they open
a security
hole.

If you have worries about spam in your organization, the Recipients Limits field can be a real plus. Check Maximum Recipients and type a number into the associated field to keep users from sending e-mails to more than a few people. In fact, you may want to make this one of the mandatory security changes for your organization to keep e-mail distribution under control and reduce the risk that an employee will use their e-mail account to send spam.

Using message size restrictions as a security aid

The Message Size Restrictions dialog box shown in Figure 6-3 may not seem like much of a security feature at first. However, you can use it as such. By limiting the size of messages that a user can receive, you can potentially eliminate some of the newer security hazards on the Internet. For example, if you set the receive size small enough, the user won't be able to receive one of those nasty new pictures that deliver a virus or other malware payload.

No, the Receiving Message Size feature doesn't provide any sizeable protection, but every little bit helps. Of course, this option won't work if your users regularly receive large files as part of your business — annoying users by not allowing them to receive their business e-mail is a good way to keep them from following the rules.

Limiting the sending message size can potentially help once the user's system is compromised by reducing the risk that a virus will send large amounts of data to the virus creator. Theoretically, the malware creator could simply send the data in smaller pieces or not send it using e-mail, but most malware doesn't have the elegant programming required to perform this task. Of course, many pieces of malware simply make a direct connection to a Web site, eliminating the need to use e-mail as a transport.

Figure 6-3:
Limiting
the mes-
sage size
can reduce
the risk of
receiving
unwanted
graphics.

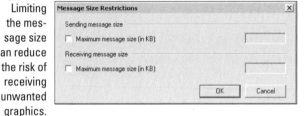

Modifying message delivery restrictions

The optimal way to control e-mail delivery is to place a restriction on it using the features found in the Message Delivery Restrictions dialog box shown in Figure 6-4. The best option when you rely on Exchange Server for internal e-mail deliver is to select the Require That All Senders Are Authenticated option. Selecting this option would disallow anyone outside the company from delivering messages to the account. Unfortunately, you won't have this option in many cases because most companies require Internet access in addition to internal access.

If you want to follow an extremely restrictive policy, you can select Only Senders in the Following List and then select the senders that the mailbox will allow. This approach is practical in only a few cases, such as an e-mail account used by a group for only group-specific messages.

The other approach is to reject messages from particular groups. You can create a list of users that can't send e-mail to a particular group. To some extent, this is a practical approach to keep unwanted e-mail at bay, but it means knowing the e-mail address of the groups you want to reject in advance. The "Understanding Content Filtering" section of this chapter provides techniques you can use for the Internet at large, where you won't necessarily know about senders before they send e-mail.

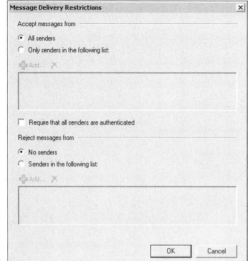

Figure 6-4:
Keep
outsiders at
bay by
disallowing
certain
kinds of
e-mail
delivery.

Modifying the Active Directory view of distribution groups

You can't access all the settings for distribution groups from within Exchange Management Console. Active Directory supports two important settings for distribution groups that you access using the Active Directory Users and Computers console found in the Administrative Tools folder of Control Panel. In most cases, you find the distribution groups in the domain Users folder, unless you specified another location when you created the distribution group. Double-click the distribution group you want to modify and you see the settings shown in Figure 6-5 on the General tab.

The Group Scope setting affects where the distribution group is used. The default setting is Universal, which means that the distribution group is accessible from any domain or forest. The Global setting limits accessibility to any domain within the current forest, while the Domain Local setting limits accessibility to just the current domain. You can see a comparison of the settings at `http://technet2.microsoft.com/windowsserver/en/library/79d93e46-ecab-4165-8001-7adc3c9f804e1033.mspx` or `http://tinyurl.com/4u9ano`. The point of this setting is to limit the availability of a distribution group to where you actually need it. Giving too much accessibility to a distribution group presents a security risk because you expose the distribution group to more potential users. In most cases, you want to change this setting to present the lowest possible accessibility.

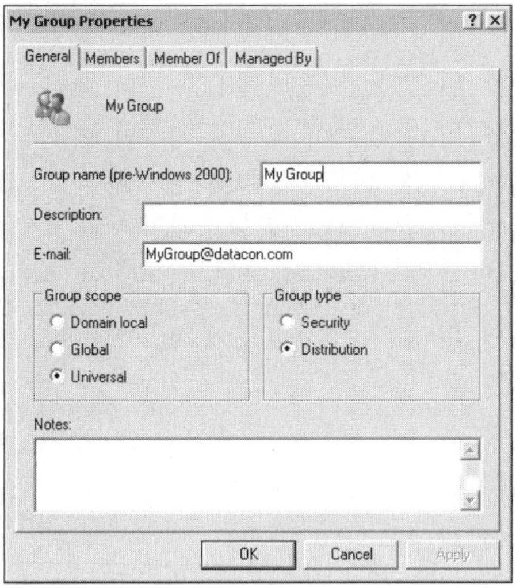

Figure 6-5:
Distribution
groups pro-
vide special
settings.

The Group Type setting affects how you can use the distribution group. The Distribution setting means that you can use the distribution group only as a means of distributing e-mail. This limitation makes the distribution group more secure because users can't use it for anything but its intended purpose of sending e-mail, rather than resources, to someone else. The Security setting has a number of implications, but the important consideration is that you can use it as an entry within a Discretionary Access Control List (DACL), which means you can use it to give someone rights. These rights can include providing access to shared resources. You can find a complete description of the additional rights at `http://technet2.microsoft.com/windowsserver/en/library/95107162-47eb-4891-832f-0c0b15b7c8581033.mspx` or `http://tinyurl.com/3gk5rt`.

Setting Mailbox Security

Exchange Server 2007 provides a significant amount of mailbox security. Every user's mailbox is essentially private at the outset. Even the administrator can't see the content of a user's mailbox. Consequently, because only the user can see the mailbox, the mailbox is about as secure as it possibly can be from prying eyes. (This section doesn't consider what the user does with the mailbox, such as loading malware onto the client system that reports the content of the mailbox through Outlook or another client application.) The administrator does have three means for modifying the security of a mailbox:

✔ **Journaling:** You use journaling to send copies of a message from the user's mailbox to a mailbox set aside as a journal store. Exchange Server makes it possible to use journaling with a single user or a group. The "Configuring a managed folder" section of Chapter 5 describes how to create a managed folder that has journaling in place. You can also double-click the managed content settings object after you create it and add journaling later by modifying the settings on the Journaling tab.

✔ **Send as permission:** This permission lets someone send messages as if he or she is the mailbox owner. In most cases, you don't want to enable this feature unless you truly want someone to respond for the mailbox owner. For example, a group leader could send messages as the entire group when needed. An assistant can respond with confirmations when someone sends e-mail to a room. However, it's usually less confusing and more straightforward for everyone to simply use their own account. The "Mail-enabling a folder" section of Chapter 5 describes how you use this feature with mail folders.

✔ **Full access permission:** The full access permission gives someone complete access to a particular mailbox. The owner of the mailbox has this permission by default. This permission gives a third party the same access. Assigning this permission is dangerous to say the least because you not only let a third party act as the owner of the mailbox but also potentially cause privacy breaches. In general, if you want to monitor a user, you should rely on journaling. One of the few occasions on which this permission is useful is when you want someone to manage a group mailbox.

You might want to provide a send as permission for a particular mailbox in certain situations. Assigning the send as permission to a mailbox after you create it requires a slightly different procedure than when you assign it during the creation process. To set the send as permission on a particular mailbox, right-click the entry you want to modify in the Recipient Configuration\Mailbox folder of Exchange Management Console and choose Manage Send As Permission from the context menu. The Manage Send As Permission dialog box appears, as shown in Figure 6-6. Click Add, choose one or more entries in the Select User or Group dialog box, and click OK.

The full access permission is required when you create a group mailbox and want one person to manage it. The only person who can normally manage a mailbox is the owner, which may not be anyone in a group situation.

To set the full access permission on a particular mailbox, right-click the entry you want to modify in the Recipient Configuration\Mailbox folder of Exchange Management Console and choose Manage Full Access Permission from the context menu. The Manage Full Access Permission dialog box appears, as shown in Figure 6-7. Note that the dialog box contains the NT AUTHORITY\ SELF entry. It's important to remember this entry because you use it to make security modifications in the Windows environment. Click Add, choose one or more entries in the Select User or Group dialog box, and click OK.

Considering the entire security picture

Many organizations view security as a yes or no kind of a setting. Unfortunately, security changes as the environment in which the server, the application, and how the user operates changes. A security setting that works fine today may not be a good idea tomorrow. Consequently, security is a continuum of the settings that work best in a particular scenario, making it very much like those psychological questions where there's no wrong answer, simply the answer that works for a particular situation.

Security isn't defined by a single piece of a solution either. You can't stop thinking about security at the border of Exchange Server or with Windows as a whole. Security requires efforts from every part of the solution: the network, operating system, application, and user. Many exploits today combine minor flaws from multiple sources. A security hole in Windows may not do the trick for a nefarious individual, but combining a minor hole in Windows with a minor hole in an application may be enough to lay your organization's data bare to an unscrupulous individual.

Even after you define a good security policy and enforce it, you can't stop thinking about security. Anyone with the proper tools can overcome the best security measures you have in place — you can't stop someone who is determined. Consequently, you must exercise constant vigilance. Inspect your network for even minor discrepancies because the smallest clue can point out a major security gap. Keep up with the latest security threats as well. It's in your best interest to provide smart security — the kind of security that requires constant effort on your part.

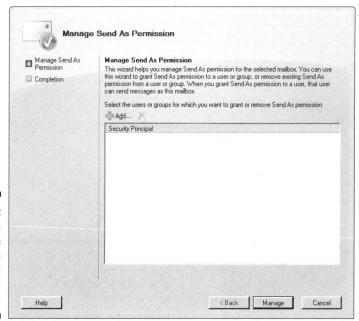

Figure 6-6:
Use the send as permission to let a third party send a message.

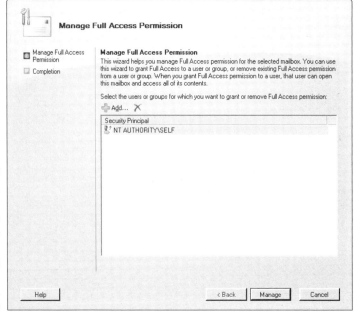

Figure 6-7:
Use the full access permission to give a third party full access to a mailbox.

You can set security also on users and groups, but the entry is actually hidden from view. To see these security settings, open the Active Directory Users and Computers console found in the Administrative Tools folder of Control Panel and choose View⊃Advanced Features. Enabling the advanced features makes additional entries available for each of the options in the Active Directory Users and Computers console. These features generally pose a significant risk when configured incorrectly, which is why Microsoft hides them from view. Always exercise caution when working in advanced features mode.

After you enable the advanced features mode, you can double-click any user or group in the Users folder and set security on the user or group. Figure 6-8 shows the My Group object defined in Chapter 5. Note that the list of users includes SELF. This is the user you should modify when you want to control access to the mailbox itself. It's interesting to go through the permissions list because you find a number of Exchange Server-specific entries, such as Read Exchange Personal Information and Write Exchange Personal Information. The permissions work just as they do for any Windows security configuration.

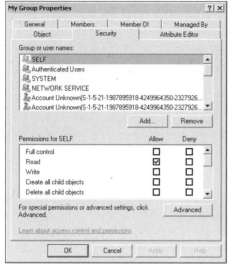

Figure 6-8:
Configure
access to
Exchange
Server
objects,
including
the SELF
object.

Auditing the User

Auditing occurs at a number of levels in Windows. Most of this auditing helps you track user activities in the system. For example, Event Viewer can provide you with important information about Exchange Server activities. Whenever someone makes a change to a user account, you see a 4662 event message, as shown in Figure 6-9. The 4662 event message replaces the older 642 event message in Windows Server 2008 (see `http://searchexchange.techtarget.com/tip/0,289483,sid43_gci1112752,00.html` or `http://tinyurl.com/4meoaq` for details). The new event message contains significantly more information as explained at `http://technet2.microsoft.com/windowsserver2008/en/library/a9c25483-89e2-4202-881c-ea8e02b4b2a51033.mspx` or `http://tinyurl.com/2xur6k`.

You can also choose to audit a particular mailbox, user, or group. A number of confusing ways for performing this task are described on the Internet. The following steps work for Windows Server 2008 and Exchange Server 2007, but may not work with other combinations of products:

1. Choose Start➪Run.

Windows displays the Run dialog box.

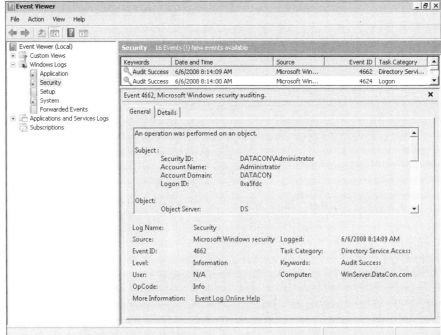

Figure 6-9:
Use Event
Viewer
to track
Exchange
Server
changes.

2. **Type** GPEdit.MSC **and press Enter.**

   Local Group Policy Editor appears. If you want to set up auditing on
   a global basis instead of the local domain, use the GPME.MSC console
   instead. The essential process is the same as using GPEdit.MSC (the
   console that's available on all versions of Windows Server).

3. **Locate the Local Computer Policy\Computer Configuration\Windows
   Settings\Security Settings\Local Polices\Audit Policy folder.**

   The Audit Policy folder shown in Figure 6-10 contains the settings for the
   auditing features of Windows. You can set the auditing policies to monitor success, failure, or both. In this case, you need to provide auditing
   for both directory service access and object access — enabling just one
   of them, contrary to the online instructions that say to enable one or the
   other, doesn't appear to work in Windows Server 2008.

4. **Double-click Audit Directory Service Access, select Success, and
   click OK.**

5. **Double-click Audit Object Access, select Success, and click OK.**

6. **Open the Active Directory Users and Computers console found in the
   Administrative Tools folder of Control Panel.**

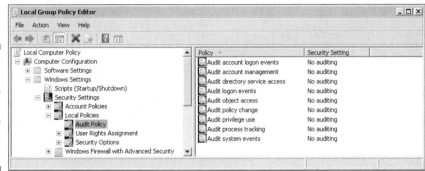

Figure 6-10:
Modify the
audit policy
as required
to verify
changes to
objects.

7. **Choose View⇨Advanced Features.**

   Enabling this option shows you features that you normally don't see in
   this console. One of these advanced features is the ability to set auditing
   on a mailbox or group.

   The Advanced Features setting can also cause problems if you change
   settings that you don't understand completely. Use this viewing mode
   with care.

8. **Double-click a user or mailbox entry in the Users folder.**

   You see a Properties dialog box that contains significantly more tabs
   than normal.

9. **Choose the Security tab.**

   Windows presents a list of security settings for the user or group that
   you've chosen to modify. Note that one of the users for a mailbox is
   SELF. This is the same SELF object that appears in the Full Access
   Permissions dialog box described in the "Setting Mailbox Security" section of the chapter.

10. **Click Advanced and then click the Auditing tab.**

    Windows presents a list of auditing options, as shown in Figure 6-11.
    These auditing options aren't available until you set the security policy as
    described in Steps 1 through 5. Consequently, if you can't access the audit-
    ing features, the Auditing tab lacks entries, or the auditing you configure
    doesn't work, you need to verify that the required policies are in place.

11. **Click Edit.**

    You see an Auditing Entry for the particular group dialog box.

12. **Click the Properties tab and select Write All Properties.**

    This selection means that Windows will audit any change made to the
    user or groups properties. You can also choose specific properties to
    monitor, but it's often easier to monitor all of them.

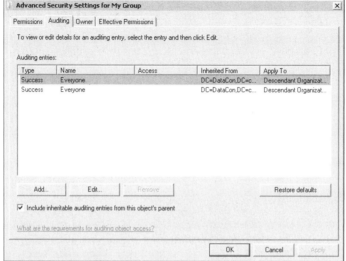

Figure 6-11:
Set the auditing features for your object.

13. **Click OK.**

    You see a new entry added to the auditing list.

14. **Click OK twice to completely close the user or group dialog boxes.**

    The auditing for this user or group is in place. Filter the Event Log for 4662 entries to see any modifications that anyone makes (including changing the auditing) to the user or group object.

Users, the weakest security link

You've heard the stories about the note (Post-It or otherwise) on the monitor and the user who gives a password out to anyone who asks. These stories, and many more, have actually happened — they aren't just tales designed to scare network administrators. The problem is that users are the weak security link in a host of other areas. All it takes is one unsecured download or a simple click on an e-mail attachment to ruin your security plans. Of course, you could simply disallow any outside access, but that strategy definitely won't work today.

The best approach for your weak link is training, written policies, and monitoring. You need all three items to reduce the user security threat. Even though most people will point to this strategy and scream, "Big Brother lives among us!" the fact is that you must maintain a secure environment that keeps the few users from ruining the experience for most users.

Considering Antispam Requirements

Any organization that interacts with the Internet requires antispam support today. Without it, users spend most of their time picking through messages of dubious origin. Of course, most e-mail client programs today have antispam features in them. In addition, an organization can rely on services such as Postini (http://www.postini.com/) to filter incoming e-mail. Although the existing solutions work well, you may want better control over the antispam functionality provided to your organization — and that's where the Exchange Server features come into play.

To provide complete antispam support for your Exchange Server setup, you must install an Edge Transport server on a separate server. In addition, the Edge Transport server must appear outside the existing Active Directory domain, and you normally separate the rest of your network from it using a hardware firewall. In short, some of the antispam features Exchange Server provides entail considerable additional setup and expense. The following sections describe the antispam features and note whether you need the Edge Transport Server to configure them.

Relying on Sender ID

Sender ID is an Edge Transport server feature that views an incoming message to determine what to do with it. The Sender ID appears as part of the header information of the message. When the Edge Transport server sees a message without a Sender ID or a Sender ID it doesn't recognize, it either rejects the message or marks it as unrecognized depending on the policy you set in place. The Edge Transport server does pass any messages with Sender ID values it recognizes. Consequently, you can choose to reject any e-mail from anyone you don't recognize.

In practice, Sender ID performs e-mail message validation. It checks with the domain from which the message was supposedly sent to verify the IP address that sent the message. If the DNS server for that domain doesn't recognize the IP address, the Edge Transport server knows that someone is trying to spoof the message (make it appear that the message comes from a location other than the actual location). Spoofing is a common practice because servers didn't validate e-mail headers in the past. You can read more about how Sender ID works at http://technet.microsoft.com/en-us/library/aa996295(EXCHG.80).aspx or http://tinyurl.com/5nuv38.

The problem with Sender ID is that it conflicts with an industry standard known as Sender Policy Framework (SPF) (see http://www.openspf.org/ for details). You can discover the difference between the two antispam techniques at http://www.openspf.org/SPF_vs_Sender_ID or http://tinyurl.com/3deg5n. The problem with the Microsoft-only solution is that your organization may have multiple e-mail server types. Fortunately, you can install SPF support on your Exchange Server using the information in the article at `http://www.msexchange.org/articles/SPF-support-Exchange-freeware.html` or `http://tinyurl.com/3f8uhr`.

Understanding Content Filtering

Content filtering isn't a new concept. Your e-mail client application likely provides content filtering in the form of rules that you create to prevent certain messages from appearing in your inbox. However, the Content Filtering feature of Exchange Server Edge Transport server adds a certain amount of intelligence to the equation. Like most server-based content filtering technologies, the Content Filtering feature uses a list of sample e-mails to determine whether the e-mail that Exchange Server receives is spam or a legitimate business message. However, unlike most content filtering, this list of messages includes real-world messages to reduce the chance of false positives. In short, Content Filtering "learns" by increasing the size of its database to consider the kind of messages your organization receives. You can read more about Content Filtering at `http://technet.microsoft.com/en-us/library/bb124739(EXCHG.80).aspx` or `http://tinyurl.com/4xlvvd`.

You can further increase the reliability of the Content Filtering feature using Outlook E-mail Postmark Validation. This technology adds a special postmark to the messages your organizations sends. When the Edge Transport server sees this special postmark, it knows that the message has come from a reliable source. Unfortunately, this feature is available only to Outlook 2007 users, which may make it less than useful for your organization. You can read about adding Outlook E-mail Postmark Validation to your server at `http://technet.microsoft.com/en-us/library/aa996016(EXCHG.80).aspx` or `http://tinyurl.com/555p3p`.

In a book, I normally don't debate the effectiveness of a technology based on my observations — I'd much prefer to provide pointers to tests run in professional labs. Unfortunately, there isn't anything on the Internet as of this writing that tells you whether the approach that Microsoft takes with content filtering does what it's supposed to do. During the time I have used Exchange Server and worked with others who have it installed, it appears that the content filtering techniques that Microsoft uses aren't any more effective than those used by other e-mail servers I've worked with, except when it comes to Outlook 2007 clients (both sender and receiver), where it seems to be considerably more effective. The point is that you shouldn't rely on Exchange Server functionality alone — you need to keep the client application features you have implemented in place. I'd love to hear about your experiences with the Exchange Server Content Filtering feature at `JMueller@mwt.net`.

Understanding spam assessment

The spam assessment that Exchange Server provides is a veritable gauntlet of software through which a message must pass before the user sees it. That any e-mail survives is almost surprising. Between the message sender and the message recipient lie eight grueling levels of checks (and still, spam managed to get through):

1. Connection filtering
2. Sender filtering
3. Recipient filtering
4. Sender ID filtering
5. Content filtering
6. Attachment filtering
7. Antivirus scanning
8. Outlook junk e-mail filtering

The output from all these checks is a Spam Confidence Level (SCL) that determines whether the user ever gets to see the e-mail. You can see all these levels in detail at `http://technet.microsoft.com/en-us/library/aa997242(EXCHG.80).aspx` or `http://tinyurl.com/5xl3jk`. Based on all the filtering that Exchange Server provides, it creates an SCL between 0 and 9. As an administrator, you control how Exchange Server reacts to that number. You could choose, for example, to discard any e-mail with an SCL greater than 8, quarantine e-mail between levels 3 and 7, and pass any e-mail with an SCL less than 2. You can discover how modify the SCL level at `http://technet.microsoft.com/en-us/library/aa995744(EXCHG.80).aspx` or `http://tinyurl.com/4ggbf6`.

Considering Antivirus and Other Malware Requirements

Nothing worse can happen to your system than to have a virus attack. A virus can destroy data, make your private data available to third parties, reduce system performance, waste user time, and generally make life miserable. As with antispam efforts, the user's e-mail application generally provides some level of antivirus support. In addition, having a good firewall in place helps reduce the ability of a virus to do its dirty work by communicating with whoever sent it. In short, the war begins on the user's machine.

The fact of the matter is that you have to start somewhere else if you expect to win the war against malware. The best tool you can have in your war on viruses and other malware is an educated user who understands the risk and chooses to act appropriately. The user can make that choice out of fear of reprisal, in expectation of a reward, or simply because it's the right thing to do. Whatever the user's reason, no matter what you do with Exchange Server, the war is lost if you don't have the user's cooperation.

As with Exchange Server antispam features, you implement Exchange Server antivirus support using the Edge Transport server. The following sections discuss the essential issues for an Edge Transport implementation. Of course, you may not want to make the investment that the Edge Transport server requires, so the following sections also include some information on potential third-party solutions that don't require such a large investment.

Considering the third-party solution

Microsoft actually does recognize that need for third-party solutions for antispam and antivirus support. You can find a list of the antispam and antivirus partners they support at `http://www.microsoft.com/exchange/partners/2007/antivirus.mspx` or `http://tinyurl.com/35pbs4`. The "Considering the Requirements for a Third-Party Add-in" section of Chapter 15 helps you make some sense out of this and other lists of helpful vendors you might want to try.

Of course, the question is whether a third-party solution can save you money over implementing a multiple-server Edge Transport server setup. The first question you must ask is whether your primary Exchange Server provides the computing horsepower required to perform all the tasks you ask of it. For many small or medium-sized organizations the answer is a resounding yes. Larger organizations may already have multiple Exchange Servers in place, so adding another server for Edge Transport won't seem like such an expense.

The second question is whether you want to potentially expose your Exchange Server to the outside world. No matter how good your setup, exposing your Exchange Server Hub Transport server to the outside world means that someone could get through without too much effort. Using multiple servers, separating them with a router, and putting out additional configuration effort doesn't guarantee that intruders won't get through, but it will slow them down considerably, which may give you the time you require to react.

A third-party solution is a great idea when cost is a concern and your data is sensitive but not world-ending sensitive. When you combine a third-party solution with user training that helps users understand the need to keep sensitive information out of e-mail, you have a winning configuration that will protect your Exchange Server setup.

Understanding Antivirus Extensibility

The Edge Transport server includes a feature called Antivirus Extensibility that makes it possible to add antivirus functionality to Exchange Server. What this feature implies is that you won't find antivirus support built into Exchange Server; you must buy it as an add-in. Microsoft hopes that you'll purchase Microsoft Forefront Security for Exchange Server and use it for your antivirus solution (see the "Using Microsoft Forefront Security for Exchange Server" section of Chapter 14 for details), but you do have alternatives. The Antivirus Extensibility feature provides four kinds of support for antivirus software:

- ✔ **Attachment filtering:** Attachments can cause untold problems for organizations, especially attachments that execute when you open them. An administrator can use the attachment filtering feature to remove all attachments or only attachments with specific file extensions. In addition, the administrator can configure these features to scan within compressed files, such as ZIP files, which makes it considerably harder for someone to send your users a file with something dangerous in it. Of course, this form of filtering can also backfire by making it impossible to use file exchanges for legitimate purposes. A good alternative is to provide a File Transport Protocol (FTP) upload site for legitimate file transfers.

- ✔ **Edge protocol rules:** Use this feature as a means of scanning for potentially dangerous files based on text patterns in the file. You use this feature only as a temporary measure until the antivirus vendor updates their signature file to incorporate the new threat.

- ✔ **Antivirus stamp:** Whenever Exchange Server scans a message for a potential virus, it adds a stamp to the message that indicates when the message was scanned and which virus checker scanned it. This stamp helps you evaluate the probability that an outside party has tampered with the message content between the time it was scanned and the time the user views it. Of course, the best approach is to provide antivirus scanning on the user's system in addition to server-based scanning.

- ✔ **Deep integration for antivirus scanning:** Developers will like this feature, but you may not even notice it. This feature tells you that Microsoft has opened more of Exchange Server for access by third-party developers, which means that the antivirus software can do a better job and provide a more seamless experience.

These features are all part of the Edge Transport server, but you need an antivirus product to make them work. Consider these features as a starting point with which the antivirus product and the Edge Transport server can work together, rather than standalone features you can implement immediately.

Considering the Use of Encryption

Encryption is the use of a mathematical process to modify a data stream into a seemingly random array of characters. *Decryption* reverses the encryption process to produce the original data stream. Some encryption techniques even use multiple levels of encryption to make it harder for someone to decrypt the message without the proper key. Triple DES is an example of multiple encryption levels (read more at `http://en.wikipedia.org/wiki/Triple_DES`).

Exchange Server provides encryption that makes it less likely that someone will monitor your communication and expose your data. It automatically encrypts any data that leaves your network and can encrypt data transferred between machines as well. The following sections describe the encryption features that Exchange Server provides.

Assume the worst and you won't be disappointed

With the number of encryption products on the market today and the availability of processing horsepower, there is no reason not to encrypt all your e-mail. If your organization deals with sensitive e-mail of any kind, you have to assume that someone is going to make that e-mail available to someone with ill intent. It's not a question of *if*, it's a question of *when*. Encrypting your e-mail at least reduces the risk that this third party will be able to read the content of that e-mail and possibly expose your company to attack.

However, encrypting just the e-mail isn't enough. You need to encrypt the user's hard drive and any device the user may rely on to transfer data. Encryption slows the system, but not enough to make it a concern in today's computing environment. The risk to your data is far higher than any lost speed. Make encryption part of your user training. Users should know how to encrypt any attachments they send to a third party. In fact, you may want to make it

company policy to encrypt all attachments with a standalone product, just to make sure that sensitive data isn't missed.

It's also important to realize that encryption isn't forever. Someone who is determined will break your encryption and read your message. At one time the Data Encryption Standard (DES) was considered unbreakable. Now you can break it in a matter of minutes with the right equipment (read more at `http://en.wikipedia.org/wiki/EFF_DES_cracker` or `http://tinyurl.com/2g6e9p`). Any encryption you use today will be broken tomorrow — count on it. What the encryption buys you is time — you need to consider how much time it will take someone to break the encryption today when you look for an encryption technology. The point is that encryption is a great way to keep someone from reading your message today. By the time they can read the message, the data it contains is likely to be irrelevant.

Using the Intra-Org Encryption feature

The Intra-Org Encryption feature ensures that messages are encrypted before Exchange Server places them on the network. The best part is that you don't have to do anything to get it — the feature is always on by default. Microsoft implements this feature using Transport Layer Security (TLS). The message traffic relies on Remote Procedure Call (RPC) for Outlook connections — third-party and Web-based clients rely on Secure Sockets Layer (SSL) instead. The Inter-Org Encryption feature

- ✔ Ensures that no one can intercept the message and read or modify it
- ✔ Provides confidentiality of message content
- ✔ Reduces the risk of man-in-the-middle attacks

Another goal of the Intra-Org Encryption feature is to enhance what Microsoft terms Information Rights Management (IRM). The basic idea behind IRM is protecting the content of e-mail in an organization. For example, you don't want an employee to see his or her performance review, and IRM helps protect that information when you send the performance review using e-mail to Human Resources (HR). You can use transport rules on the Hub Transport server to implement IRM based on subject, content, or a combination of sender and recipient. You can read more about IRM at `http://office.microsoft.com/en-us/help/HA101029181033.aspx`.

Considering the use of opportunistic TLS encryption

When a client application supports TLS, Exchange Server automatically detects the support and uses TLS for all communication. TLS is inherently more secure than SSL, which is why you should use it. Some misinformed people have said that TLS and SSL 3.0 are precisely the same, but they aren't. The differences between TLS and SSL 3.0 are significant enough that the two encryption techniques won't interoperate. Fortunately, TLS does support a mode in which it loosens its encryption to support SSL 3.0. Don't rely on the less-than-stellar third-party information available on this topic on some Web sites — use the standard found at `http://www.ietf.org/rfc/rfc2246.txt` for information instead.

TLS support extends to Unified Messaging. You can tell Exchange Server to encrypt all your Voice Over IP (VOIP) communications to keep their content confidential. See the article at `http://technet.microsoft.com/en-us/library/bb124092(EXCHG.80).aspx` or `http://tinyurl.com/4actev` to discover more about this topic. VOIP actually relies on Mutual Transport Layer Security (MTLS) to perform the encryption. It's important to note that the device must support encryption to make this feature work.

Understanding that SSL certificates are automatically installed

Exchange Server automatically creates and installs a self-signed SSL certificate for you. This certificate makes it possible for Exchange Server to sign all e-mail messages. Of course, you may not want to use the self-signed certificate, so Microsoft provides the means for you to reconfigure the SSL certificate support as needed. The "Defining the Secure Sockets Layer (SSL) configuration" section of Chapter 4 provides details on this process.

Using S/MIME encryption for messages

The Secure Multipurpose Internet Mail Extensions (S/MIME) standard makes it possible for any e-mail client to send encrypted and signed e-mail to another client. Some people confuse encryption and signing. *Encrypted* e-mail has the content scrambled in a manner that makes it impossible for someone to see the content without a lot of extra effort. However, once someone breaks the encryption, he or she can modify the content of the message without detection. That's where signing comes into play. *Signing* makes it possible for the recipient to identify the sender with complete confidence; it also provides the means for the e-mail client to detect changes to the message.

Combining signing and encryption greatly enhances the security of your message. Even if someone does manage to read the content and change it, the e-mail client application will detect the change. The tradeoff for this security is speed. Encryption and signing both use processing cycles and system resources, so you give up efficiency for security when you use encryption, signing, or both to secure a message.

It doesn't matter what kind of client you use. However, the important feature in Exchange Server is that you can control the use of S/MIME to some extent. For example, you can force Outlook Web Access (OWA) users to rely on S/MIME. See the article at `http://technet.microsoft.com/en-us/library/bb738151(EXCHG.80).aspx` or `http://tinyurl.com/4sals9` for details on this topic.

Chapter 7

Interacting with Clients

· ·

· ·

You've installed, configured, and secured your Exchange Server. At this point, you want some clients, other than Outlook Web Access, to interact with Exchange Server. The "Connecting to Exchange Server with a Client" section of Chapter 4 describes how to connect to Exchange Server using Outlook. However, you can do a lot more than simply connect to Exchange Server — and that's what this chapter is about. This chapter describes how to get more value out of the Exchange Server you just created.

Part of the Exchange Server experience is making use of the various data stores that Exchange Server provides. For example, an administrator can create a safe sender list that affects the entire enterprise. This chapter addresses this and many other Outlook configuration issues.

Outlook 2007 provides some special features. You've already read about a few of these features in other chapters. For example, Chapter 6 tells you about the Outlook E-mail Postmark Validation feature. This chapter also provides you with a special Outlook 2007 section that describes more of these features and tells you how to use them.

Working with Outlook

Outlook 2003 and 2007 both provide a number of interesting features when you connect them to Exchange Server 2007. Although this book isn't a comprehensive guide to working with Outlook, the following sections do describe a few of the more interesting features. Make sure you look through the "Understanding the Service Pack 1 (SP1) Differences" section of Chapter 1 for features that apply only when you install SP1. The material in this section assumes that you've created an Exchange Server account in Outlook, rather that relying on the POP3 or IMAP4 support that Exchange Server provides.

Accepting Safe Sender List Aggregation

The Safe Sender List Aggregation feature provides *white listing*, which is a method of saying a particular sender isn't dangerous. It's important to know about this feature because it affects the way in which Outlook interacts with the Edge Transport server. In this case, when a user makes a connection to the server, a feature called EdgeSync sends the user's safe sender list to the Edge Transport server. The Edge Transport server respects this list to reduce the potential for false positives. In other words, if a sender appears on the user's safe sender list, the Edge Transport server will send the message to the user's inbox, even if the message wouldn't normally pass the Spam Confidence Level (SCL) tests. (See the "Understanding spam assessment" section of Chapter 6 for additional details.)

A potential problem with this feature is that the user could create a safe sender entry for someone who isn't particularly safe. The user may see the content provided by the sender as safe, or at least desirable, but in reality, the content the sender provides isn't safe at all. For example, a user may accept e-mail from a site that provides access to downloadable music and that site might send a keylogger to the user's e-mail. Because the site appears on the user's safe sender list, the Edge Transport server could send the tainted e-mail. This particular problem points out the need for multiple layers of security. The user's system must include spam and virus checking functionality. This issue also points out a potential area to troubleshoot when you try to locate the source of contamination on your network.

Many administrators don't completely understand two issues about Safe Sender List Aggregation. The first issue is that Safe Sender List Aggregation is on a per-user basis. If one user has a safe sender and the other doesn't, the first user will receive e-mail from that sender but the second user may not, depending on the sender's SCL value. The second issue is that the Edge Transport server respects only safe senders — it doesn't respect blocked senders. Consequently, if a user has blocked a particular sender, but that sender's SCL value is low enough, Exchange Server will still send it to the user's inbox. Outlook will block the sender, however, so the net effect is that the sender is still blocked. The difference is that the sender's e-mail will consume the resources required to transport it from the Edge Transport server to the Hub Transport server to the user's inbox.

Understanding the Anti-spam Stamp

The Anti-spam Stamp feature is the result of a check that Exchange Server performs on each incoming e-mail message. This stamp tells you how the Edge Transport server views a particular message. You see results of tests it performs. For example, you can determine whether the message has a Sender ID attached to it and what value the Edge Transport server provided by the Phishing Confidence Level (PCL). (A *PCL* is essentially the same as an SCL — it provides a value between 0 and 9 that tells you how certain the Edge Transport Server is that a particular message contains phishing content.) You can easily view the Anti-spam Stamp in Outlook using the following procedure:

1. **Right-click the message you want to view and choose Options from the context menu.**

   You see the Message Options dialog box shown in Figure 7-1. This dialog box contains a number of pieces of information, but the most important in this situation is the Internet Headers field.

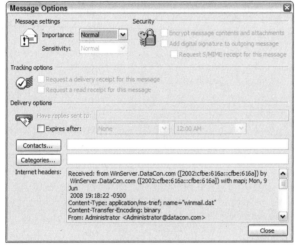

Figure 7-1: Locate the Exchange Server entries for a message to see the Anti-spam Stamp.

2. **Scroll through the list of Internet headers until you see the X-MS-Exchange-Organization headers.**

   You should see up to a total of three headers. The content of these headers tells you about how the antispam functionality provided by the Anti-Spam Stamp feature works. The following list describes each of them. The article at `http://technet.microsoft.com/en-us/library/aa996878(EXCHG.80).aspx` provides details about each of the entries and how you should interpret them:

   - **X-MS-Exchange-Organization-PCL:** Shows the PCL value that the Edge Transport server assigns to the message.

   - **X-MS-Exchange-Organization-SCL:** Shows the SCL value, from 0 to 9, that the Edge Transport server assigns to the message.

- **X-MS-Exchange-Organization-Antispam-Report:** Displays an encoded report that contains one or more of the following items: the Sender ID (SID), DAT file version (DV), signature action stamp (SA), signature DAT file version (SV), PCL, SCL, custom weight of the message (CW), pre-solved puzzle (PP), timestamp, and Multipurpose Internet Mail Extensions (MIME) stamp. The report can also contain a number of other fields depending on optional content and checks that the Edge Transport server performs.

You can use a special process to add all antispam features of Exchange Server to a Hub Transport, rather than rely on an Edge Transport. You use Exchange Management Shell to perform this task. The "Installing and configuring antispam agents" section of Chapter 12 describes how to add and configure antispam support to your single server Exchange Server setup.

Considering the Two-Tiered Spam Quarantine

The Two-Tiered Spam Quarantine feature makes it possible to reduce the risk of borderline messages reaching the user's inbox. Exchange Server uses a set of rules that may not always accurately identify spam. In these situations, Exchange Server can place the message in the Spam Quarantine mailbox, which is a special mailbox that only the administrator can access.

The administrator can delete the message or send it to the user after reviewing it. Exchange Server places the reviewed message in the user's Junk E-mail folder. This placement alerts the user to the fact that the message may contain unusable material. In addition, Exchange Server contains the message to plain text, which reduces the potential for contamination on the user's machine.

The quarantine process does present a few problems, the most important of which is that any dynamic content is stripped, along with attachments. The user sees only the original text content, which can make the message useless for anything other than determining who sent the message. The best way to handle this situation is to place the sender in the safe sender's list, restart Outlook, and ask the sender to transmit the message again. Because the sender now appears on the user's safe sender list, the Edge Transport server will deliver the message intact.

Outlook 2007 users have some additional choices when it comes to processing quarantined messages. It's possible to recover the original message from the Spam Quarantine mailbox. Unfortunately, the process is relatively complex, so using the standard Outlook 2003 process of having the sender transmit the message a second time probably works better. You can read about this process at `http://technet.microsoft.com/en-us/library/aa998920(EXCHG.80).aspx`.

Understanding attachment filtering

Attachment filtering is the act of removing attachments, extra content in the form of a file, from messages. Most e-mail servers today have this feature, so it isn't surprising that Exchange Server also supports attachment filtering. Of course, you must consider the Exchange Server extras. For example, the Safe Sender List Aggregation feature affects how attachment filtering works — safe senders don't have their attachments filtered in many situations.

When people collaborate through e-mail, it often involves the use of attachments. Someone sends a document to someone else so they can create it and provide comments. The problem is that attachments can also contain viruses and other malware, so attachments make administrators nervous. For some administrators the answer is clear: simply remove all attachments and you won't have any problems. Unfortunately, this shortsighted viewpoint hinders user productivity and can make it nearly impossible in some cases. A better method of addressing this issue is to consider individual circumstances and filter as needed. When working with Exchange Server, you have the following filtering options:

✓ **Filename or file extension:** Defines a filename or a file extension to filter. For example, you can filter out a single filename using something like `BadFile.EXE`. Entering a value of *.EXE filters all files with an EXE file extension. Using a file extension filter can backfire. For example, many people exchange compressed files in the ZIP format, so providing an entry of *.ZIP could cause problems for users who rely on this format.

✓ **Multipurpose Internet Mail Extension (MIME) type:** The MIME type defines the kind of content that the file contains. For example, a MIME type of text/plain is probably safe, but a MIME type of application/octet-stream (an executable) could present problems. You can find a list of common MIME types at `http://www.w3schools.com/media/media_mimeref.asp`.

The default attachment scanner provided with Exchange Server doesn't let you scan within files. Using a compressed file scan means that you can allow ZIP files as long as they don't contain executables. Microsoft suggests using its Forefront Security for Exchange Server product to add this capability. The "Using Microsoft Forefront Security for Exchange Server" section of Chapter 14 describes this product.

When Exchange Server detects a message with an attachment that you've defined as unsafe, you need to decide what to do with that attachment. Automatically deleting every attachment is excessive and counterproductive in many situations. Of course, you do want to get rid of any attachments that promise to trash your system immediately. You can choose any of the following actions when working with attachments in Exchange Server:

✔ **Block the message and attachment:** The system blocks the message and attachment, which means that the user doesn't see either of them. However, the user does receive a Delivery Status Notification (DSN) message. This message tells the user that the system blocked the message and provides a reason for blocking it. The user can ask the administrator to release the message, which saves time asking the sender to transmit the message again. Use this option when you feel that both the message (the message may contain scripts) and attachment could present a problem, but you aren't completely certain because there are exceptions that you want the user to receive.

✔ **Strip the attachment from the message but allow the message to pass:** The system sends the message to the user but strips the attachment from it. In this case, the system deletes the attachment and you can't recover it. The system replaces the attachment with a text file that tells why the system stripped the attachment. If a message also includes allowed attachments, those attachments appear with the message. Use this option when you know an attachment, such as an executable, is unsafe but still want the user to receive any other content provided with the message. This is the default option.

✔ **Silently delete both the message and attachment:** The system deletes both the message and the attachment without sending any notification to either the sender or receiver. You should view this option as the option of last resort. The only time this option makes sense is when you need to consider social issues (such as users who don't understand the need for the deletion or a sender who simply wants to know that the e-mail address is active) as well as guard your system from attack. In most cases, this option will garner user hostility once users discover that the system is simply deleting their messages without any notification whatsoever.

Understanding the Multi-Mailbox Search feature

Exchange Server 2007 automatically indexes every message in every mailbox, making it possible to search for messages using a number of criteria. The most interesting use of this indexing capability is the Multi-Mailbox Search feature. You use this feature to locate any message in a group of mailboxes that matches specific criteria. For example, you can search for all users who have had discussions with a particular client within a specific timeframe. Exchange Server makes it possible to output the results of such a query to any of the following:

✔ Microsoft Windows SharePoint Services site

✔ New or existing local PST file

✔ Mailbox

The best part of the Multi-Mailbox Search feature is that you don't have to do anything special to obtain the required capability. However, you do have to do something special to make the query. You always perform a multimailbox search using Exchange Management Shell. The "Performing a multimailbox search" section of Chapter 12 describes how to perform a search using this feature.

Considering the use of transport rules

Transport rules will have a strong effect on communication in your organization. You must consider how they affect the client application and the users that rely on the client application. An administrator can choose to create a rule that prevents communication between various departments in an organization.

In some cases, the administrator must create a rule to meet legal or other requirements. However, some rules are in place simply because of company needs or requirements. For example, an organization could have two groups working competitively on a project and want to keep them from exchanging e-mail. The "Working with the organization-level Hub Transport" section of Chapter 3 provides details on how transport rules fit in the scheme of the Hub Transport server. The following steps describe how to create a new transport rule:

1. **Select the Organization Configuration\Hub Transport folder. Click the Transport Rules tab.**

   Exchange Server doesn't come with any transport rules configured, so you won't see any entries in the Results pane the first time you create a transport rule. Otherwise, you see all of the transport rules you created in the past.

2. **Click New Transport Rule in the Actions pane.**

   Exchange Management Console displays the New Transport Rule dialog box shown in Figure 7-2.

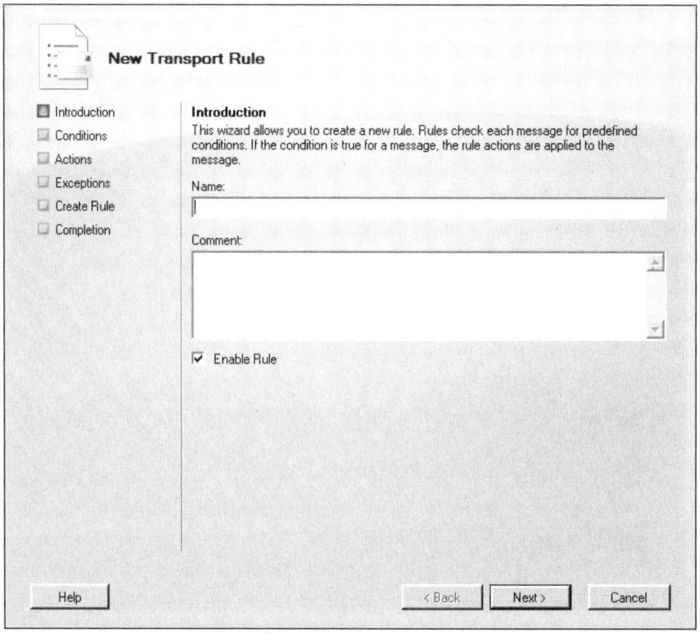

Figure 7-2:
Define
transport
rules as
needed to
maintain
correct mail
flow.

3. **In the Name field, type a name for the transport rule in the Name field.**

4. **(Optional) Type a comment for the transport rule.**

   In most cases, you want to provide a comment that explains the purpose of the transport rule. A complete comment can help avoid confusion later, especially if another administrator must discover the purpose of the rule.

5. **Select or deselect Enable Rule as needed. Click Next.**

   The wizard presents a host of conditions, as shown in Figure 7-3. A transport rule can use as many of these conditions as needed to define the rule completely. A single condition usually won't provide discrete message selection, and overly broad rules can prove problematic because they trap more messages than intended.

6. **Scroll through the list and select a condition that matches a requirement.**

   The wizard places the condition in the lower window shown in Figure 7-3. Notice that the condition normally has a link associated with it. When you click this link, you see any of a number of dialog boxes asking for additional information to define the condition. For example, when you select the From People condition, you see a link for People. Click this link and you'll see a Select Senders dialog box, where you define the people to whom the rule applies.

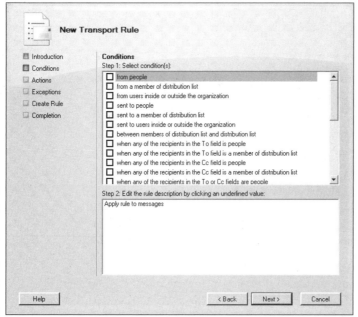

Figure 7-3:
Use
conditions
to define
the limits of
a transport
rule.

7. **Click the link associated with the condition, provide the required information in the dialog box you see, and click OK.**

8. **Perform Steps 6 and 7 for as many conditions as required to define the transport rule.**

9. **Click Next.**

   The wizard displays a number of actions, as shown in Figure 7-4. The actions define how the transport rule reacts when a message meets the conditions you define. You can provide as many actions as needed to provide complete support for the rule requirements.

10. **Scroll through the list and check an action that matches a requirement.**

    As with a condition, you see a link associated with the action. Click this link to define the action completely.

11. **Click the link associated with the action, provide the required information in the dialog box you see, and click OK.**

12. **Perform Steps 10 and 11 for as many actions as required to describe what to do with a message meeting the transport rule conditions.**

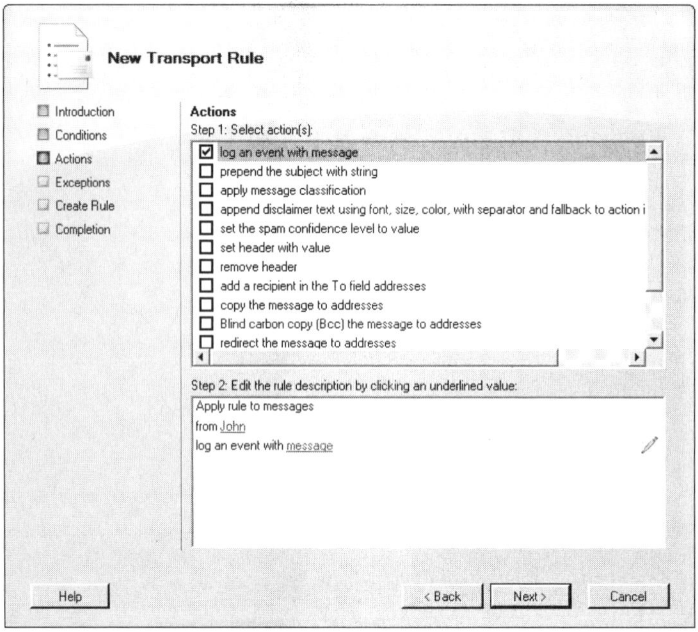

New Transport Rule

- Introduction
- Conditions
- Actions
- Exceptions
- Create Rule
- Completion

Actions
Step 1: Select action(s):

☑ log an event with message
☐ prepend the subject with string
☐ apply message classification
☐ append disclaimer text using font, size, color, with separator and fallback to action i
☐ set the spam confidence level to value
☐ set header with value
☐ remove header
☐ add a recipient in the To field addresses
☐ copy the message to addresses
☐ Blind carbon copy (Bcc) the message to addresses
☐ redirect the message to addresses

Step 2: Edit the rule description by clicking an underlined value:

Apply rule to messages
from John
log an event with message

Help   < Back   Next >   Cancel

Figure 7-4:
Use actions
to define
what task
to perform
with the
message.

13. **Click Next.**

    The wizard displays a number of exceptions, as shown in Figure 7-5. You don't have to define any exceptions. This is an optional part of the transport rule creation process. When you do define an exception, the exception tells Exchange Server to perform the action except when a particular condition occurs. Consequently, exceptions are a negative kind of condition.

14. **(Optional) Scroll through the list and select an exception that matches a requirement. Click the link associated with the exception, provide the required information in the dialog box you see, and click OK. Perform this step as needed for any exceptions you want to define.**

15. **Click Next.**

    You see a summary of the conditions, actions, and exceptions you defined for the rule.

16. **Click New and then click Finish.**

    Exchange Server creates the new transport rule for you.

Rules have a priority. The first rule you create has priority 0, the second has priority 1, and so on. Exchange Server executes the rules in the order in which they appear. Consequently, the order of the transport rules is important because one rule may override another rule in some situations. To change the priority of a rule, highlight the rule in the list and click Change

Priority in the Actions pane. Type a new priority in the Change Rule Priority dialog box and click OK. Exchange Server will move the rules around as required to ensure that each rule priority is unique.

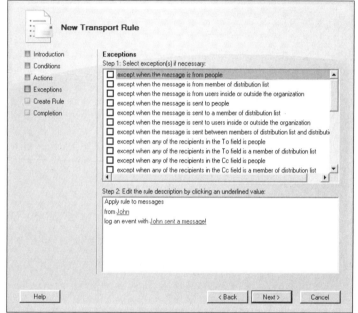

Figure 7-5:
Use exceptions to define when the transport rule doesn't apply.

Considering Personal Store Requirements

The term personal store could have a number of meanings. However, for this book, a *personal store* is a secure location for the digital certificates of the current user. Digital certificates provide a means of verifying the identity of a sender, encrypting or decrypting messages, and signing your messages before you send them. In short, digital certificates are an identity feature that protects communication between a message sender and recipient and also provides protection between a user and Exchange Server.

A user can obtain a digital certificate in a number of ways. However, the digital certificates you use with Exchange Server are obtained either from a certificate server on the network or through a third party such as VeriSign (`http://www.verisign.com/`). For the digital certificate to have any meaning, it must rely on a trusted Certificate Authority (CA). Consequently, a digital certificate used for external e-mail normally comes from a third-party CA rather than a network CA.

When you want to use digital certificates with devices that don't have an account, such as a router, you must install the Network Device Enrollment Service. In some cases, Exchange Server provides access to network devices that require digital certificates, so you may need this service to provide a complete end-to-end solution. You can discover more about this feature at http://technet2.microsoft.com/windowsserver2008/en/ library/569cd0df-3aa4-4dd7-88b8-227e9e3c012b1033.mspx.

The digital certificate is also part of the S/MIME support provided by Exchange Server SP1. To use S/MIME to encrypt and digitally sign messages, users must have a digital certificate installed on their system. The following sections describe the Exchange Server-specific tasks that you perform with the user's personal store to ensure that a usable digital certificate is in place and to safeguard that certificate against loss.

Verifying the presence of a digital certificate

It's important to verify the existence of a digital certificate on the client machine. Of course, you could go to each client machine in turn, open the e-mail client, and use whatever commands are needed to verify the certificate, but this approach is time consuming and error prone. An easier way to perform the task is to use one of the methods described in the following sections.

You can't directly connect to a remote system and see the digital certificates for a particular user. It's possible to see the machine digital certificates from a remote location, but the digital certificates used for Exchange Server are user-specific. Consequently, you must create a connection to the remote system using an application such as Remote Desktop. The "Interacting with the Client Machine Using Remote Desktop" section of Chapter 14 describes how to use Remote Desktop.

Using Microsoft Management Console (MMC) to view the digital certificate

Using MMC is nice because it provides a graphical interface. Unfortunately, you won't find a tool in the Administrative Tools folder of Control Panel to work with MMC — you must create a new console instead. The following steps describe how to create the required console and then view the digital certificates of the user you specify:

1. **Create the Remote Desktop (or other) connection to the remote machine.**

2. **Choose Start⇨Run.**

   Windows displays the Run dialog box.

3. **Type** MMC **in the Open field and click OK.**

   MMC opens a blank host application where you can create a console to view certificates. If you want, you can save the console to a file after you create it. To reopen the console, simply type the console name followed by the MSC extension, such as ViewCerts.MSC, in the Open field of the Run dialog box.

4. **Choose File⇨Add/Remove Snap-in.**

   MMC displays the Add/Remove Snap-in dialog box.

5. **Click Add.**

   You see the Add Standalone Snap-in dialog box shown in Figure 7-6, where you can choose from a list of snap-in objects. Most of these snap-ins, such as Computer Management, already appear as part of a console in the Administrative Tools folder. However, it's interesting to scroll through the list to see if your machine includes snap-ins that aren't part of the established consoles.

Figure 7-6: The Add Standalone Snap-in dialog box contains a list of snap-ins you can use.

6. **Highlight Certificates and click Add.**

   The snap-in wizard asks you to provide a certificate source. Although the machine and services do have certificates and you might want to view them at some point, the certificates on which Exchange Server relies exist in the user store.

7. **Choose My User Account (that is, the account you're using on the remote machine) and click Finish.**

   The wizard adds the Certificates snap-in to the Standalone tab of the Add/Remove Snap-in dialog box.

8. **Click Close to close the Add Standalone Snap-in dialog box and OK to close the Add/Remove Snap-in dialog box.**

   The console now contains a root folder named Certificates – Current User. When you expand this root folder by clicking the plus sign next to Certificates – Current User, you see a list of certificate stores, as shown in Figure 7-7.

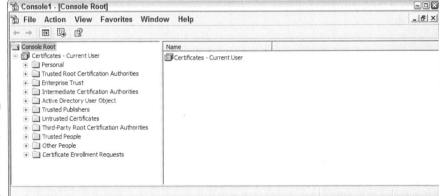

Figure 7-7: Every user has multiple certificate stores.

9. **Select Personal\Certificates.**

   You should see one or more certificates in the list. However, a user might not have any certificates at all.

10. **Double-click each certificate in turn. Click the Details tab. Locate the Subject field.**

    The Certificate dialog box shown in Figure 7-8 displays the Subject field details. You should see one certificate for each e-mail account that the user possesses. When working in a large organization, the user may only have one e-mail address for Exchange Server. Smaller organizations may have two e-mail addresses, one for the public Internet and another for the local Exchange Server.

At this point, you can save the console by choosing File⇨Save. Fill in a name for the console and click Save. You can find an MSC file by that name on the user's hard drive and access it whenever you need to verify the status of certificates on the user's machine. Copying the MSC file to other machines makes the console available on those machines too.

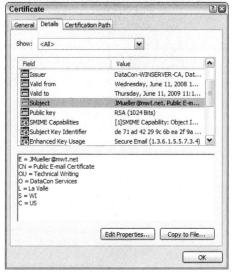

Figure 7-8:
Verify that
the user
has a
certificate
for each
e-mail
address.

Using Windows PowerShell to view the digital certificate

Sometimes using a command line interface is significantly faster than using a graphical alternative. In this case, you can type a single command to see all the personal certificates a user has. As with the MMC console, you must create a connection to the user's machine using Remote Desktop or some other remote management application. To view the certificates on a particular machine, type

```
Get-ChildItem Cert:\CurrentUser\My | fl
```

and press Enter. You see a listing of certificates like the one shown in Figure 7-9. The Subject field tells you which e-mail account the certificate addresses. The user must have one certificate for each e-mail account.

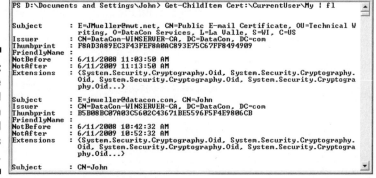

Figure 7-9:
Using the
command
line option
displays all
certificates
at once.

Using the digital certificate

Simply having a digital certificate on your system doesn't do much. The digital certificate must appear as part of the e-mail client application or the application won't interact with Exchange Server in a secure manner. In most cases, the e-mail client application provides a specific way to add digital certificate support. The following steps describe how to use a digital certificate with Outlook 2003 (the process for Outlook 2007 is similar):

1. Choose Tools⇨Options. Click the Security tab.

Outlook displays the Options dialog box shown in Figure 7-10.

Figure 7-10:
The security settings appear on the Security tab of the Options dialog box.

2. Click Settings. If this is an additional security setting, click New to create a new security setting.

You see the Change Security Settings dialog box shown in Figure 7-11.

3. Type a name for the settings in the Security Settings Name field.

If you have multiple e-mail accounts, make sure you type a name that reflects the e-mail account you want to configure. You need separate security settings for each e-mail account because the security settings offer support for only one digital certificate.

4. Click Choose in the Signing Certificate field.

Outlook displays the Select Certificate dialog box, which contains a list of e-mail compatible certificates on the system. If you don't see a certificate in the list, it means that the certificates on your system aren't configured for use with e-mail.

Figure 7-11:
Add a
security
setting for
each e-mail
account.

5. **Highlight the e-mail digital certificate associated with the account you're configuring and click OK.**

   If you need help choosing the right certificate, click View Certificate. The Certificate dialog box (refer to Figure 7-8) presents complete information about the certificate's use. Note that Outlook uses the certificate to fill in the Signing Certificate and Encryption Certificate fields.

6. **Click OK.**

   Outlook adds the security settings to the client.

7. **Repeat Steps 2 through 6 if you need to configure additional security settings for other accounts.**

Importing and exporting the digital certificate

Digital certificates are unique. Even if you replicate the content of a digital certificate completely and give it precisely the same name, the digital certificate that a CA generates is different from any other digital certificate. In fact, it's the unique nature of digital certificates that gives them value in making the connection between sender and receiver secure.

The messages you sign and encrypt with a digital certificate are also unique. You can't open a message encrypted with one digital certificate using another digital certificate. If you could, using a digital certificate would be useless because the digital certificate wouldn't actually lock anything. The combination of a unique digital certificate and the requirement to use a particular digital certificate to interact with messages means that you must create a backup of the digital certificate you use to sign and encrypt a message or you lose access to that message.

Always store your digital certificates in a safe location other than the host system (such as on a CD stored in a vault somewhere). Otherwise, a hard drive failure will cause you to lose both your data and your digital certificate. Exchange Server doesn't store a copy of the user's digital certificate on the host server because doing so would cause a security breach. In fact, the only place you find the digital certificate is in the secure storage area provided by Windows. Use the following steps to import or export a digital certificate using Outlook:

1. **Choose Tools⇨Options. Click the Security tab.**

   Outlook displays the Options dialog box (refer to Figure 7-10).

2. **Click Import/Export.**

   Outlook displays the Import/Export Digital ID dialog box shown in Figure 7-12.

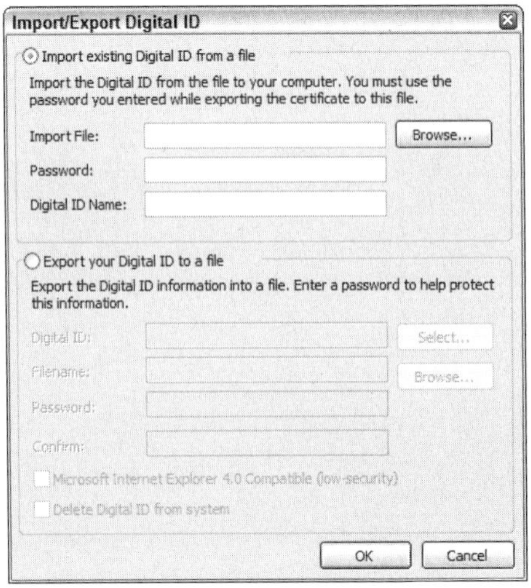

Figure 7-12:
Create a backup of your digital certificate to ensure you can access secure e-mail later.

Import/Export Digital ID

⊙ Import existing Digital ID from a file

Import the Digital ID from the file to your computer. You must use the password you entered while exporting the certificate to this file.

Import File: _____ [Browse...]

Password: _____

Digital ID Name: _____

○ Export your Digital ID to a file

Export the Digital ID information into a file. Enter a password to help protect this information.

Digital ID: _____ [Select...]

Filename: _____ [Browse...]

Password: _____

Confirm: _____

☐ Microsoft Internet Explorer 4.0 Compatible (low-security)

☐ Delete Digital ID from system

[OK] [Cancel]

3. **Select the correct option for importing or exporting the digital certificate.**

4. **When you want to export a digital certificate, click Select to choose the digital certificate you want to export.**

5. **Type the password associated with the digital certificate.**

   When exporting a certificate, make sure that you use a secure password that includes numbers, special characters, uppercase letters, and lower-case letters.

6. **When you want to import a digital certificate, type a name for the certificate.**

   Outlook uses this name to identify the certificate in Windows.

7. **Click OK.**

   Outlook imports or exports the digital certificate.

Chapter 8

Creating Custom Forms

● ●

In This Chapter

▶ Using Details Templates Editor

▶ Modifying a template

▶ Using tools to add controls

▶ Changing control behaviors

● ●

*E*xchange Server uses a number of forms to help you fill out information. For example, when you edit a user's mailbox entry, you see a User form (Outlook presents the form in its own dialog box). These forms provide a specific appearance — they offer generic entries that may not even apply to your organization. For example, the Phone/Notes tab contains an entry for a pager. Many organizations have exchanged their pagers in favor of a cellular telephone. Consequently, you might want to replace this field with a cellular telephone number. Exchange Server provides access to six templates that you can edit (as described in the "Opening Details Templates Editor" section of the chapter).

Fortunately, you can change the forms that Exchange Server uses to obtain information. Details Templates Editor provides access to all default forms that Exchange Server uses to obtain information. You can modify these forms to meet your needs. This editor also provides the means to change forms back to their original form when you make a mistake and want to start over again. You can even add custom data to the forms so that they reflect your organization's particular needs. (This second action isn't approved of by Microsoft.)

This chapter discusses both templates and forms. A *template* is a blueprint — it tells how to create a form. A *form* is a particular instance of a template. When using the Details Templates Editor console, you see a list of templates. On the other hand, when you are viewing a particular user in Outlook, you are seeing a form.

The changes you make to these forms affect only the Offline Address Book (OAB) entries and other Exchange Server data. The user's personal address book and local data are unaffected. Consequently, you should set the user's system to use the OAB as a default if you want to be sure that user's have access to the form changes you make. The following sections describe how to work with Details Templates Editor to provide customized forms for the user.

Creating the Details Templates Editor console

Exchange Server 2007 SP1 provides access to Details Templates Editor through the Toolbox folder. However, if you're using an older version of Exchange Server 2007, you can still obtain access to this valuable tool by creating your own console. The "Using Microsoft Management Console (MMC) to view the digital certificate" section of Chapter 7 tells how to create a new MMC console. Instead of adding the Certificates snap-in, you add the Details Templates Editor snap-in. The resulting console works precisely the same as the one you access from the Toolbox folder. Some screenshots will look slightly different if you're using an older version of Exchange Server, but the essential functionality is the same.

Opening Details Templates Editor

The Details Templates Editor console is where you make changes to the forms that Exchange Server provides for entering data into the system. Figure 8-1 shows the initial displays for this console. Depending on how you open the Details Templates Editor console, you may have to select the Details Templates entry in the left pane as shown in the figure to see the list of templates that Exchange Server uses.

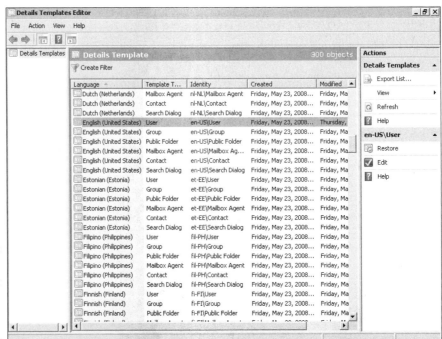

Figure 8-1: Select one of the templates to modify.

The center pane contains a list of default templates. Every language includes six template types. Exchange Server supports 50 languages, so the center pane contains a total of 300 entries. The templates you can modify include

- ✔ **Contacts:** Provides information about someone who lacks an Exchange Server account on the local server. Normally, this is someone outside the company.

- ✔ **Users:** Provides information about someone who has an Exchange Server account on the local server.

- ✔ **Groups:** Defines a group of mailboxes. The mailboxes can be any kind of mailbox that Exchange Server supports.

- ✔ **Mailbox Agents:** Interacts with the user to deliver specialized Exchange Server information. For example, the Quota Message Service (`http://www.microsoft.com/downloads/details.aspx?FamilyId=EB52F6AB-E07A-476C-B32B-145AF6EA970C`) tells the user when a mailbox has exceeded a specified size.

- ✔ **Public Folders:** Contains publicly accessible data and message stores.

- ✔ **Search Dialogs:** Helps the user locate information found on Exchange Server.

In addition to the language and template type, you see the template identity, when the template was created, and the last time someone modified the template. The creation date always remains the same. Consequently, by comparing the creation date with the modification date, you can determine whether someone has modified a template without actually opening it.

This chapter discusses two editors with similar names. The Details Templates Editor console displays a list of all templates available on Exchange Server. The Details Template (singular) Editor console shows the details of a single template.

Editing a Template

Details Template Editor helps you modify the content of a particular template. To open this editor, double-click any of the entries shown in Details Templates Editor. You see a display associated with a particular language and a particular template type, as shown in Figure 8-2. In this case, you see the English (United States) language version of the User template.

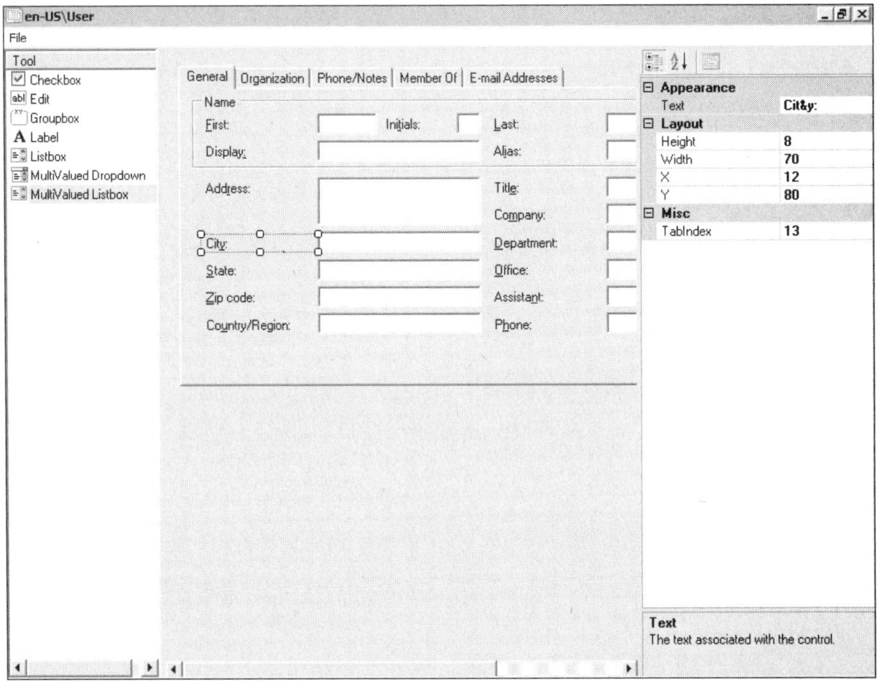

Figure 8-2:
A single
template
contains
all of the
information
required for
a particular
language.

The display shown in Figure 8-2 contains three panes. Each pane has a
particular purpose, as described in the following list:

- ✔ **Tool pane (left):** Contains a set of controls (tools) you can use to add
  content to a template. Each of these controls provides access to a
  particular kind of data. The "Working with Tools" section of the chapter
  describes the Tool pane in detail.

- ✔ **Designer pane (middle):** Shows how the form created with the template
  will look. You won't see any data entries in the Designer pane. The purpose of this pane is to help you design template content. The "Working
  with Tools" section of the chapter shows how to place controls on the
  Designer pane.

- ✔ **Properties pane (right):** Provides the means to modify the way in which
  the controls interact with the user. The Properties pane shows the properties (attributes) for the selected control. Each control has unique properties, so you may see entries other than the ones shown in Figure 8-2 in
  this pane. To see the properties for another control, simply select another
  control in the Designer pane. The "Considering the use of properties for
  controls" section of the chapter describes how to modify properties in
  detail.

Changes you make to a template won't automatically appear in Outlook. You must close your copy of Outlook and reopen it to see the changes you make. It's important to keep this in mind when you make user-requested changes to forms. Make sure you tell the users to close their copy of Outlook and reopen it to see the changes you make.

The changes you can make to a template depend on the template that you're working with. Some templates have specific requirements, and Microsoft makes many of the controls uneditable because changes to the controls will result in data errors or application failure. These uneditable controls act as a failsafe so that you can't make a modification to a critical control. In short, Details Template Editor provides a safe environment in which to work.

If you ever make a mistake with a form, you can reverse your changes by right-clicking the template in Details Templates Editor and choosing Restore from the context menu. However, this feature is a double-edged sword because it can also cause you to lose changes. It's essential to remember that all edits are a one-way process in both Details Templates Editor and Details Template Editor. Neither editor has an undo button, so you need to make changes with care.

Working with Tools

When you open a template for editing, you see a Details Template Editor display that contains a Tool pane. The Tool pane contains a number of controls that you use to create new content for a form. A control has a physical appearance, such as a check box or list box. In addition, it has one or more *values* or *properties* that determine how Exchange Server reacts to the control. Finally, a control often has one or more *actions* or *methods* associated with it that determine what happens when the user changes the control's values. Each control has a different purpose as described in the following list:

- ✔ **Check box:** Provides the means for accepting true/false values. When the user selects a check box, the associated value is true. You can also view the value as selected or on when it's checked. The point is that the user wants the action specified by the check box to occur.

- ✔ **Edit text box:** Accepts freeform text input. A user enters a value that you can't define in advance. Use the edit text box carefully because it can cause gaps in your security. A user can enter any value in an edit text box, which means that users will enter both correct and incorrect values, some of which can have unpredictable results. Whenever possible, rely on predefined values provided by the check box, list box, multivalued drop-down box, or multivalued list box to exclude unacceptable values.

✔ **Group box:** Combines a group of controls into a cohesive whole for logical or presentation reasons. For example, you might want to group into one area all controls that define a contact's name. Using this approach makes it easier for the users to see that the controls belong together and that they should fill out the controls as a single unit (such as first name, middle initial, and last name). The group box normally includes a value that defines why the controls are grouped together.

✔ **Label:** Defines the purpose of other controls. The user can't interact with a label or change its value. You use labels to tell the user how to work with a control and what to provide as input to it.

✔ **List box:** Displays a list of acceptable values from which the user can choose. For example, you might use a list box to display a list of states or countries. A list box lets the user choose only one value, so you use it in places where there's only one acceptable answer out of a group of answers.

✔ **Multivalued drop-down box:** Displays a list of acceptable answers in a compact form. The user clicks the down arrow next to the control, chooses one or more entries, and clicks the up arrow next to the control to move to the next control. This control can accept one or more selections. The user must use Ctrl+Click or Shift+Click to select multiple values.

✔ **Multivalued list box:** Displays a list of acceptable answers in an open format. This control can accept one or more selections. The user must use Ctrl+Click or Shift+Click to select multiple values. Many users find that this control is easier to work with than the multivalued drop-down box because they can see all or at least a number of the selections at one time. However, this control consumes a lot of space, and you may find that it doesn't provide efficient use of screen real estate.

Not every control is available for every template. For example, when working with the Search Dialog template, you have access to only the edit text box, group box, and label controls.

To add a control to a template, simply drag the control from the Tool pane and place it on the template. Details Template Editor will help you place the control by providing alignment marks, as shown in Figure 8-3. In this case, the template contains a new label and a multivalued drop-down box control. The multivalued drop-down box control appears as a dark box because I haven't dropped it on the form yet. Note the two alignment marks. The horizontal mark shows that the multivalued drop-down box control is aligned with the bottom of the label control. The vertical mark shows that the multivalued drop-down box control is aligned with the edit text box controls above it.

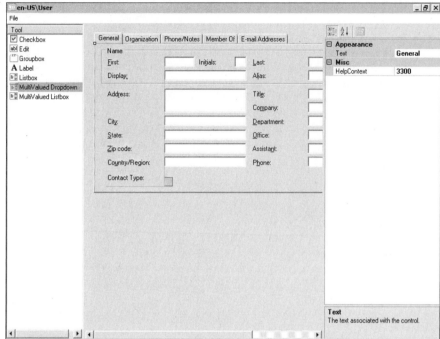

Figure 8-3:
Add controls as needed to define new content.

Developers will notice that Details Template Editor lacks a lot of the controls that you find in a programming product such as Visual Studio. For example, there's no command button, so you can't add custom actions. Details Template Editor provides a means for administrators to modify existing forms without resorting to using a full-fledged programming language. If you want to interact with Exchange Server at a lower level, you must work with the Exchange Server Application Programming Interface (API), which is described at http://msdn.microsoft.com/en-us/exchange/default.aspx. Working with the API is outside the scope of this book. For more details on Exchange Server development, check out *Mastering Microsoft Exchange Server 2007* by Barry Gerber and Jim McBee (published by Sybex).

Modifying Behaviors

Templates provide specific behaviors. Let's say you don't like the current User template and want to make some changes to it. Behavior changes come in three forms:

✔ **Deletion:** The existing control doesn't apply to your organization and you don't want users wasting hard drive space filling it out. In this case, you can simply remove the control and the user won't see it. To delete the control, select it in the Designer pane and press Delete. Although you can recover controls you deleted using the restore feature, it's better to ensure that the user doesn't need the control before you delete it. In some cases, you can simply make the control read-only so that the user can see it but not change it.

✔ **Addition:** The template doesn't provide space for a particular kind of data. For example, your company may want to know whether a particular contact is a vendor, a customer, or both. The current User template doesn't provide a space for this kind of information, but you can add it if desired.

✔ **Modification:** The controls don't work the way that you want them to work or contain incorrect information. By modifying controls you can change how the template works. For example, the User template contains a number of read-only fields. You may not want to allow users to modify the username, but you may want to let them change the user's address when necessary. Of course, you could ask them to head to the administrator's office for every change to ensure that the change is correct, but most administrators don't have the time for this.

The following sections describe all three forms of template behavior modification. Along the way, you also discover both properties and attributes. The attributes are especially important because they control what the user sees in the forms created from the templates you design. You also find out how to create new attributes by modifying the Active Directory schema (design) using Active Directory Services Interface Editor (ADSI Edit).

Considering the use of properties for controls

A property defines the characteristics of a control. For example, the size of the control is the result of two property values: Height and Width. The position of the control on the template is the result of two other property values: X and Y. You can see all four of these properties in Figure 8-2. These four properties define the physical characteristics of the control.

In some cases, you find that you can't modify every property for every control. For example, when you work with the Mailbox Agent template, the controls on most of the tabs have no editable properties. In addition, you can't remove most of the existing controls. However, you can add new controls, and all the properties on the new controls are fully editable.

Some properties define how the control works in relation to the rest of the template. For example, the `TabIndex` property shown in Figure 8-2 tells the order in which a user will access the control when pressing Tab. There's one exception to this rule — even though the label control has a `TabIndex` property, the user can't select it using either the mouse or the Tab key.

The first value property you see for a control is the `Text` property. This property defines the text that the label displays to the user. Notice the ampersand (&) before the *y* in Figure 8-2. The ampersand has a special purpose in making the control next to the label easy to access. The user can press Alt+y to access this control. If you want to display an ampersand, type two ampersands (&&) together.

Most controls have additional properties you need to consider. The edit text box control has the most additional properties, as shown in Figure 8-4.

Figure 8-4:
Properties
determine a
wide range
of actions
and
behaviors.

Behavior	
MaxLength	**64**
Multiline	False
ReadOnly	**True**
UseSystemPasswordChar	False
Layout	
Height	**12**
Width	**37**
X	**83**
Y	**13**
Misc	
AttributeName	**Given-Name**
ConfirmationRequired	**False**
TabIndex	2

The `MaxLength` property determines the maximum number of characters that the user can type. Setting this property correctly can reduce the security risk of using an edit text box control by reducing the opportunities to inject false data into the system. The `Multiline` property determines whether the content appears on multiple lines. You use this property for notes and other long content. When the `ReadOnly` property is set to `True`, the user can see the data but not edit it. Finally, the `UseSystemPasswordChar` property tells the control to display the default password character (usually an asterisk, *) instead of the text the user types to keep the information secret. The "Understanding the use of attributes" section of this chapter describes the use of the `AttributeName` and `ConfirmationRequired` properties.

Understanding the use of attributes

The forms that Exchange Server creates using the templates you design aren't standalone — they work with other elements of Exchange Server and Windows. The values that you see in the form are stored in Active Directory, which is essentially a huge database. The `AttributeName` and `ConfirmationRequired` properties define how the control interacts with Active Directory. The `AttributeName` property determines what data appears in the control, and the `ConfirmationRequired` property determines whether the system asks for confirmation before making a change.

The attribute names you see depend on the Active Directory schema. A *schema* is a description of the Active Directory organization. If you want to see an address field, the schema must contain a definition for an address field.

The `AttributeName` property drop-down list box displays the attributes you can use to fill the field. When a user displays the form, the system retrieves the value for that field from Active Directory and displays it on-screen. If the user makes a change to the field, Exchange Server retrieves the new value and sends it to Active Directory. Consequently, any changes you make using a form affect Active Directory content and appear in any application that relies on that content.

The kind of control you add to a template determines the attributes you can access. For example, an edit text box control can access the Address attribute, but you can't access the Address attribute using a multivalued drop-down box. However, the multivalued drop-down box can access the `Business-Category` attribute. When you don't see the attribute you need with one control type, try another control type to see whether the attribute appears in the list.

Setting attribute security using the ADSI Edit console

Microsoft locks down security for Active Directory with good reason — you really don't want everyone to make any kind of change to records that Active Directory contains. When it comes to user objects, Active Directory lets authenticated users read the records but not write to them. Unfortunately, this means that any changes you'd like users to make in Outlook aren't doable because Outlook will simply tell the users that they don't have the permissions required to make the changes. What you're encountering here is the tough balance of making contact information maintainable and secure.

If you choose to let users make changes to account information, you must do so in a controlled manner. You use the ADSI Edit console in the Administrative Tools folder of Control panel to make security changes. When you open this console, you see what amounts to a blank screen. Use the following procedure to make security changes:

1. **Right-click ADSI Edit and choose Connect To from the context menu.**

   ADSI Edit displays the Connection Settings dialog box shown in Figure 8-5. You want the Default Naming Context, as shown in the Select a Well-Known Naming Context field. Depending on which server you want to access, you may need to choose a different computer.

Figure 8-5:
Create a
connection
to Active
Directory.

2. **Click OK.**

   You see a connection added for the Default Naming Context.

3. **Locate the CN=Users entry in the Active Directory Hierarchy.**

   Figure 8-6 shows the location of this entry on my server. Your server will likely contain different entries, but Figure 8-6 shows basically where to look. Notice the list of user objects in the Details pane.

4. **If you want to provide access to all user objects, right-click the CN=Users entry. Otherwise, right-click the CN=<User Object> you want to change. Choose Properties from the context menu and click the Security tab.**

   You see a list of security principles for the object you selected. This dialog box should look familiar because it's the same dialog box you use to set security anywhere else in Windows.

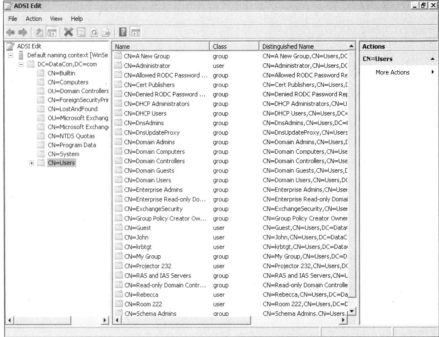

Figure 8-6:
Locate
the list of
users in
your Active
Directory
setup.

5. **Select the Read and Write options for the Authenticated Users entry.**

   The Authenticated Users security principle is the one that Exchange
   Server uses when accessing an object in Active Directory.

6. **Click OK.**

   As with all security changes, the user must log out of and back into the
   system to receive the benefits of the security change.

Creating a new attribute using the ADSI Edit console

Attributes appear as part of the Active Directory schema, not as part of the
Active Directory data. Consequently, if you want to add a new attribute to an
Outlook template, you must use the Active Directory schema to do it.

Microsoft doesn't support adding new attributes to your template. They want
you to use only the attributes they supply. The procedure in this section
isn't supported or encouraged by Microsoft and they may very well make it
unusable in some future version of Exchange Server.

Before you can create a new attribute, you need a unique identifier for it called an Object Identifier (OID). You can obtain the base OID value from Microsoft at `http://msdn.microsoft.com/en-us/library/ms677620.aspx`. The process involves copying a script from the Web site at `http://www.microsoft.com/technet/scriptcenter/scripts/ad/domains/addmvb03.mspx` and running it on your system. To ensure that you can copy the base value, type **CScript <Script Name>** at the command line and press Enter. The number you obtain is the OID root value for your company. Add a period and then an additional number to the base value when creating your attribute. For example, if your base value is 2.5.5.4, you might use 2.5.5.4.1 for the first attribute you create. Every attribute must have a unique value.

To make schema changes, you use the ADSI Edit console in the Administrative Tools folder of Control panel. When you open the ADSI Edit console, you see what amounts to a blank screen. The following steps describe a typical attribute addition. Modify the steps as needed to create the attribute you need:

1. **Right-click ADSI Edit and choose Connect To from the context menu.**

   ADSI Edit displays the Connection Settings dialog box (refer to Figure 8-5). Depending on which server you want to access, you may need to choose a different computer.

2. **Choose Schema in the Select a Well-Known Naming Context field and click OK.**

   You see a connection added for the Schema context.

3. **Locate the CN=Schema,CN=Configuration,<Your Domain Information> entry.**

   ADSI Edit shows a list of objects, as shown in Figure 8-7. You should scroll through this list to ensure that the new attribute you want to create doesn't already exist.

4. **Right-click the CN=Schema,CN=Configuration,<Your Domain Information> entry and choose New⇨Object from the context menu.**

   You see the Create Object wizard.

5. **Highlight attributeSchema and click Next.**

6. **Type a common name for the new attribute and click Next.**

   The common name is the name you see when working in Details Template Editor.

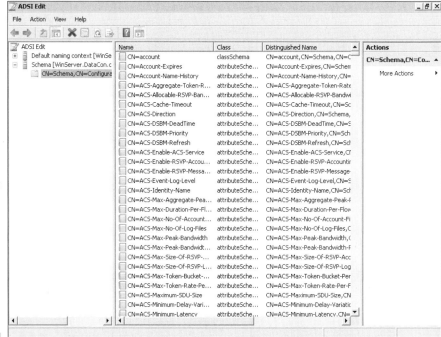

Figure 8-7:
The schema
listing
shows
objects
you can
interact with
in Active
Directory.

7. **Type an oMSyntax value and click Next.**

The oMSyntax value defines the kind of data that the attribute contains. For example, if you want to create a new string, you'd type a value of 64. Of course, you need a list of types from which to choose; you can find them at `http://www.microsoft.com/technet/prodtechnol/ windows2000serv/reskit/distrib/dsbe_ext_dghb.mspx`. In most cases, you use one of these types:

- **1:** Boolean (true or false) — use this type for the check box control
- **2:** Integer (32-bit)
- **64:** Unicode string
- **65:** Large integer (64-bit)

8. **Type a Lightweight Directory Access Protocol (LDAP) display name and click Next.**

In most cases, this is a form of the common name. For example, if the common name is ContactType, the LDAP display name is contactType. Notice that the first letter is always lowercase by convention.

9. **Type** TRUE **or** FALSE **in the Is-Single-Valued field and then click Next.**

This field determines whether the attribute accepts one entry or multiple entries. Type TRUE for a single value control, such as an edit text box control. Type FALSE for a multiple value control, such as a list box, multivalued drop-down box, or multivalued list box control.

10. **Type an attribute syntax value and click Next.**

The attribute syntax value defines how Active Directory stores the data. You want an attribute syntax value that matches the kind of data you create. The Web site at `http://www.microsoft.com/technet/prodtechnol/windows2000serv/reskit/distrib/dsbe_ext_dghb.mspx` provides a complete list of attribute syntax values. Here are the most common values:

- **2.5.5.8:** Boolean (true or false) — use this type for the check box control

- **2.5.5.9:** Integer (32-bit)

- **2.5.5.12:** Unicode string

- **2.5.5.16:** Large integer (64-bit)

11. **Type the unique attribute ID you created earlier and click Next.**

The Create Object wizard asks whether you want to create any additional attributes.

12. **Click More Attributes and follow Steps 1 through 11 if you want to create more attributes. Otherwise, click Finish.**

ADSI Edit creates the new attribute for you. Right-click ADSI Edit and choose Refresh from the context menu to see your new attribute.

Unfortunately, you still can't see your new attribute in Details Template Editor. You must make one additional change. The attribute must have a mAPIID value associated with it. Unfortunately, if you double-click your new attribute now, Active Directory won't let you change the mAPIID value. To add the mAPIID value, you must make a system change using the LDP utility. The following steps tell how to perform this task:

1. **Choose Start⇨Run. Type** LDP **in the Open field and click OK.**

You see the LDP utility.

2. **Choose Connection⇨Connect.**

You see the Connect dialog box.

3. **Type the name of your server and click OK.**

LDP makes a connection to your server.

4. **Choose Connection⇨Bind.**

   You see the Bind dialog box.

5. **Enter the credentials required to log onto the server as a schema administrator and click OK.**

6. **Choose Browse⇨Modify.**

   You see the Modify dialog box.

7. **Type** schemaUpgradeInProgress **in the Attribute field.**

8. **Type 1 in the Value field.**

9. **Click Enter, and then Run.**

   LDP makes the required change to the system status. At this point, you can modify the mAPIID value for your attribute.

10. **In the ADSI Edit console, double-click your new attribute.**

    ADSI Edit displays the properties dialog box for your attribute.

11. **Double-click the mAPIID value.**

    You see the Integer Attribute Editor.

12. **Type a unique value higher than 32,768 and click OK twice.**

    Unfortunately, Microsoft doesn't provide a guideline for this value. It must be unique and it must not be a value that Microsoft Exchange is already using. Microsoft Exchange currently doesn't use any value higher than 32,768.

13. **In the LDP utility, type 0 in the Value field.**

14. **Click Enter and then Run.**

    The attribute is ready for use in Details Template Editor.

Part III

Advanced Techniques

"Our automated response policy to a large company-wide data crash is to notify management, back up existing data and sell 90% of my shares in the company."

In this part . . .

Accidents happen! Errors occur despite your best efforts to prevent them. Sometimes you simply make a mistake with your Exchange Server setup. Chapters 9, 10, and 11 help you prevent, locate, and fix potential Exchange Server errors. Chapter 11 is especially important because it helps you overcome problems — to plan for them to happen so that when they do occur, it's not a major problem.

Everyone wants to work faster. Chapters 12 and 13 introduce you to the command line, where you can work considerably faster than when you use the GUI. The tradeoff is that this environment can introduce the potential for making additional errors, so you should gain experience with Exchange Server before working with the command line.

Chapter 9

Troubleshooting Your Configuration

*E*ven the best setup will experience configuration problems at some point. A new piece of software or hardware or failing software or hardware can cause problems. You may decide to add new features, such as support for mobile devices. Errors can creep in from outside Exchange Server too. Something as a simple Domain Name Server (DNS) configuration error can ruin your day. In short, configuration errors have many causes and you need to know how to troubleshoot them all.

It's within the realm of possibility that you might not even know a problem exists. Unless you are extremely perceptive or have users who really understand how Exchange Server is supposed to work, a small problem can go unnoticed for a long time without anyone reporting it. For example, a template may have a field that is incorrectly formatted or points to the wrong attribute. All of the forms that rely on that template will input incorrect information into Active Directory — information errors that you later need to fix. Your first line of defense against the kind of problem that corrupts your database or causes other problems in the background is monitoring, the first topic of this chapter.

After you discover a problem, you need to consider a fix for it. Sometimes the problem is outside your control and you need to obtain a solution from Microsoft to repair it. When the problem is definitely one of local origin, you may need the assistance of Microsoft Exchange Troubleshooting Assistant to find it. Sometimes locating the problem is a matter of old-fashioned troubleshooting techniques. While this last category falls into the minority of problems you see, a problem of this sort can consume considerable time to locate and understand.

Once you locate the problem, you need to repair it. Although this chapter can't discuss all possible problems you see and definitely not all potential solutions, it does provide you with the information you need to locate problems and their solutions on your own. Chapter 10 builds on the information in this chapter to help you recover from mail-specific problems with greater ease.

Testing Your Configuration

One of the most common administrator tasks for Exchange Server once you configure it is performing testing. Tests help you monitor the health of your configuration. When you begin to see a drop in test results, you know that something is wrong with the configuration, even if you can't see it by using the Exchange Server features. The time to catch problems is before the user can see them. When you catch errors early, the user may not even know they're present and you'll save a lot of time handling support issues in addition to fixing errors.

Considering user setup issues

User setup issues can be one of the more difficult testing issues because this is essentially an end-to-end test. A user setup includes the client application, connectivity between the workstation and the server, the mailbox, and everything in-between. However, you can create a simple test to check for user setup issues. Begin by creating a test user — a mailbox for someone who doesn't actually exist. The "Adding a user" section of Chapter 4 tells you how to perform this task.

It's important to consider the consequences of creating a test user. Because this user doesn't actually exist, you don't have to worry about any user-caused errors getting in the way. Using a test user lets you separate errors caused by misconfiguration on user machines from errors on the server. However, you also don't want someone using this account for illegitimate purposes. Consequently, you give this test user the lowest possible rights on the server. If you can send a message to this user and receive a message from this user, you know that overall Exchange Server security isn't a problem either. In short, relying on a test user helps you eliminate potential cause for problems on your system while checking connectivity.

After you create the test user, check connectivity to and from Exchange Server by sending messages to the test user and receiving messages from the test user. It's important to check message flow in both directions. You need to perform this check from at least one workstation on the network. If your network has multiple segments, you must perform the test from each segment to ensure there are no connectivity issues. When users rely on

Outlook Web Access (OWA), it's also essential to check connectivity using a browser connected from outside of the network so you can verify the firewall configuration works as intended.

In addition to simple e-mail, you should also try other message types. Try making an appointment. Accept and decline appointments to ensure that functionality works as well. It's essential to verify the operation of the Offline Address Book (OAB) because this is one area where users may not notice a flaw. Try accessing public folders and using the client in every other way that you expect users to work with the client. This test may not seem very important, but sometimes users don't report the flaws they see and an administrator account has a habit of making some problems simply disappear. You should create a checklist for performing this test to ensure every feature is tested every time.

After you complete the checks you want to perform, delete the test user account. You want to start with a clean account every time you test to ensure that no configuration errors creep into your test setup. Deleting the test user account also helps reduce potential security risks. If the test user account doesn't exist after the test, you don't have to worry about someone using it for nefarious purposes.

Considering mailbox issues

Mailbox issues can prove difficult to troubleshoot because you don't have access to the content of the mailbox in most cases. Yes, you can tell the user that Exchange Server should provide complete and unhindered access to the mailbox, but you can't explain why the user can't see a particular message or interact with other users until you work with the user's mailbox data. In most cases, locating the source of a problematic mailbox means sitting at the user's machine and working through the problem without the normal administrator tools.

It's essential to eliminate every other potential source of problems before you work with a user's mailbox. A connectivity problem requires that you review connectivity issues, rather than look at the mailbox as the source of the problem.

The following sections help you narrow an error to the content of the user's mailbox. After you use this information to determine that everything outside the mailbox works, you usually have to visit the user's machine to learn more about the problem message. In many cases, you discover that the problem makes sense. For example, the system deleted some message material because you have a transport rule in place that shows the material is unacceptable. An executable attachment normally falls into this category. Unless you work with a knowledgeable user, even discovering an illegal attachment can prove elusive until you make the trip to the user's machine.

Using Outlook logging to your advantage

One of the best tools you have for testing Outlook functionality is the logging feature that Outlook provides. This feature makes it possible to track Outlook activity as you perform tasks such as checking availability information or sending e-mail. Both Outlook 2003 and Outlook 2007 use the same set of steps to enable this functionality as described in the following steps:

1. **Choose Tools➪Options and click the Other tab.**

   You see the Options dialog box.

2. **Click Advanced Options.**

   Outlook displays the Advanced Options dialog box shown in Figure 9-1.

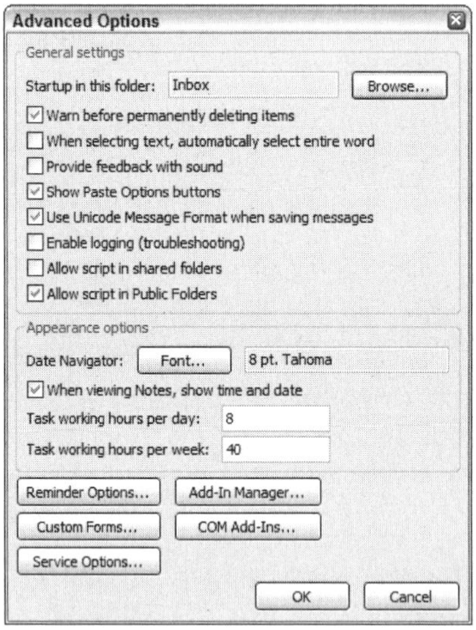

Figure 9-1:
Enable logging to discover the source of errors.

3. **Select Enable Logging (Troubleshooting) and click OK.**

4. **Click OK to close the Options dialog box.**

5. **Restart Outlook.**

6. **Perform any actions required to duplicate the error.**

   Outlook creates a log as you perform the tasks.

7. **Choose Tools➪Options and click the Other tab.**

   You see the Options dialog box.

8. **Click Advanced Options.**

   Outlook displays the Advanced Options dialog box (refer to Figure 9-1).

9. **Select Enable Logging (Troubleshooting) and click OK.**

10. **Click OK to close the Options dialog box.**

11. **Close Outlook.**

The log file you just created appears in a log file in the `\Documents and Settings\<User Name>\Local Settings\Temp` folder on your hard drive. The log file you need depends on the Outlook function you troubleshoot. For example, you track e-mail messaging using the `OPMLog.LOG` file for POP3 and the `IMAP0.LOG` file for IMAP4, and you track availability using the `OLKDisc.LOG` file.

Open the log file using an application such as Notepad. The contents contain step-by-step information on the tasks that Outlook performs to complete each of the tasks you request. It's important to keep the log file as small as possible to make debugging easier. You can find a list of common Outlook error codes and associated solutions at `http://www.balasai.com/esupport/index.php?_m=knowledgebase&_a=viewarticle&kbarticleid=88`.

Troubleshooting the Availability and Autodiscover services

The Availability service provides secure, consistent, and up-to-date access to free and busy times between Outlook users. However, the technique you use to troubleshoot the Availability service depends on the client the user has.

To find the availability information, Outlook 2007 uses the Autodiscover service to determine the URL to use for the Availability service. In fact, in most cases you must also configure the external URLs for the OAB and Unified Messaging (UM) correctly to obtain a working solution. Consequently, you normally troubleshoot the Availability and Autodiscover services together for Outlook 2007 configurations. Read more about the Availability service at `http://technet.microsoft.com/en-us/library/bb232134.aspx` and the Autodiscover service at `http://technet.microsoft.com/en-us/library/bb124251(EXCHG.80).aspx`.

Outlook 2003 users don't rely on the Autodiscover service. These older clients rely on the public folders you configure for availability information instead. In short, it's essential to know the kind of client that the user has when looking for availability problems with Outlook. The "Providing an Offline Address Book (OAB)" section of Chapter 4 describes the differences between configuring OAB for Outlook 2007 and Outlook 2003.

After you ensure that the Availability service is running and that either the Autodiscover or public folder configuration is correct, you check client functionality using the logging technique described in the "Using Outlook logging to your advantage" section. Try to access availability information for a number of users to determine whether the problem is a particular user (in which case, a transport rule may be the source of the problem) or all users (in which case the client may have configuration issues). You can find a list of common Availability service error codes at `http://technet.micro-soft.com/en-us/library/bb397225(EXCHG.80).aspx`.

Outlook 2007 users can have a number of problems with the Autodiscover service that affect the Availability service that don't affect Outlook 2003 users. The article at `http://blog.shijaz.com/2008/05/problems-with-exchange-server-2007.html` describes the primary suspect in this case, a certificate with incorrect information. The author discusses the problem, a diagnostic you can use to detect it, and a solution.

Overcoming HTML problems with OWA

OWA can suffer from any of the problems that occur with its desktop counterpart. Consequently, before you begin looking for an OWA-specific problem, determine whether the problem is more generic by accessing the mailbox with a desktop client such as Outlook. If you can access the mailbox properly using the desktop client, the problem likely lies with OWA.

The browser that the user relies on to access the Web site can have configuration issues. When the user complains of OWA access, make sure you check the browser configuration first. For example, most browsers today won't work with OWA using their default configuration because OWA requires the use of scripts. The first step is to ensure that the OWA site is on the browser's safe sender list. A firewall can also cause problems by OWA blocking content. In short, look for any browser configuration problems that could also prevent the browser from accessing other secure Web sites that rely on scripted content.

It's also possible for a user to experience some problems that aren't easily resolved. For example, Microsoft includes filtering in Exchange Server that could make it impossible to send certain types of content to an OWA client. In this case, you need to configure a secure network share to allow content exchange as described in the Knowledge Base article at `http://support.microsoft.com/kb/899394/en-us`. Fortunately, many of these problems also have software fixes as described in the Knowledge Base article at `http://support.microsoft.com/kb/912939/en-us`.

Some administrators will walk away from a fix when they don't think about the conditions under which OWA executes, even on Windows Server 2008. OWA always relies on IIS 6.0 functionality. That's why you need to install the IIS 6.0 features on Windows Server 2008 to run it. Consequently, when you see troubleshooting techniques such as the Knowledge Base article at `http://support.microsoft.com/kb/301428`, it applies to IIS 7.0 users as well. Unfortunately, you have to figure out how to apply the repair steps to the IIS 7.0 console, rather than using IIS 6.0 equivalent. I hope Microsoft remedies this situation soon.

Catching connectivity problems

For many administrators, testing connectivity is difficult at best. The problem is that connectivity involves a mix of hardware and software. A bad router can cause connectivity problems. Network Interface Cards (NICs) do go bad and they usually don't go completely bad. Because of the way network hardware encounters problems, you may see the network deliver messages more slowly but not stop delivering them. Fortunately, most network hardware comes with testing aids; all you have to do is run them.

Monitoring doesn't always mean performing a test. In some cases, monitoring means using Event Viewer or other software that Microsoft provides as part of Windows.

The user testing you perform in the "Considering user setup issues" section of the chapter can help you detect connectivity problems. You may find that the e-mail works, but not as quickly as you expect. After you eliminate performance issues, such as the user watching the basketball game over the network connection, you should consider breaking out the testing disk for your hardware. Verify that you can run the test using a live connection. Some tests require that you use a loopback (a kind of closed circuit) connection to perform the test.

Thinking outside the configuration issue box

In most cases, you need to test more than just Exchange Server to ensure that your setup continues to run trouble-free. The entire Exchange Server environment, connections to other systems, and the state of the Internet all affect how your setup runs. Consequently, in addition to testing Exchange Server, you need to check these elements for flaws using the vendor instructions:

- ✔ Windows as a whole
- ✔ All your hardware, especially hard drives
- ✔ Network connections
- ✔ Routers and other external connectivity
- ✔ Connections to your Internet Service Provider (ISP)
- ✔ Workstation hardware
- ✔ Client applications

Any of these sources can cause significant problems for your Exchange Server setup. Besides these sources, you also need to consider any partners that you work with because a problem on a partner system will also affect your setup. It always pays to look for malware when you suspect a problem. You must check every system that has a connection to your server to ensure that malware isn't a problem.

Obviously, this section gives you a lot of ground to check, and most organizations simply don't have the resources to perform checks on these sources every day. You should begin testing on the local server and move out from there as time permits. In some cases, little issues you notice on your server point to bigger issues somewhere else, and you can use these little issues as a guide to finding the true source of the problem. When it comes to something as large as Exchange Server, you must test the obvious first and then move on to areas that are outside the usual realm of configuration issues.

Performing Required Updates

You can add Exchange Server to the list of items that Windows Update checks automatically. These updates will keep Exchange Server itself ready for use. If you used the "Performing the Installation" section of Chapter 2 to install Exchange Server on your machine, you already have this support in place. Otherwise, you can pop the installation media into your DVD drive and choose Option 5 on the list of items that you see when the startup program completes its initialization process.

The Exchange Server software isn't the only part of Exchange Server you need to update. Interestingly enough, the spam support requires a separate update. Consequently, if you're updating only Exchange Server, your system may still experience all kinds of problems. The Knowledge Base articles at `http://technet.microsoft.com/en-us/library/bb125199(EXCHG.80).aspx` and `http://technet.microsoft.com/en-us/library/bb124241(EXCHG.80).aspx` provide details on configuring Exchange Server to support automatic spam updates.

Using the Exchange Processes Are Failing Tool

The Exchange Processes Are Failing tool helps you locate and diagnose problem processes. In some cases, you may not even know that there is a problem because the process may not affect an Exchange Server feature you work with directly. However, you normally have a clue that something is wrong. If you don't see a direct failure of Exchange Server functionality, such as lost mailbox features, Event Viewer will display the problem in a log.

You may wonder where this tool comes from since it doesn't appear in the Toolbox folder of Exchange Management Console. The tool actually appears as part of Microsoft Exchange Troubleshooting Assistant (ExTRA), which doesn't appear anywhere in the Start menu. Microsoft Exchange hides a number of tools in the \Program Files\Microsoft\Exchange Server\ Bin folder of your machine, so you want to be sure to look in this folder when you have a need that doesn't seem to appear in any of the other tools discussed in this book. The following steps describe how to use the Exchange Processes Are Failing tool to locate errors on your system:

1. **Choose Start⇨Run.**

   Windows displays the Run dialog box.

2. **Type** ExTRA **and click OK.**

   Windows starts Microsoft Exchange Troubleshooting Assistant.

3. **Click Select a Task in the Welcome screen.**

   You see a list of Microsoft Exchange Troubleshooting Assistant tasks, as shown in Figure 9-2.

4. **Click Exchange Processes Are Failing.**

   The wizard asks you to provide a name for the scan. In addition, you must choose how to identify the servers for the scan.

5. **Type a name for the scan in the Enter an Identifying Label for this Analysis field.**

6. **Choose an option in the How Do You Want to Specify the Server to Scan field.**

   Choose Select Exchange Servers to Scan for Failure Events when working with multiple servers. If you have only one server or want to scan only one server, choose the Scan a Specific Server for Failure Events option. This procedure assumes that you've selected the Scan a Specific Server for Failure Events option.

7. **Type the name of the server in the Select Server field.**

8. **Click Start Scanning Server.**

   The display initially shows the scanning process. After this process is finished, the display automatically shows that it's preparing the report for you. Finally, you see a View Results display like the one shown in Figure 9-3.

Figure 9-2:
Microsoft
Exchange
Trouble-
shooting
Assistant
provides
access to a
number of
tools.

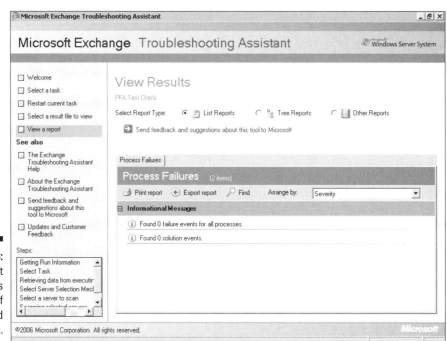

Figure 9-3:
The result
of a scan is
a listing of
any failed
processes.

Performing Database Recovery Management

The Database Recovery Management tool appears in the Toolbox folder of Exchange Management Console. When you double-click this entry, you see Microsoft Exchange Troubleshooting Assistant. Figure 9-4 shows what this tool looks like.

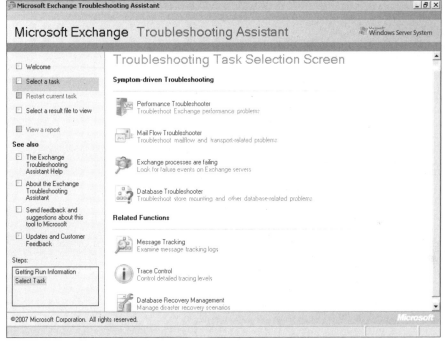

Figure 9-4: Microsoft Exchange Trouble-shooting Assistant provides a number of useful tools.

When you first start Microsoft Exchange Troubleshooting Assistant, you see the usual update display. After a version check online and possible update, you see the Enter Server and User Information window shown in Figure 9-5.

In most cases, all you need to provide is a name for your organization in the Enter an Identifying Label for This Activity field and an Exchange Server name in the Exchange Server Name field. After you enter these two values, click Next, and Microsoft Exchange Troubleshooting Assistant tries to make a connection to Active Directory. When working with complex setups, you may need to provide a different domain controller name and even provide different credentials. After Microsoft Exchange Troubleshooting Assistant makes the Active Directory connection, it displays a list of tasks you can perform, such as repairing a database, as shown in Figure 9-6.

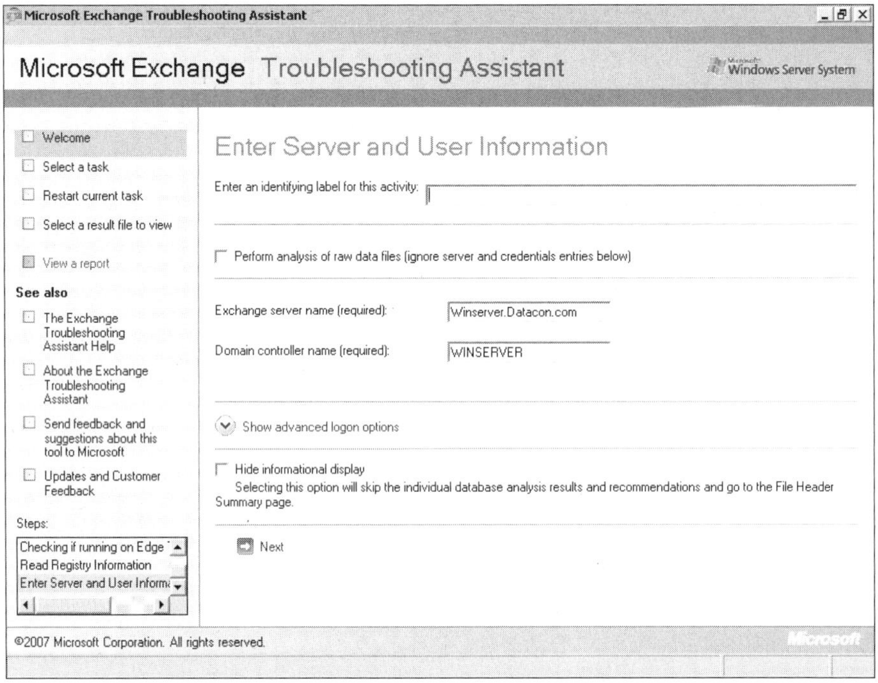

Figure 9-5:
Provide the
required
server and
user infor-
mation to
log onto the
system.

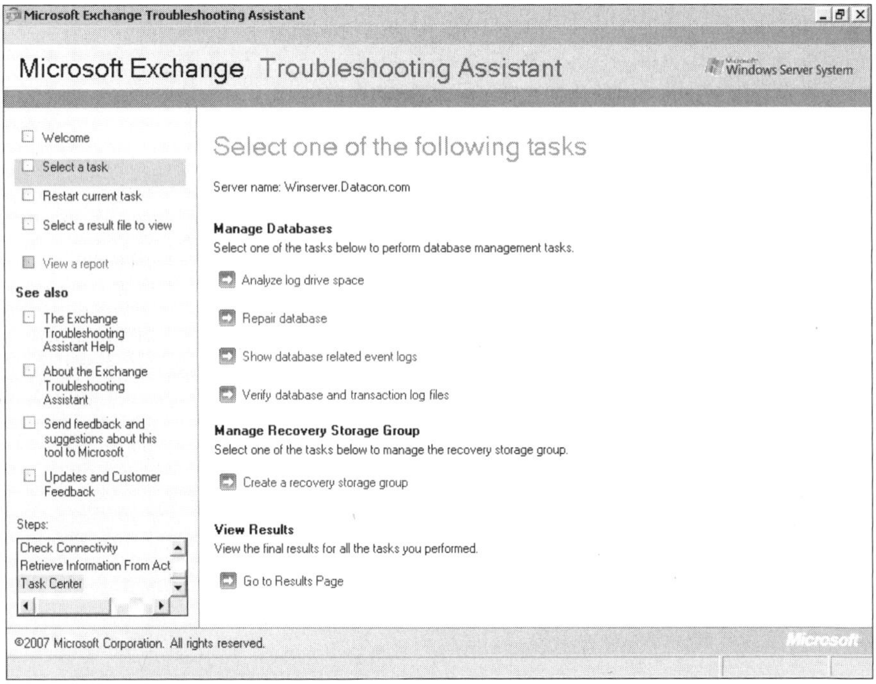

Figure 9-6:
Database
manage-
ment
involves
performing
a number of
tasks.

Each of the management options shown helps you discover facts about the Exchange Server database. The following list provides an overview of each of these tasks:

- **Analyze Log Drive Space:** Displays a list of the storage groups and their associated logs. You see the amount of space used by the logs and how much space the logs can use to grow. Most important of all, Exchange Server shows an estimate of the number of days before the log will run out of space so you can make adjustments as necessary.

- **Repair Database:** Starts a wizard that helps you repair a database. You choose the storage group that you want to work with and one or more databases within that storage group that you want to repair. This is the last option you should use to fix a database. Microsoft recommends that you restore the database from a backup as an alternative. The repairs performed using this approach are significant, and you must make a backup of the database immediately after you complete this task to ensure that you have a new, compatible database backup. Depending on the size of your database, this task could require hours, and you should always perform this task with all users logged off Exchange Server.

- **Show Database Related Event Logs:** Obtains all database event log entries no matter where they appear. Use this feature to ensure that you see all event log entries. When you initially select this option, Microsoft Exchange Troubleshooting Assistant asks how many hours of event log entries you want to see. If you type **0**, you see all event log entries.

- **Verify Database and Transaction Log Files:** Performs a check of database and transaction log files to ensure that the database is clean and that you don't have to apply log entries to the database to update it before you mount it. You can only perform this check on dismounted databases. To dismount a database, right-click its entry in the Server Configuration\Mailbox folder of Exchange Management Console and choose Dismount Database. Users can't access dismounted databases, so make sure you perform this task only when users aren't connected to the system.

- **Create a Recovery Storage Group:** Creates a recovery storage group that holds the content of the databases found in the storage group you choose. You use the recovery database to restore the database after errors occur. The recovery storage group acts as a kind of backup. You should view it in the same way as you view Windows restore points.

Using Database Troubleshooter

Database Troubleshooter looks for error information about the databases on your system and provides a detailed report on the database condition. Use this tool when you want to check the overall state of the database, including server status and other external conditions that could affect the database. You begin using this tool in the Toolbox folder of Exchange Management Console. The following steps describe how to create the Database Troubleshooter report:

1. **Double-click Database Troubleshooter in the Toolbox folder.**

   Exchange Server displays Microsoft Exchange Troubleshooting Assistant, which begins by checking for updates online. After the tool installs any required updates, you see a status message.

2. **Click Go to Welcome Screen.**

   You see the Enter Server and User Information window (refer to Figure 9-5). This window is your assurance that you're working with the correct version of Microsoft Exchange Troubleshooting Assistant.

3. **Type a name for your organization in the Enter an Identifying Label for This Activity field.**

4. **Type an Exchange Server name in the Exchange Server Name field.**

5. **Click Next.**

   Microsoft Exchange Troubleshooting Assistant tries to make a connection to Active Directory. After the Active Directory connection is complete, you see a Select Event Log Detect Option window.

6. **Type a value for the event log detection in the field provided.**

   Use a value of 0 for all event log entries. A positive value indicates the number of minutes that you want to retrieve, with 120 minutes (2 hours) as the default.

7. **Click Retrieve Event Logs.**

   Microsoft Exchange Troubleshooting Assistant analyzes the system and application event logs for potential database entries. Eventually, you see an Event Log Scan Results dialog box, which provides a quick overview of the event log entries that Database Troubleshooter found. In most cases, you see a message saying simply that it didn't find any entries.

8. **Click Go to Results Page.**

   You see a report similar to the one shown in Figure 9-7 that tells you about any database errors that Database Troubleshooter found. Drill down to the various levels to see detailed information about any errors.

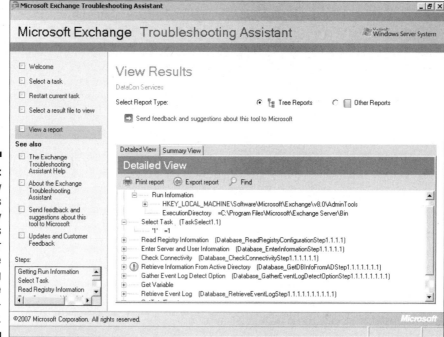

Figure 9-7:
View
reports
about any
errors
in your
database
using
Database
Trouble-
shooter.

Chapter 10

Recovering from Mail-Specific Problems

*T*his chapter discusses a considerable number of issues that affect the use and performance of Exchange Server. All of these issues are important, but no issue is more important than the e-mail that users create. The data contained in mailboxes will cause more problems and is worth more than any other single area of Exchange Server. In fact, you can lose your entire Exchange Server configuration and it won't cause the amount of problems that the loss of the data in a single mailbox will cause. Consequently, in some respects, this is the most important chapter of the book because it describes how to work through some common mail-specific problems.

Fortunately, Microsoft recognizes the difficulty of locating e-mail problems because the company provides a number of tools to help you overcome them. This chapter shows how to use Mail Flow Troubleshooter, Message Tracking, Queue Viewer, and Routing Log Viewer — all valuable tools in your fight to keep the messages moving. Each tool has a specific purpose, so the chapter also emphasizes when you use one tool over another to accomplish a particular task.

It's best to have a copy of the e-mail a user needs, even when an outage is unavoidable. Replication represents the best way to try to maintain updated backups of user e-mails because it works automatically and continuously. However, you also need to perform regular backups because replication doesn't protect you from major damage such as a failed hard drive.

Consequently, you need to couple the procedures found in this chapter with the maintenance tasks described in Chapter 11. A well-maintained Exchange Server setup is less likely to cause significant problems and will let you get that weekend off that you deserve.

Using Mail Flow Troubleshooter

Mail Flow Troubleshooter is a type of diagnostic aid that helps you understand a problem. It begins by asking you some questions about the problems you see with Exchange Server and then helps you locate the source of those problems. Consequently, this tool is a kind of diagnostic aid in which you participate, rather than let the software do all the work. You use this tool when users report problems sending or receiving e-mail or other message types (such as schedules) but you can't find anything wrong using the diagnostic aids described in Chapter 9.

The following steps show how a typical session works — your particular experience will differ based on answers you provide and the actual cause of problems on your system:

1. **Double-click Mail Flow Troubleshooter in the Toolbox folder.**

   Exchange Server displays Microsoft Exchange Troubleshooting Assistant, which begins by checking for updates online. After the tool installs any required updates, you see a status message.

2. **Click Go to Welcome Screen.**

   You see the Exchange Mail Flow Troubleshooter window shown in Figure 10-1.

3. **Type a report title in the Enter an Identifying Label for This Analysis field.**

4. **Select one of the entries from the What Symptoms Are You Seeing drop-down list box.**

   Often, the list won't contain all potential problems you see. Select an entry that closely matches the problem, rather than looking for a specific match in every situation.

5. **(Optional) Select Hide Informational Display when you don't want to see intermediate test results.**

   Although it may be cumbersome to review all intermediate results, you can often use them to help you better understand the process Mail Flow Troubleshooter is using to help you locate a problem. If you don't receive satisfactory results the first time you run this wizard, try running it a second time with the informational displays intact.

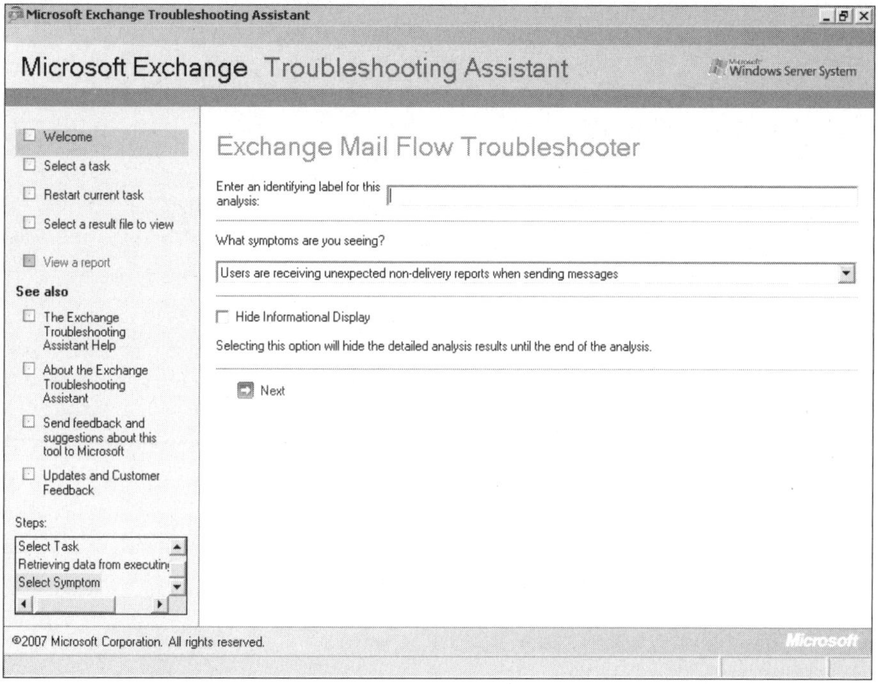

Figure 10-1:
The initial
window
asks for
a basic
problem
definition.

6. **Click Next.**

   The wizard displays the Enter Server and User Information window shown in Figure 10-2. The wizard uses this information to determine which Exchange Server to check.

7. **Type an Exchange Server name in the Exchange Server Name field.**

8. **(Optional) Type the name of a global catalog server in the Global Catalog Server Name field.**

   In most cases, the name you see in the Global Catalog Server Name field is the correct one for the local server. You need to change this field only when you want to work on another server. You may also need to provide additional credentials when working with another server, as shown in Figure 10-2.

9. **Click Next.**

   The wizard retrieves information about Exchange Server and tells you about any errors it sees when you have the Hide Informational Display option cleared (the default setting). In most cases, you see a list of informational messages that tell you about the mail flow on your server, which can be interesting to read. If you have the Hide Informational Display option selected, proceed to Step 11.

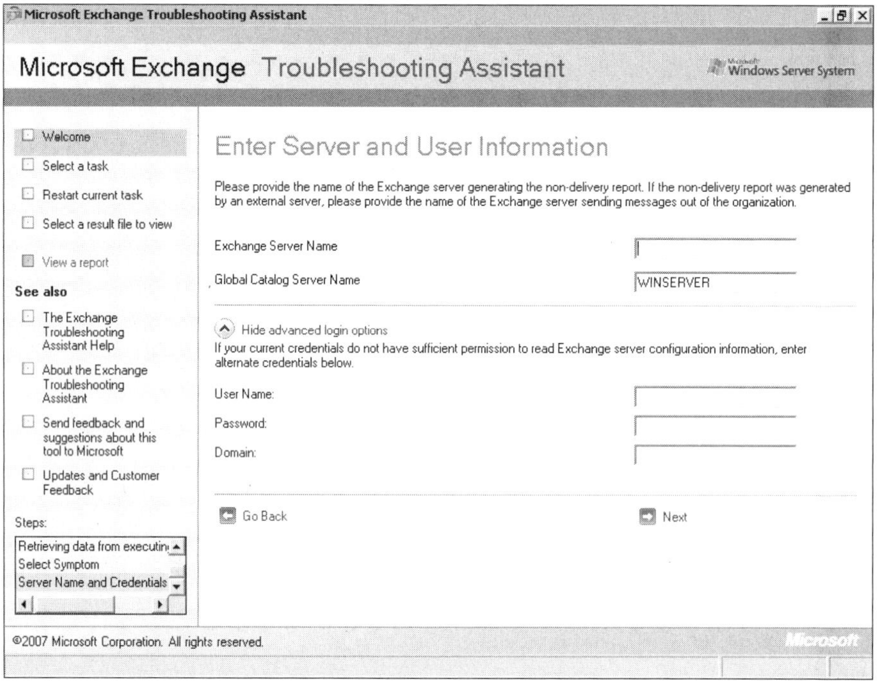

©2007 Microsoft Corporation. All rights reserved.

Figure 10-2: Log into the Exchange Server you want to work with.

10. **Click Next.**

    You see the Enter Delivery Status Notification Code window.

11. **Select one of the codes listed in the Delivery Status Notification Code drop-down list box.**

    These codes define the problem that you're seeing with the message. In most cases, the message has an error statement. At the end of the message, you see the server URL, followed by a message code such as 4.4.7. This is the notification code that the wizard expects you to enter.

12. **Click Next.**

    The wizard retrieves the delivery status notification code information. If you have the Hide Informational Display option selected, the wizard scans the Exchange Server logs and you see the View Results window. If the Hide Informational Display option is deselected, you see the human readable information associated with the delivery status notification code.

13. **Click Next.**

    The wizard scans the Exchange Server logs. After the scan is complete, you see the View Results window shown in Figure 10-3.

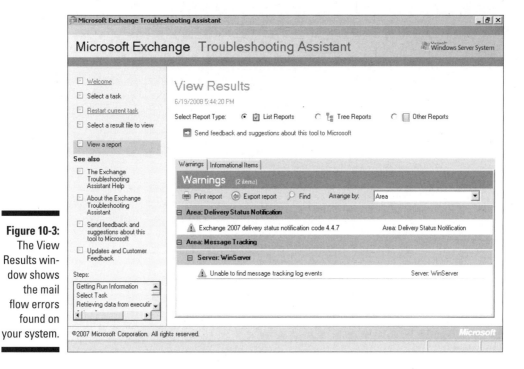

Figure 10-3:
The View Results window shows the mail flow errors found on your system.

Performing Message Tracking

Message Tracking helps you locate an e-mail message event no matter where it is. It can appear in any mailbox and you can track the message across servers. Consequently, you can find any message event anywhere, as long as you have specific criteria to use. A message event tells you about the message, such as whether the message transfer succeeded. The message event doesn't display the content of the message.

The key term to keep in mind when making a search is *specific.* A search can produce a huge number of results, which can require hours of additional searching on your part when you don't provide specific enough criteria. Telling Exchange Server to look for all messages from Jerry will almost certainly not produce the results you want. Adding criteria to the search will slow the search down because you're asking Exchange Server to do more work. However, what you must consider is that Exchange Server is doing the work instead of you. Even so, adding too many criteria to the search can produce unacceptably large search times.

Searches use Exchange Server resources. If your server's already heavily loaded, adding a search to the burden will almost certainly slow everything to a crawl. Perform searches when they are least likely to cause system problems. For example, a complex search works better after hours, when no one is using a system. You could perform a simple search on a lightly loaded server during work hours, but do so carefully. The best approach is to perform searches when users are away from their machines.

Now that you have a better idea of what Message Tracking is about, it's time to configure Message Tracking on your system. The following steps describe how to use Message Tracking:

1. **Double-click Message Tracking in the Toolbox folder.**

   Exchange Server displays Microsoft Exchange Troubleshooting Assistant, which begins by checking for updates online. After the tool installs any required updates, you see a status message.

2. **Click Go to Welcome Screen.**

   You see the Message Tracking Parameters window shown in Figure 10-4.

Message Tracking Parameters

Select check boxes to include criteria in the message tracking search.

Recipients	☑	Jerry	Resolve Recipient
Sender	☑	Ann	Resolve Sender
Server	☑	MyServer	Server from Sender
EventID	☑	RECEIVE	
MessageID	☑		
InternalMessageID	☑		
Subject	☑		
Reference	☑		
Start	☑	Friday , June 20, 2008 11:47 AM	
End	☑	Friday , June 20, 2008 11:57 AM	

Exchange Management Shell command

get-messagetrackinglog -Recipients:Jerry -Sender "Ann" -Server "MyServer" -EventID "RECEIVE" -Start "6/20/2008 11:47:00 AM" -End "6/20/2008 11:57:00 AM"

⬅ Go Back   ➡ Next

Figure 10-4: Define any parameters that you want to use to perform a search.

3. **Select any criteria you want to use for the search. Type any information in the associated fields required for the search.**

Even though Figure 10-4 shows all of the fields selected for clarity, you normally use fewer fields. The content of the Exchange Management Shell Command field changes as you change criteria. You can save this command for later use in duplicating the search at the command line. Highlight the text, press Ctrl+C, and paste the command in Notepad or some other application where you can save it as a file. When you need to troubleshoot e-mail, select the FAIL option in the Event ID field.

4. Click Next.

Message Tracking searches the event logs for events that contain the information you specify. Depending on the complexity of the search criteria you provided, the current load on the server, and the size of the log files, the search may take a while. Even a simply search requires 30 or more seconds to complete, so don't worry if you see the search window displayed for what seems like a long time. Eventually, you see a list of message events that match the criteria you specify, as shown in Figure 10-5.

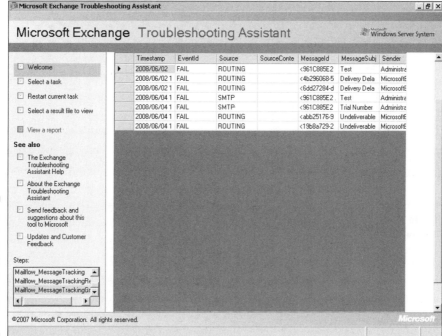

Figure 10-5: The output tells you about messages that fit the criteria you specify.

Interacting with Queue Viewer

The Queue Viewer tool helps you see the message queues used to direct messages and the messages that the queues contain. You can see any number of queues for Exchange Server, but a simple setup normally contains two queues: one to accept messages and another to output messages. Start Queue Viewer by double-clicking Queue Viewer in the Toolbox folder. Figure 10-6 shows a typical Queue Viewer display.

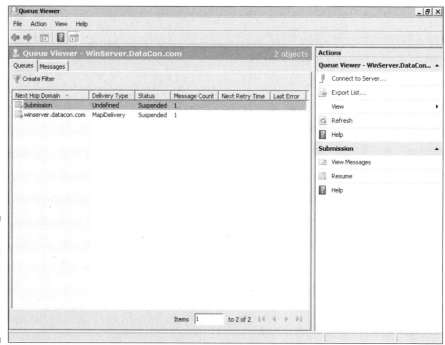

Figure 10-6: Use Queue Viewer to see queues and messages within queues.

Working with queues

Sometimes messages can arrive at Exchange Server faster than the server can process them. If the messages went directly to the processing portion of Exchange Server, users would experience timeframes when they couldn't upload messages. Because these times occur when Exchange Server and the users are busiest, the delays reduce user productivity significantly. To combat this problem, all messages go to a queue. As its name implies, a *queue* is a location in memory where Exchange Server holds messages until it can process them. In many cases, the queues won't contain any messages because Exchange Server can process them immediately.

If you don't see the queues you expected to see, look at the top of the Actions pane, which tells you the name of the current server. If you need to change servers, click Connect to Server. You see the Connect to Server dialog box. Click Browse, locate the server you want, and click OK. Click Connect to make the server connection.

The Submission queue shown in Figure 10-6 receives messages. The messages aren't sorted in any way — all messages go to this queue. After Exchange Server performs checks on the messages and determines where they should go, it sends them to the delivery queue. In this case, the winserver.datacon.com queue is the only delivery queue for the server.

The display shows the queue name, delivery type, status, message count, next retry time, and last error message. The delivery type is undefined for the Submission queue because it receives messages of all types. The winserver.datacon.com queue delivers only Messaging Application Programming Interface (MAPI) messages. If you wanted to deliver another kind of message, the display would show another queue entry. The status column reads Suspended for both queues. That's because I wanted to trap some messages to display. Normally, the status column reads Ready. Click Resume in the Actions pane to restart a queue if you ever see the Suspended indicator.

The Message Count column is the one you should watch. This column tells you how many messages Exchange Server hasn't processed yet. Under ideal circumstances, this column would always read 0 or 1. However, conditions are seldom ideal. If this number becomes overly large, you need to start determining why so many messages remain in the queue. The Last Error column can help, but often you must view individual messages using the Messages tab, which is described in the next section.

Working with messages

The Messages tab, shown in Figure 10-7, displays the messages contained in every queue that Exchange Server can access. The message entries tell you the message sender, current status, size, Spam Confidence Level (SCL), queue identifier, message source name, subject, and any error associated with that specific message. Using this information helps you determine whether a particular message has a problem associated with it and whether you need to act on that message or let Exchange Server handle it (such as when Exchange Server must retry sending a message).

If you want to see the messages in a specific queue, highlight the queue entry in the Queues tab. Click View Messages in the Actions pane. You see another tab that contains the name of the queue and contains only messages from that queue. The content of the queue-specific tab is the same as the content shown in the Messages tab.

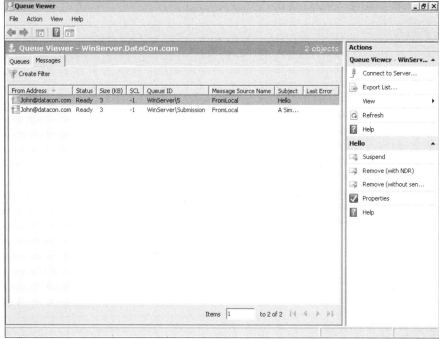

Figure 10-7:
The
Messages
tab shows
all pending
messages
on the
server.

Even if a queue is suspended, messages can have a Ready status indicator.
Exchange Server sets the individual message status based on that message's
content and deliverability, rather than on the queue's status. If you see a
Suspended indicator, you can attempt to deliver the message by highlighting
its entry and clicking Resume in the Actions pane.

A problem message can clog the queue. In some cases, messages are unde-
liverable or have other problems. You have two options when working with
problem messages.

- **Remove (with NDR):** Choosing this option removes the message from
  the queue (deleting it) and sends a Non-Delivery Report (NDR) to the
  sender. The NDR tells the sender why the message is unacceptable and
  provides an opportunity to send it again.

- **Remove (without sending NDR):** Choosing this option removes the message from the queue without sending an NDR. You choose this option
  when a message comes from a source that you don't want to support,
  such as spam or a virus. In fact, sending the NDR when working with
  spam can tell the sender that the server is active and perhaps that the
  account is usable.

Unlike queues, messages provide you with additional information when you need it. To see this additional information, highlight the message and click Properties in the Actions pane. You see a message Properties dialog box like the one shown in Figure 10-8.

Figure 10-8:
Message details tell you more about the message and its potential content.

Some of the content of this dialog box, such as the subject, is the same as the information you see in the Messages tab. However, this dialog box contains a few entries worth noting, such as the message recipient. In fact, the Recipients tab provides complete status information about the recipient, including whether the recipient is active. The Source IP field is another good value to look at because it tells you the source of the message, and you can use this information to determine whether the source is trustworthy.

Understanding Replication

Replication is a kind of backup for your Exchange Server. However, instead of the backup occurring at a specific time each day, replication occurs constantly. As changes appear in one location, they also get sent to a secondary location for safe keeping. Replication doesn't necessarily provide complete safety — it's possible to lose a message or two because the replication doesn't occur simultaneously with the original message processing; however, replication is so fast that the probability of losing a particular message is extremely small.

You must choose the kind of replication that matches your server requirements. Exchange Server 2007 SP1 supports three kinds of replication:

- ✔ Local Continuous Replication (LCR)
- ✔ Cluster Continuous Replication (CCR)
- ✔ Standby Continuous Replication (SCR)

Of the three, SCR is new to SP1, so you can use it only in this environment. Older versions of Exchange Server 2007 have access to both LCR and CCR.

Some administrators feel that replication is the complete answer to backup — but it isn't. Replication provides an extremely fast response to a localized calamity; it helps you get up and running quickly when the only problem is that the server has failed for some reason. Replication won't help you when natural disasters or other issues strike. If both the default and backup servers fail, replication won't help you. In short, if you count exclusively on replication to provide data backup, you may not lose your data immediately, but you'll lose it eventually.

The most important issue for an Exchange Server configuration is determining whether you need replication. Using replication means adding hardware (normally a server) to your system, and your organization may not be able to afford a multiserver setup. In this case, performing regular backups will provide you with some measure of safety. If the server fails, you lose only the new messages since the last backup.

If you decide to use replication, you must decide which kind of replication works best for your organization. The following sections describe the three kinds of replication and provide a few tips on choosing the right replication for your organization.

Considering LCR

The LCR option is the closest to performing a backup and is the least expensive of the three options. This is also the easiest option to implement on any system. When using this option, you create a replicated copy of the Exchange Server databases on another drive of the local system or on a Storage Area Network (SAN) or Network Area Storage (NAS). See `http://compnetworking.about.com/od/networkstorage/f/san-vs-nas.htm` for a comparison of SAN and NAS configurations.

An LCR configuration protects you from a hard drive failure but not a server failure. If the server fails and the Exchange Server replicated database is on the local server, you still won't have access to your e-mail. However, because hard drive failures are on the top of the list of bad things that happen to servers, this is a good option for a company on an extreme budget that has an extra disk in their server.

The SAN or NAS option is better. If the server fails and you have a second server with access to the SAN or NAS, you can bring the server online and restore e-mail access in a matter of minutes in many cases. However, users will still experience a gap in e-mail coverage. In addition, if the second server isn't a dedicated Exchange Server setup, users will experience slow response times, which always causes problems for the administrator. The following steps describe how to enable LCR for any Exchange Server Setup:

1. **Choose the Server Configuration\Mailbox folder in Exchange Management Console.**

2. **Highlight the storage group you want to replicate.**

   Replication works only on storage groups, not individual databases within the storage group. Consequently, you must have enough disk space for the entire storage group.

3. **Click Enable Local Continuous Replication on Selected Object.**

   You see the Enable Storage Group Local Continuous Replication wizard. The initial dialog box shows the storage group name and any databases within the storage group.

4. **Click Next.**

   The wizard displays the Set Paths dialog box shown in Figure 10-9.

5. **Click the Browse button for the Local Continuous Replication System Files Path field, locate the path you want to use for storage, and click OK.**

   The default setting places the replicated copy on the same hard drive as the Exchange Server setup. This location doesn't make any sense because a hard drive failure will knock out the replicated copy as well. You must choose another storage location on a different drive to make replication worthwhile.

6. **Click the Browse button for the Local Continuous Replication Log Files Path field, locate the path you want to use for storage, and click OK.**

   Choosing an entirely different drive for the log files will provide a performance boost for your system. The use of multiple storage paths reduces the latency normally found in hard drives. As with the system files, you must choose another drive to store the replicated copy; otherwise Exchange Server won't be able to recover from a hard drive failure.

7. **Click Next.**

8. **You see a mailbox Database dialog box for one of the databases in the storage group.**

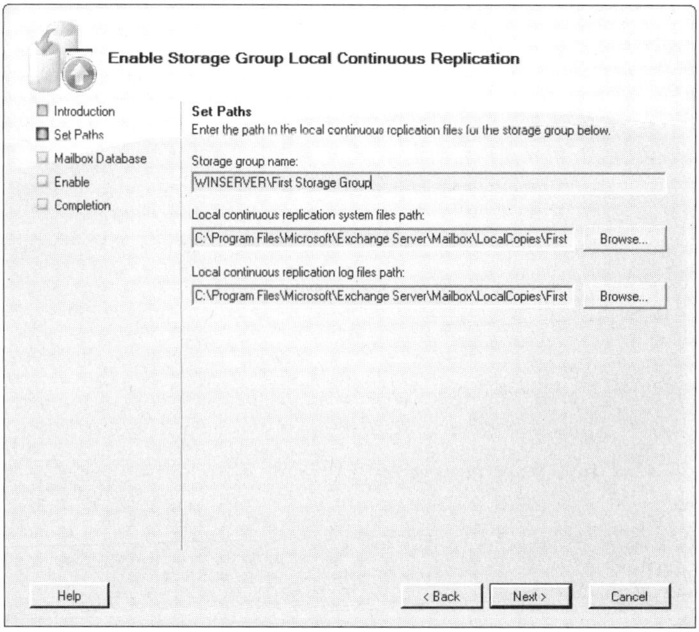

Figure 10-9:
Provide the
replication
storage
paths.

9. **Click the Browse button for the Local Continuous Replication Exchange Database File Path field, locate the file path you want to use for storage, and click Save.**

   In this case, you supply both a path and filename for storage. Don't use the default setting because Exchange Server defaults to using the local drive. The default filename consists of the mailbox name followed by the EDB (Exchange DataBase) file extension. For example, if the name of the mailbox is MyMailbox, the default filename is MyMailbox.EDB. Using the default filename makes it easier to recover from an error later.

10. **Perform Steps 7 through 9 for each mailbox in the storage group.**

11. **Click Next.**

    You see a summary dialog box that describes the steps that the wizard will perform.

12. **Click Enable.**

    The wizard performs the required replication. This step can require several minutes to complete. Eventually, you see a Completion dialog box.

13. **Click Finish.**

    The Copy Status field for the storage group changes from Disabled to Healthy.

Considering CCR

The CCR option requires that you have a full cluster setup for your network. In this configuration, a server acts as the active node — the node that services message requests directly. All other servers in the cluster act as passive nodes. They copy the data from the active node continuously so that the replication process is ongoing and doesn't rely on the active node server for the replication process. The advantages of this configuration are many:

- ✔ No single failure point
- ✔ No special hardware required
- ✔ No shared storage requirements (such as a SAN or NAS)
- ✔ Deployable in one or two datacenter configurations
- ✔ Reduced maintenance requirements

The ability to deploy this setup in two datacenters means that you can replicate the Exchange Server database in two physical locations. You still need to make backups of your Exchange Server database, but you can safely reduce the frequency at which you make the backup.

This configuration comes with two major disadvantages. The first is cost — this is the most expensive replication option because you must buy dedicated servers and extra software. The second is complexity. Even experienced administrators fear configuring a cluster because the process has many potential failure points.

Microsoft intends the CCR setup for large organizations with a number of Exchange Servers and a host of Active Directory domains. This is the option for General Motors, not Joe's Candy Store. Configuring this form of replication is outside the scope of this book.

Considering SCR

The SCR option is new to SP1. This option offers true standby replication for medium to large organizations. When a failure occurs, the standby server takes over immediately. As with CCR, this option requires that you provide multiple servers. However, the servers need not appear as part of a cluster. The terminology is a bit different for SCR. The default server is called the *source,* and any servers that replicate data on the default server are *targets.* SCR has these advantages of its predecessors:

✔ **Multiple replication targets per storage group:** When working with an LCR or a CCR configuration, you can create only one replication target (see the procedure found in the "Considering LCR" section of the chapter). By allowing multiple targets, SCR improves reliability and makes it considerably less likely that a failure will cause mailbox damage or unavailability.

✔ **Configurable replication delay:** If the default database becomes corrupted, you don't want to copy that corruption to the replicated copy. An administrator can add a replication delay to SCR that makes it possible to disable the default database before corruption can spread to the replicated copies. The downside is that more delay means more lost records in the replicated copy. Consequently, this feature helps you balance individual data loss against complete corruption of an entire database.

One of the potential problems with SCR is that you manage it completely with Exchange Management Shell. Microsoft seems to think that this is a feature, but really, whether using Exchange Management Shell is a feature depends on the abilities of the administrator. To use this form of replication, you must be completely comfortable at the command line. A single typo can cause considerable problems for your server setup. Consequently, Microsoft has hung a sign saying, "Advanced Administrators Only" for this form of replication.

Working with Routing Log Viewer

Routing Log Viewer provides a means of seeing how Exchange Server moves data from one location to another. Double-click Routing Log Viewer in the Toolbox folder to start this utility. Figure 10-10 shows a typical view of the content of this utility. (The utility doesn't have a log open when you start it; you must open the log file using the procedure in the "Opening log files" section.)

The four tabs you see in Figure 10-10 describe various routing elements. For example, you might want to know where messages go after they leave the organization. The following list describes the purpose of each of these tabs:

✔ **Active Directory Sites & Routing Groups:** Provides a listing of Active Directory sites and the servers in those sites. Each of the servers in the Servers list is associated with a link. Click the link to see specifics about the server.

✔ **Servers:** Displays Exchange Server specifics about each server, including the Exchange Server version, as shown in Figure 10-10. You can also discover particulars of Mailbox DataBases (MDBs). Notice that all entries provide fully qualified Active Directory paths, making it easy to locate additional information about each object.

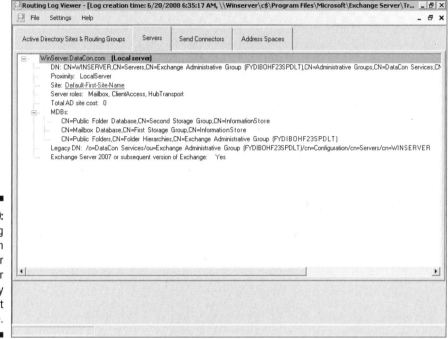

Figure 10-10:
Find routing
information
for your
server
and any
problems it
may have.

✔ **Send Connectors:** Provides particulars about each of the send connectors configured on the system. For example, you can determine the maximum message size that the send connector supports and whether it has Domain Name System (DNS) routing enabled.

✔ **Address Spaces:** Shows all address spaces configured for the system and the send connectors that support them. Click a send connector link to view details about that send connector.

Now that you have a better idea of the task that Routing Log Viewer performs, it's time to look at the methods for using it. The following section describes essential tasks you can perform with Routing Log Viewer.

Opening log files

Routing Log Viewer begins with an empty display — you must open a log file to view it. Use the following procedure to open a log file:

1. **Choose File⟹Open Log File.**

   You see the Open Routing Table Log File dialog box.

2. **Click either Browse Server Files or Browse Local Files.**

   Clicking Browse Server Files displays a list of log files on the transport server you specify. If you don't specify a transport server, you see the local log files. Clicking Browse Local Files always displays the local files. In either case, you see the Open dialog box shown in Figure 10-11.

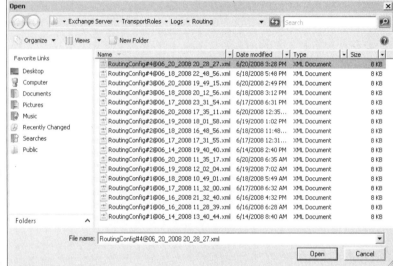

Figure 10-11:
Choose the file you want to open.

3. **Highlight one of the files in the list.**

   Each routing log uses a special format so you can easily identify it. The filename begins with RoutingConfig#<Number>. The log file number updates after the system or you make changes to the configuration. The next set of numbers is the log date. Finally, you see the log time.

4. **Click Open.**

   Routing Log Viewer displays the log file you requested.

Comparing two log files

Sometimes you want to compare two log files so you can see their differences. For example, you may want to know precisely what happened to the routing configuration during an earlier change in the day because your Exchange Server setup suddenly stops sending messages. The following steps show how to perform a comparison:

1. **Open the initial log file using the procedure found in the "Opening log files" section of the chapter.**

2. **Choose File⇨Compare Log Files.**

   You see the Open Routing Table Log File dialog box.

3. **Click either Browse Server Files or Browse Local Files.**

   You see the Open dialog box (refer to Figure 10-11).

4. **Highlight one of the files in the list and click Open.**

   Routing Log Viewer displays the differences in the two logs or tells you that there aren't any differences. Figure 10-12 shows a typical example of a change between two logs.

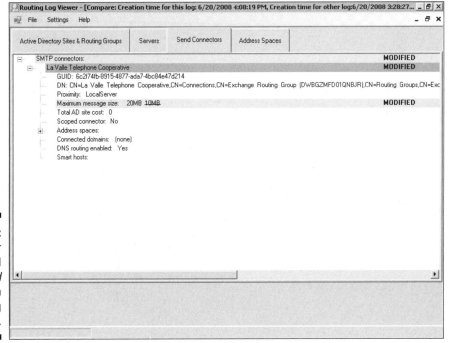

Figure 10-12: Look for the word *Modified* when viewing changes.

Chapter 11

Performing Maintenance Tasks

. . . .

. . . .

Maintenance is an essential part of any computing activity, including working with Exchange Server. Features such as replication help keep maintenance lower, but you still have to perform some level of maintenance to get the most out of Exchange Server and to ensure the safety of your data. Efficiency and data safety are the essential reasons to perform maintenance.

Many administrators know that efficiency and data safety are important, but many of them put maintenance off anyway. Fortunately, you have other reasons to perform maintenance on Exchange Server:

✔ Locate potential incursions by people of ill intent, whether internal or external to the company

✔ Remove old accounts and other objects

✔ Identify potential hardware deficiencies and looming failures

✔ Reduce support time by eliminating sources of use irritation

✔ Define potential failure points that don't appear during Exchange Server usage

The following sections describe various maintenance tasks you perform when working with Exchange Server. These tasks are in addition to the other administrative tasks you perform. For example, this chapter doesn't discuss adding new users, even though you perform that task as part of administering Exchange Server. These maintenance tasks are what most administrators would consider extra work. Even though Exchange Server will work fine for some amount of time if you don't back it up, all it takes is one failure to emphasize the need to perform this extra work.

Creating a Data Store Backup

Backups are essential and, in some cases, mandatory. You must back up your data to reduce or eliminate data loss, and yet administrators fail to perform backups. There are so many stories about failed data backups that even end users have heard more than a few of them. The act of performing a backup is relatively simple and the consequences of not performing this task are so dire that you would think no one would fail to perform backups. The problem is not one of desire, in most cases, but one of technique — selecting the right data and ensuring that the data truly is backed up. The following sections describe how to work with Exchange Server data.

This chapter doesn't tell you how to perform a backup of Windows or of any other applications you've installed under Windows. To ensure the safety of your data, you must create a complete backup of everything, including your Windows configuration. Otherwise, you might find that you have difficulty using the Exchange Server backup you create. Don't forget to back up all certificates on your system. Creating a new certificate with the same name won't work — you must have the original.

Defining backup requirements

Exchange Server is a big product with lots of features and complexities. It may initially appear that attempting to create a backup is also a complex undertaking, but you need to consider only these items in your backups:

- ✔ Mailboxes (found in the `\Program Files\Microsoft\Exchange Server\Mailbox\` folder)
- ✔ Public folder databases (found in the `\Program Files\Microsoft\Exchange Server\Mailbox\` folder)
- ✔ Offline Address Book (OAB) (found in the `\Program Files\Microsoft\Exchange Server\ExchangeOAB` folder)
- ✔ Client access settings (found in the `\Program Files\Microsoft\Exchange Server\ClientAccess` folder)
- ✔ Windows registry (the `HKEY_LOCAL_MACHINE\SOFTWARE\Microsoft\Exchange` and `HKEY_LOCAL_MACHINE\SYSTEM\currentcontrolset\Services` keys)
- ✔ Security certificates

As long as you create backups of these elements, you have everything needed to recreate your Exchange Server installation. Although the mailboxes and public folder databases appear in the `\Program Files\Microsoft\Exchange Server\Mailbox\` folder of your system by default, you can choose any alternative location, so you must know where the data is stored on your system. The same holds true for any other data folder you create. The "Importing and exporting the digital certificate" section of Chapter 7 describes how to export the digital certificates on your system to create a file you can back up. Make sure you back up all server, administrator, and user certificates; otherwise you may find that you can't access some types of data.

Of course, many organizations also create backups of optional elements. It's possible to recreate an Exchange Server installation by performing a complete setup, but performing this task is daunting, so many organizations also create backups of the Exchange Server configuration files. These optional elements are helpful, but not mandatory. Theoretically, you could create a backup of the entire `\Program Files\Microsoft\Exchange Server` folder to reduce your installation and setup time, but this backup isn't mandatory.

You may have noticed that this section doesn't mention anything about Active Directory. Exchange Server relies heavily on Active Directory, but you back up this element as part of Windows. If you don't perform proper Windows back-ups you won't have an Active Directory backup, and many Exchange Server elements, such as user account information, will be lost. In short, you now have another reason to perform a good backup of Active Directory.

It's never necessary to back up some Exchange Server elements such as the mailbox queues. The data in the queues is transitory, so any backup you make now will be useless a few seconds from now. That said, some organizations do back up the queues as part of their data. You can find a complete listing of both mandatory and optional data backup elements for Exchange Server 2007 at `http://technet.microsoft.com/en-us/library/bb124780(EXCHG.80).aspx`.

Understanding the use of faster and fewer backups

Backups are resource intensive. Consequently, making a backup in the middle of the day is probably going to incite users to riot because they won't be able to access their e-mail. You won't be able to do anything about the problem because the backup is in process and there isn't any way to force the backup application to use fewer resources. In short, making multiple backups during the day to reduce data loss probably won't work. That's why you use replication to fill in the gaps during the day. The "Understanding Replication" section of Chapter 10 describes replication.

If you're using replication, you should also back up the replication databases. Having both the original and replicated data in the backup provides additional reliability. It's unlikely that both the original and replicated database will have an error, so you have two opportunities to restore all data on your system intact.

Understanding backup types

Exchange Server supports two kinds of backup. The first is the older Extensible Storage Engine (ESE) backup that NTBackup and many third-party vendors support. The technology behind this kind of backup is mature and well tested. It offers the security of having appeared with all previous versions of Exchange Server and is probably the best option for small- and medium-sized companies.

The second kind of backup is the newer Volume Shadow copy Service (VSS). This backup first appeared in Windows Server 2003. The new Windows Server 2008/Vista backup program uses VSS, but you won't find many third-party generic solutions that support it. Microsoft introduced VSS to let you perform an Exchange Server-aware backup in which the system can help ensure that you back up all Exchange Server data. VSS backups are almost mandatory for large organizations.

Either technique will produce an acceptable backup. However, using ESE is more work and is more error prone as the size of your Exchange Server setup increases. The article at `http://msexchangeteam.com/archive/2004/06/25/166104.aspx` explains why using VSS is the best option for larger organizations.

To avoid the dirty backup scenario described in the article, you need to shut down Exchange Server and then perform the backup. Shutting down Exchange Server closes all databases and ensures that the data is in a stable state. Otherwise, Exchange Server must attempt to restore pending database changes using the log files. Although this option is feasible for small- and many medium-sized organizations, it isn't possible for large organizations.

Depending on the size of your organization, you may have to track the cycles of usage on your system and determine a best-fit backup time. A smaller organization will have an actual workday where you can make the backup in the evening, after normal work hours when no one should be using e-mail. A larger organization may simply have to choose a time of day when traffic is low and provide support with the information required to help users through any temporary slowness.

Choosing a backup application

Windows Server 2008 comes with a useless image backup; you should rely on it only as a last resort. The Windows Server 2008 backup creates an image of the entire disk. If a part of your Exchange Server installation fails, you can't use the backup to restore just that part of the application — you must restore the entire drive. If you're using Windows Server 2003, the old NTBackup application will work as a means for creating an Exchange Server 2007 backup.

You do have many third-party options from which to choose. If you have a large Exchange Server setup and want to ensure that everything is backed up properly, you might want to invest in an Exchange Server-specific backup product. Microsoft provides a listing of Exchange Server 2007 compatible products at `http://www.microsoft.com/exchange/partners/2007/backup.mspx`. Use these products in addition to any Windows backup you perform.

Many organizations combine their Exchange Server backup with a Windows backup. In this case, you may want to use a generic backup application. For example, many smaller organizations use Nero (`http://www.nero.com/eng/backup.html`). The company has a free trial version you can use to determine whether Nero is for your organization. Any backup solution you choose for Windows Server 2008 must support the new Windows Server 2008 features if you want to make a complete backup of the entire server. You can obtain a quick overview of these requirements at `http://searchdatabackup.techtarget.com/tip/0,289483,sid187_gci1316363,00.html`.

Monitoring Exchange Server Performance

Performance is a measure of the reliability, security, and speed of an Exchange Server. A server performs well when the reliability, security, and speed factors are balanced to provide the best overall server usability. You observe and interact with server performance through monitoring, testing, and troubleshooting. *Monitoring* is a continuous process in which you observe overall performance factors to judge whether the server requires testing and, ultimately, troubleshooting. The following sections describe monitoring, the first level of performance assessment for your Exchange Server setup.

Monitoring large Exchange Server setups

The performance monitoring that Exchange Server natively provides works well for smaller organizations. However, if you have multiple Exchange Servers and several client locations, you need something more than these native capabilities. The Microsoft solution to the large Exchange Server configuration management process is using System Center Operations Manager (SCOM). You can discover more about this process at `http://www.msexchange.org/articles_tutorials/exchange-server-2003/monitoring-operations/managing-exchange-2003-scom-2007-part1.html`. You obtain the Exchange Server 2007 Management Pack (MP) for SCOM at `http://www.microsoft.com/downloads/details.aspx?FamilyId=1A83E112-8677-4E03-83C3-F1B7EBFC3A4B`.

Creating Performance Baseline Health Check

Performance Baseline Health Check begins very much like any other Exchange Best Practices Analyzer check. The "Using Best Practices Analyzer" section of Chapter 4 provides you with the essentials you need to know to perform a basic health scan. However, in this case, you check the Performance Baseline (2 Hours) option in the Health Check Options field as shown in Figure 11-1. This test requires two hours at a minimum to run, and it does affect system performance, so you don't want to run this check during peak usage hours on a weekday.

Always perform all required maintenance on your system before you begin this check. At a minimum, perform a backup of the system to ensure that you have a copy of your data available for restoration should an error occur. It's also important to perform any required updates to ensure that you check against the latest Exchange Server software. After you've accomplished these prerequisites, you can run Performance Baseline Health Check without problems.

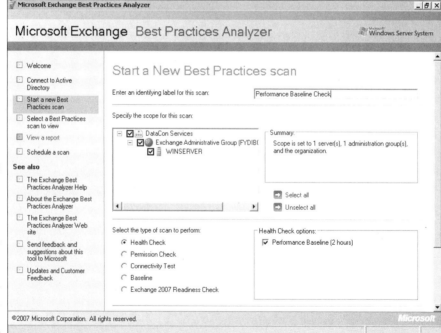

Figure 11-1:
Create a performance baseline for your system so you can monitor changes to it.

Determining how often to check performance

Performance isn't something that degrades immediately or suddenly — it's a process. If you're working with a large network, it's possible to find a performance problem every day, but a smaller network may not see a performance problem for months. Consequently, the size of your network determines how often you need to run Performance Baseline Health Check on your system. A larger network requires more frequent checks. Considering that the check requires two hours to complete, there's a point where the network size becomes large enough that you can't run the check and you must rely on continuous monitoring with a product such as SCOM.

The reliability of the hardware and software in your server also determines how often you must perform this check. Higher-quality products generally require fewer checks. Maintaining a log of maintenance items will help you determine the overall reliability of your server and help you establish a monitoring interval that makes sense.

Usage trends also help you define how often to check performance. As the load on the server increases, reliability decreases, which means the server becomes more vulnerable to issues that could affect overall performance. A server that has a larger load should receive more frequent checks.

 A good rule of thumb to follow is that even the smallest organization should check performance monthly. Checking less often than a month invites disaster because you can't see any trends for your system. Once you start checking your system more often than once a week, you should consider moving to a constant monitoring product such as SCOM.

Considering the use of dynamic distribution groups

Dynamic distribution groups can greatly reduce the amount of work that an administrator must perform to configure distribution groups. The standard practice for creating distribution groups is to create an actual list as described in the "Configuring Distribution Groups" section of Chapter 5. A dynamic distribution group relies on an Active Directory query for configuration, so all you need to worry about is creating the right query, and the distribution group configures itself. Using dynamic distribution groups is a performance option because they help the administrator create distribution groups quickly and potentially with fewer errors.

A problem with dynamic distribution groups is that you must create the right query. The query relies on Active Directory objects. For example, you can easily create a dynamic distribution group for all people who reside in office 200. Of course, this query works only when all recipients actually reside in office 200. Most organizations are managed by exception. For example, you may want to create a distribution group that includes everyone in office 200 except Joe Smith, but the manager forgets to tell you that Joe is in that office, so you create a query that includes Joe by accident. If you'd configured the distribution group manually, the error probably wouldn't have occurred. Consequently, dynamic distribution groups work great as long as you're good at creating concise and accurate queries.

Using dynamic distribution groups also requires that you populate the various objects with information. An organization may not include every vital piece of information about a user within Active Directory. You can't create a query based on the user's location unless you include location information in Active Directory for every user. Inconsistent entries are worse than none at all because you can end up with dynamic distribution groups that contain incomplete membership.

All of these caveats aside, dynamic distribution groups are a boon for the administrator. When someone leaves the organization and you delete his or her record, the user's membership in a dynamic distribution group is also deleted. Likewise, when you add someone with the right values, the person automatically appears in the dynamic distribution group. The automation makes dynamic distribution groups good for security, reliability, and speed. The following steps describe how to create a dynamic distribution group:

1. **Choose the Recipient Configuration⇨Distribution Group folder in Exchange Management Console.**

2. **Click New Dynamic Distribution Group in the Actions pane.**

   You see the New Dynamic Distribution Group dialog box shown in Figure 11-2.

3. **Type a name for the dynamic distribution group in the Name field.**

   The wizard automatically creates an Alias field value for you. In most cases, you want to retain this name unless doing so would result in a duplicate alias value.

4. **Click Next.**

   You see the Filter Settings dialog box shown in Figure 11-3. This is where you choose the filter used to create the dynamic distribution group. The filter removes potential candidates from the dynamic distribution group, but it doesn't provide the query used to create the dynamic distribution group. Consequently, you may find that you use the All Recipients Types option most often.

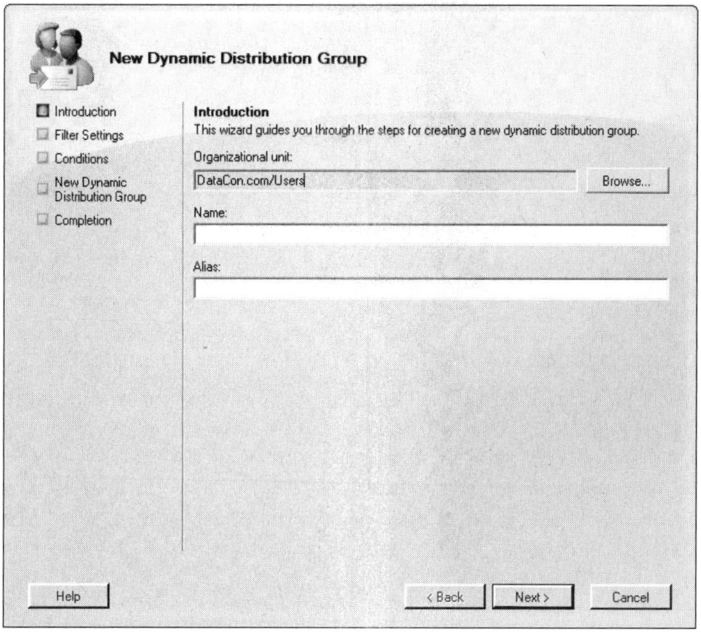

Figure 11-2:
Add a new
dynamic
distribu-
tion group
to your
Exchange
Server
setup.

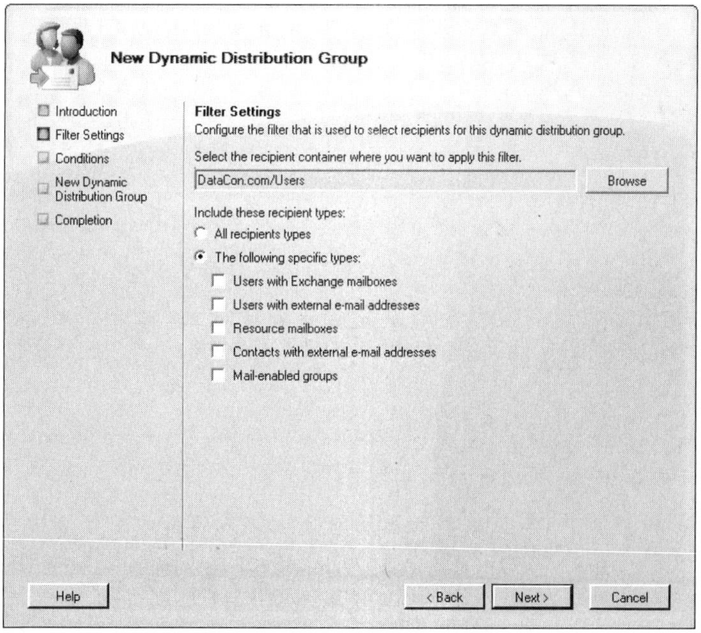

Figure 11-3:
Choose
the Active
Directory
objects that
receive
e-mails in
the group.

5. **Choose the All Recipients Types option or filter the output by choosing The Following Specific Types. If you choose The Following Specific Types, you must also select one or more of the type options.**

6. **Click Next.**

You see the Conditions dialog box shown in Figure 11-4. This is where you choose the Active Directory objects used to create the query.

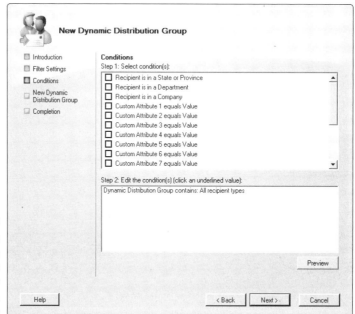

Figure 11-4:
Define one
or more
query
conditions.

7. **Select a condition.**

The wizard adds a new condition entry in the Step 2 field.

8. **Click the link for the condition, provide one or more condition values, and click OK.**

9. **Perform Steps 7 and 8 for each condition you want to add.**

10. **Click Next.**

The wizard displays a summary of the new dynamic distribution group.

11. **Click New.**

Exchange Server creates a new dynamic distribution group based on the entries you provide.

12. **Click Finish.**

Testing Performance Using Performance Monitor

The second phase of performance assessment is testing through real-time monitoring. Performance Monitor provides a means for testing performance by checking actual statistics during usage. For example, when you monitor the CPU, you see the number of processing cycles used for specific tasks. You've probably used Performance Monitor for other tasks in Windows. When you double-click Performance Monitor in the Exchange Management Console Toolbox folder, you see an initial display similar to the one shown in Figure 11-5. The difference for Exchange Server is that you can monitor specific Exchange Server features in addition to the normal Windows and hardware statistics.

The operation of Performance Monitor is the same when working with Exchange Server as it is when working with hardware, Windows, or any other application. Performance Monitor works by checking the application for objects that have counters. In some cases, the counters have instances that you can check. Figure 11-6 shows the Add Counters dialog box you use to add new counters to Performance Monitor to test Exchange Server performance. The Exchange Server application elements all begin with the word *MSExchange*. The objects begin with *MSExchange ActiveSync*.

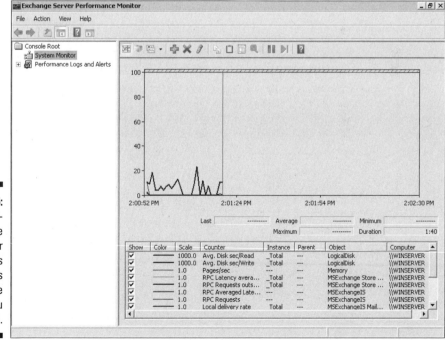

Figure 11-5: Performance Monitor displays statistics about the object you choose.

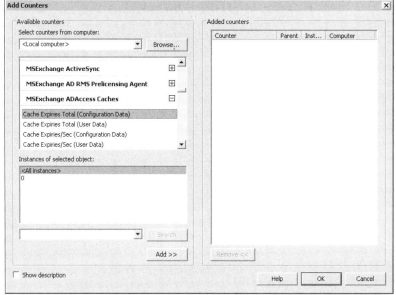

Figure 11-6:
Microsoft
Exchange
provides a
wealth of
counters
you can use
to test per-
formance.

Figure 11-6 shows a typical view of Exchange Server objects. The following list provides a quick overview of Performance Monitor terminology as it relates to Exchange Server:

- ✔ **Application:** Defines one or more executables that constitute a cohesive group. When working with Exchange Server, you find only one application, MSExchange. Every MSExchange entry in the Available Counters field shown in Figure 11-6 belongs to Exchange Server.

- ✔ **Object:** Describes a particular feature in the application. In Figure 11-6, ActiveSync, AD RMS Prelicensing Agent, and ADAccess Caches are objects. The Add Counters dialog box always displays MSExchange and the object name together so that you know the two are related.

- ✔ **Counter:** Provides a count of a particular object property. For example, Cache Expiries Total (Configuration Data) is a counter in Figure 11-6. A counter counts the occurrence of a particular event for a given time span. The resulting number appears on the display shown in Figure 11-5.

- ✔ **Instance:** Defines the number of counters available for a particular object. For example, a server includes one instance of the % Idle Time counter for each CPU or CPU core installed on a server. In some cases, you see instance values even if the counter has only one instance. Figure 11-6 shows that the Cache Expiries Total (Configuration Data) counter can have multiple instances, even though it has only one instance for this setup.

Exchange Server comes with a host of counters you can use to test performance. The Web site at `http://technet.microsoft.com/en-us/library/aa996329(EXCHG.80).aspx` provides a complete list of these counters and tells you how they measure Exchange Server performance. You should also review the list of key common counters described at `http://www.windowsnetworking.com/articles_tutorials/Key-Performance-Monitor-Counters.html` to ensure that you provide complete Exchange Server performance testing.

When working with Exchange Server, using fewer counters is better. Otherwise, the output can become confusing and you may find that you tweak the wrong element, making things worse. For example, even though you can add all counters for a particular object, it's better to add only the counters or counter instances you require to locate a problem. Remove wrong guesses by clicking Delete on the toolbar before you add new counters. You can find a basic tutorial on using new Windows Server 2008 features at `http://searchsystemschannel.techtarget.com/generic/0,295582,sid99_gci1266845,00.html`. If you want more in depth coverage, consider getting my book, *Windows Server 2008 All-in-One Desk Reference For Dummies* — Book III, Chapter 5 provides some great information about measuring Windows Server 2008 reliability and performance.

Locating Resource Hogs Using Performance Troubleshooter

The third phase of performance assessment is locating and diagnosing performance problems. You begin this phase by double-clicking Performance Troubleshooter in the Exchange Management Console Toolbox folder. Exchange Server starts Microsoft Exchange Troubleshooting Assistant. After the initial update check, you see the usual update messages. The following steps tell you how to initiate a troubleshooting session:

1. **Click Go To Welcome Screen.**

   You see the initial display shown in Figure 11-7.

2. **Type a name for the analysis in the Enter an Identifying Label for This Analysis field.**

3. **Select Troubleshoot New Performance Issue.**

   The wizard also gives you the option of analyzing previously collected data that you saved during a previous session.

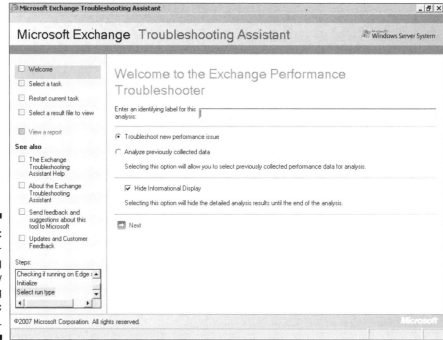

Figure 11-7:
Start a trou-
bleshooting
session by
providing
some basic
information.

4. **(Optional) Deselect the Hide Informational Display option.**

   Clearing this setting will display all intermediate analysis steps, which
   can help you diagnose difficult problems. Try keeping the intermediate
   steps hidden at the outset so you get to the summary faster.

5. **Click Next.**

   The wizard asks you which symptoms you're seeing.

6. **Select a symptom from the list.**

   In some cases, you won't see a precise symptom that matches what you
   see on the server. Select the symptom that matches most closely to the
   systems you see.

7. **Click Next.**

   The wizard asks you to provide a server name and global catalog server
   name.

8. **Type the server name in the Server Name field.**

9. **Type the name of the server that hosts the global catalog in the Global
   Catalog Server Name field.**

10. **Click Next.**

    You see the Configure Data Collection dialog box shown in Figure 11-8.

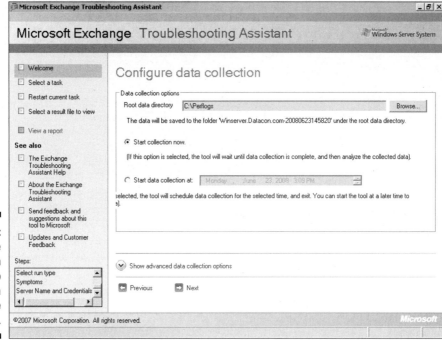

Figure 11-8:
Provide
information
on when to
collect data
and where
to store it.

11. **(Optional) Click Browse, choose a new folder location in the Browse for Folder dialog box, and click OK.**

    Normally you rely on the default storage folder to make it easier to find the data later.

12. **Choose Start Collection Now.**

    It's also possible to collect the data after hours using the Start Data Collection At option. However, in most cases, you need the data immediately to locate the source of a problem.

13. **Click Next.**

    Exchange Server creates a data folder and performs the required analysis. The analysis phase requires several minutes to complete because Exchange Server must check a number of system objects. This may be a good time to get a cup of coffee. Eventually, you see a View Results display like the one shown in Figure 11-9.

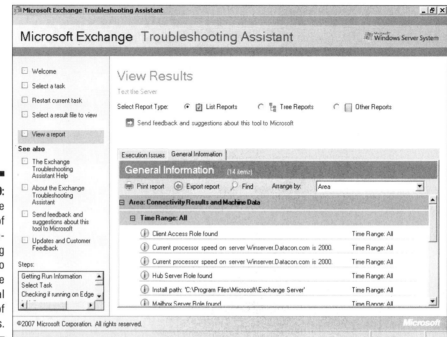

Figure 11-9:
View the
output of
the trouble-
shooting
session to
determine
potential
sources of
problems.

Chapter 12

Using Exchange Management Shell

*M*icrosoft keeps coming up with different names for essentially the same thing. If you've worked with computers for a while, you know about the command prompt. Originally, it appeared as the Disk Operating System (DOS). The command prompt is simply a version of the command processor that runs under Windows. After many years, Microsoft has introduced the Windows PowerShell, which is amazingly like the command prompt, only it relies on managed code rather than the old DOS executables to perform work. Even so, from an administrators perspective, not much is different. This chapter is about Exchange Management Shell, which as you may have guessed by now, is simply a fancier version of Windows PowerShell. So, this chapter is essentially about a specialized form of the command prompt you've probably used for many years to manage applications using text commands, rather than relying on mouse and menus.

Windows PowerShell offers a lot of features not found in the command prompt. For example, it offers better security. The applications you run in Windows PowerShell have security embedded in them too, which means that between Windows PowerShell and the applications it runs, you run a smaller risk of modifying something without having the proper rights to do so. This chapter provides an overview of the most interesting new Windows PowerShell features, and it also helps you understand what Exchange Management Shell adds to Windows PowerShell to make it a better choice for working with Exchange Server.

Windows Server 2008 and Vista place additional restrictions on the command prompt and Windows PowerShell. You must have administrator privileges to perform many tasks. Consequently, this chapter tells you how to create an administrator-level Windows PowerShell session (the same technique works for the command prompt).

One of the enhancements that Windows PowerShell provides is better help. The help is a little more descriptive, consistent, and easier to access. The next section of the chapter shows how to get help at the Windows PowerShell prompt.

Once you understand how to work with Windows PowerShell, it's time to start using the Exchange Management Shell version to perform tasks with Exchange Server. Microsoft places a strong emphasis on working with Exchange Server using Exchange Management Shell, and you often find that the Exchange Server help files offer no other solution for some problems. The rest of this chapter is devoted to demonstrating how to perform some essential tasks with Exchange Management Shell.

Understanding Windows PowerShell

Windows PowerShell is a new kind of command prompt. When you open it, you see a prompt, just like you do when you open the Start⇨Programs⇨ Accessories⇨Command Prompt application. The difference is that Windows PowerShell relies on managed, rather than native, code. *Managed code* is the kind of executable supported by .NET Framework. It's not important to know the low-level details of managed code; simply know that it's an improvement over the command prompt. Here are some things to consider when thinking about Windows PowerShell.

- ✔ Windows PowerShell provides a greater level of reliability than the command line.
- ✔ Using the Windows PowerShell improves security because you need the required credentials to execute commands.
- ✔ Windows PowerShell helps the administrator obtain the full resources of .NET Framework without becoming a programmer.
- ✔ In many cases, the commands are easier to remember and use because they rely on human readable terms (the older commands are also available, for the most part, should you decide to employ them).
- ✔ Scripting is considerably more powerful in Windows PowerShell, albeit not always as easy as working at the old command prompt.
- ✔ Instead of using plain text for data, Windows PowerShell uses .NET objects, which means you can obtain consistent output of complex data.

Windows PowerShell has quite a bit to offer. The following sections describe the essentials of Windows PowerShell.

Considering the need for Windows PowerShell

The fact that .NET Framework hasn't taken over yet may leave some people considering not using Windows PowerShell today. It's true; you can work with Windows XP, Windows 2003, Vista, and Windows Server 2008 at the command line without ever looking at Windows PowerShell. Microsoft doesn't throw out old technology very quickly. However, they do throw it out. With Exchange Server, Microsoft is doing some serious housecleaning at the command prompt, and you need to keep on top of it. Exchange Server requires an investment in Windows PowerShell if you want to complete tasks in a timely manner. However, there are many other reasons to use Windows PowerShell, as described here:

- ✔ It provides better automation features so you can do more with less effort.
- ✔ You can create scripts more quickly in many cases.
- ✔ Scripts created with Windows PowerShell tend to execute faster for a given task than performing the task at the old command line.
- ✔ Using Windows PowerShell reduces potential mistakes.
- ✔ You get more information from Windows PowerShell than you do from the command line utilities of the past.
- ✔ It's easier to obtain usable help in Windows PowerShell than it is at the command prompt (which sometimes doesn't provide any help).

Of course, this begs the question of whether you should just throw away that old command prompt. Unfortunately, you can't do that either. Many individuals and most companies have a significant base of existing batch files and scripts that they aren't going to be willing to throw away. Unfortunately, this established base might not run very well under Windows PowerShell for the very reasons that you want to use it — improved security and reliability. Consequently, during this transitional phase, you'll probably have to use both the command line and Windows PowerShell for maximum productivity. To make the transition smoother, you may want to begin moving those old batch files and scripts to Windows PowerShell as time permits.

A number of people are starting to compare the Windows PowerShell interface to the interface provided with Linux. You can find an interesting article on the topic at http://arstechnica.com/guides/other/msh.ars. Most people who've used both Windows PowerShell and Linux agree that Microsoft has taken a significant step in the right direction by making the command line easier to use overall and more object oriented. The result is that you have a more consistent interface to work with, even if it's significantly different from what you used in the past.

Considering the Exchange Management Shell difference

The Exchange Management Shell is indeed simply Windows PowerShell in disguise. However, you do find differences. For example, when you open Windows PowerShell, you see a simple prompt. When working with Exchange Management Shell, you see some introductory help information, as shown in Figure 12-1. The Tip of the Day changes each time you start Exchange Management Shell.

In addition to this cursory change, the Exchange Management Shell loads a number of shell extensions. These extensions come in the form of *cmdlets*, which are small applications that work essentially the same as those found at the DOS command line with the important differences noted earlier in this chapter. The cmdlets help you administer Exchange Server. You see how to use a number of these cmdlets as the chapter progresses. For right now, simply consider them as little applications that you use to manage Exchange Server.

Exchange Management Shell loads the Exchange Server cmdlets you need automatically. Windows PowerShell is extensible. You can make it perform additional tasks by loading additional cmdlets. Consequently, although you could manage Exchange Server using a standard Windows PowerShell prompt, it's much easier to use Exchange Management Shell because it performs all the required preliminary work for you.

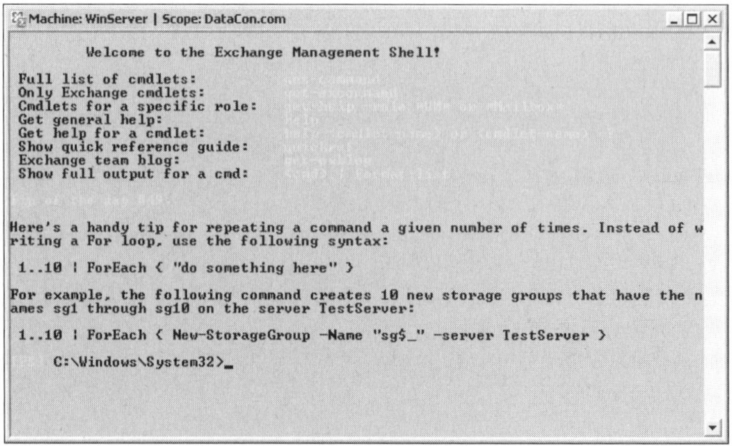

Figure 12-1:
Exchange Management Shell provides some introductory help when you open it.

```
Machine: WinServer | Scope: DataCon.com                                    _ □ ×

              Welcome to the Exchange Management Shell!

Full list of cmdlets:
Only Exchange cmdlets:
Cmdlets for a specific role:
Get general help:
Get help for a cmdlet:
Show quick reference guide:
Exchange team blog:
Show full output for a cmd:


Here's a handy tip for repeating a command a given number of times. Instead of w
riting a For loop, use the following syntax:

1..10 | ForEach { "do something here" }

For example, the following command creates 10 new storage groups that have the n
ames sg1 through sg10 on the server TestServer:

1..10 | ForEach { New-StorageGroup -Name "sg$_" -server TestServer }

     C:\Windows\System32>_
```

Opening an Administrative PowerShell Prompt

When working with older versions of Windows, you simply opened a command prompt and started typing commands. You can still work with Windows XP at the command prompt without thinking about security at all. However, starting with Vista, Microsoft made the decision to treat administrators as standard users. Consequently, administrators now have to think about privilege elevation to perform certain tasks. The following sections discuss why you need an administrative Windows PowerShell prompt, how to obtain one, and how to determine whether you have it by executing a simple command.

Understanding the need for an administrative prompt

Microsoft has made the claim that Vista and Windows Server 2008 are more secure than any previous version of Windows. In fact, if you use all the security features in these operating systems and don't disable the features Microsoft includes for system protection, you'll find that the entire environment is more secure. The changes are welcome in a world filled with all kinds of nefarious individuals, adware, viruses, and spyware.

The plus side of the increased security is that you might not have to worry as often about users creating havoc and destroying everyone's computer data with the latest attachment in an e-mail that somehow gets through your filtering process. The negative side is that you'll face those annoying User Access Control (UAC) prompts far more often than you might like.

Part of the reason for increased command line security is the need to reduce errors (both intended and unintended). For example, deleting all temporary files on a drive might seem like an innocuous task and it is. However, deleting system files will produce terrible results and perhaps make the system unusable. Working with Windows PowerShell, you'll see a message about the pending deletion. You must give Windows PowerShell permission to elevate your rights and perform the act you requested. If you're like many advanced users, the warning is going to be incredibly annoying and you might simply disregard it.

The administrative prompt is a way around Windows security in general and Windows PowerShell security in specific. What you're doing is telling Windows that you want to elevate your rights for a particular application, Windows PowerShell in this case, so that you don't have to contend with the UAC prompts. The administrative prompt comes with the warning that you're circumventing controls designed to keep you from shooting yourself in the foot. In short, you're trading convenience for security.

Opening the administrative command prompt

You can open any application in administrative mode. Although this section shows how to open Exchange Management Shell in administrative mode, you can use this technique with any application. The following steps tell how to perform this task:

1. **Choose Start⇨Programs⇨Microsoft Exchange Server 2007.**

2. **Right-click Exchange Management Shell and choose Run as Administrator from the context menu.**

3. **If you aren't part of the Administrators group, you may see a UAC prompt asking you to provide a name and password of an administrator account. Provide the name and password as requested. Click OK.**

   Windows opens Exchange Management Shell in administrator mode.

Understanding the Windows PowerShell difference

After you open Exchange Management Shell in administrator mode, you might want to try a command or two. Most commands and many utilities don't work the same when using Windows PowerShell. For example, say you want to locate all temporary files on your system and place the results in the Temp.TXT file. Using the old command prompt method, you would type **Dir *.TMP /S >> Temp.TXT** and press Enter.

The old techniques don't work under Windows PowerShell. Instead, you type **get-childitem -Include *.TMP -Recurse >> Temp.TXT** and press Enter. The results are similar; the syntax is completely different. You can substitute Dir for get-childitem, but that's about the limit of the similarities. The Dir command does work differently under Windows PowerShell. The output appears in Figure 12-2. Notice the use of the get-childitem command. You could substitute Dir *.TMP and obtain the same results.

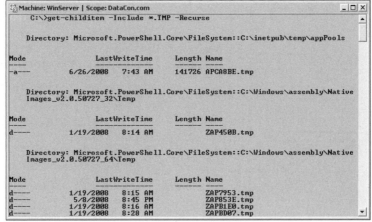

Figure 12-2:
The output of the directory command, no matter which syntax you use, differs in Windows PowerShell.

All of the tools provided with Exchange Server are for the 64-bit environment. Your workstation may rely on a 32-bit version of Windows, so you need 32-bit tools. It's possible to download a copy of the 32-bit version of the Exchange Server utilities at `http://www.microsoft.com/downloads/details.aspx?FamilyId=6BE38633-7248-4532-929B-76E9C677E802`.

Getting Windows PowerShell Help

If you've ever used the old command prompt, you know that help was uneven, unhelpful, and difficult to find, even when the command or utility provided help. (Some of those old utilities didn't provide any help, so you had to discover how to use them through arcane texts online.) Windows PowerShell partially fixes the problems with the old help. This section describes how to discover the cmdlets (the new name for utilities) that Windows PowerShell supports and how to obtain help for them.

Locating the cmdlets you need

Windows PowerShell uses a wealth of new names for old commands. For example, the CD command from days past is now the set-location command. You can see a list of the Windows PowerShell commands by typing **Help *** and pressing Enter. Figure 12-3 shows part of the list. You can scroll the list one item at a time by pressing Enter. Scroll the list one page at a time by pressing the spacebar. If you don't want to see any more of the list, press Ctrl+C.

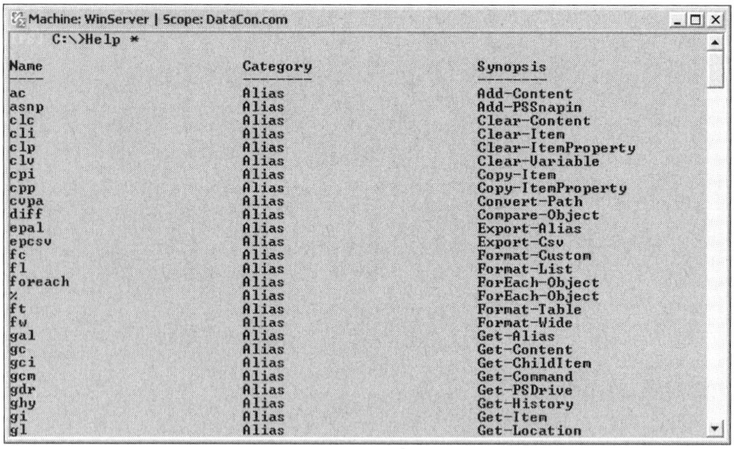

Figure 12-3:
Before you
begin using
Windows
PowerShell
in earnest,
you'll want
to review
the com-
mand list.

This list might look a little daunting at first. However, it represents a major change in the way that the command shell works with commands from ancient Unix to a more modern object-oriented methodology. Instead of guessing which commands you can access, you now get a complete list with a simple command. The bottom line is that Windows PowerShell provides a wealth of new commands, many of which don't appear in the old command prompt; however, you must learn a new way of working with those commands.

However, let's say you don't want to see the entire list; you just want to see mailbox commands. In this case, you type **Help *Mailbox*** and press Enter. Windows PowerShell displays a list of the cmdlets that contain the word *Mailbox* anywhere in their title. These commands are added by Exchange Management Shell — you won't see them if you open Windows PowerShell directly. The asterisk (*****) is a wildcard character. It represents any number of characters in the position you place it. If you want to see all cmdlets that end in *Mailbox*, you type **Help *Mailbox** and press Enter instead.

Another wildcard character is the question mark (**?**). The **?** represents a single character. Consequently, when you type **Help *Mailbox??????** and press Enter, you see all of the cmdlets that have six letters after *Mailbox*, such as Remove-UMMailboxPolicy and Get-MailboxServer. However, you don't see Get-MailboxDatabase because it contains more than six letters after the word *Mailbox*. Use combinations of keywords and wildcard characters to locate the cmdlets you need.

Obtaining help for a specific cmdlet

After you find the cmdlet you want to use, you need to know how to use it. The Help command can help you here too. Simply type **Help** followed by the name of the cmdlet you want to read about. For example, type **Help Get-MailboxServer** and press Enter to see more information about the Get-MailboxServer cmdlet, as shown in Figure 12-4.

The information you receive is relatively complete. You see a synopsis of the cmdlet, the syntax for using it, and a detailed description. In many situations, this is enough information to get you going with the cmdlet. However, it may not be enough information when you haven't used the cmdlet before. In this case, you can use the -Detailed command line switch to obtain additional information. For example, when you type **Help Get-MailboxServer -Detailed** and press Enter, you see all of the information you saw before, plus an overview of each of the command line arguments.

If this still isn't enough information, then you can use the -Full command line switch. For example, when you type **Help Get-MailboxServer -Full,** you see all the information that Microsoft can provide about the Get-MailboxServer cmdlet. This time, you obtain detailed information about each command line argument, including the values that the cmdlet allows for each argument. In addition, you see usage examples. However, now you're looking at four screens of information, which can make the detailed information cumbersome to use.

This chapter doesn't provide every detail about using Help. Type **Help Help** and press Enter to discover more information about using Help. For example, if you want to know only the syntax of a cmdlet such as Get-Mailbox Server, you can type **(Get-Help Get-MailboxServer).Syntax** and press Enter (Get-Help is the full name for Help). In short, you can be very specific about what you want Help to provide as output.

Figure 12-4: Help provides information about any cmdlet.

```
Machine: WinServer | Scope: DataCon.com                              _ □ ×
       C:\>Help Get-MailboxServer

NAME
      Get-MailboxServer

SYNOPSIS
      Use the Get-MailboxServer cmdlet to return a mailbox server object and all
      its attributes. If no parameter is specified, a complete list of the mailbo
      x servers in the entire Microsoft Exchange Server organization is returned.

SYNTAX
      Get-MailboxServer [-Identity <MailboxServerIdParameter>] [-DomainController
      <Fqdn>] [-Status <SwitchParameter>] [<CommonParameters>]

DETAILED DESCRIPTION
      To view all the Mailbox server attributes that this cmdlet returns, you mus
      t pipe the command to the Format-List cmdlet.
      The ExchangeVersion attribute that is returned is the minimum version of Mi
      crosoft Exchange that you can use to manage the returned object. This attri
      bute is not the same as the version of Microsoft Exchange that is displayed
       in the Exchange Management Console when you select Server Configuration.
      To run the Get-MailboxServer cmdlet the account you use must be delegated t
      he following:
      * Exchange View-Only Administrator role
      For more information about permissions, delegating roles, and the rights th
      at are required to administer Exchange Server 2007, see Permission Consider
      ations.
```

Executing Cmdlets

Cmdlets contain the code required to perform tasks using Exchange Management Shell. As mentioned, Exchange Management Shell is actually a specialized form of Windows PowerShell. In addition to the standard Windows PowerShell cmdlets, you obtain the specialized Exchange Server cmdlets. The following sections describe how to execute cmdlets. You see some of the most essential cmdlets that Exchange Server has to offer for the administrator. If you want a more complete description of cmdlets, see *Professional Windows PowerShell for Exchange Server 2007 Service Pack 1 (Programmer to Programmer)* by Joezer Cookey-Gam, Brendan Keane, Jeffrey Rosen, Jonathan Runyon, and Joel Stidley (Wrox).

Setting mailbox configuration with the Set-CASMailbox cmdlet

The Set-CASMailbox cmdlet helps you configure client access for Microsoft Exchange ActiveSync, Outlook Web Access (OWA), Post Office Protocol version 3 (POP3), and Internet Message Access Protocol version 4 (IMAP4) for a specified user. The help for this cmdlet is huge, but don't let that frustrate you. The Set-CASMailbox cmdlet doesn't require that you use a lot of command line switches. In fact, one or two are all you usually need. That said, you can control a lot of different user settings using this one cmdlet.

The first task is to determine the name (identity) of the mailbox you want to configure. You can look for the mailbox using Exchange Management Console. However, the easier way to perform this task at the command line is to use the Get-Mailbox cmdlet. Just type **Get-Mailbox** and press Enter to see a list of mailboxes. The Get-Mailbox cmdlet supports a host of filters you can use to limit the number of results. For example, if you type **Get-Mailbox -Identity A*** and press Enter, you see just the mailboxes that begin with the letter A such as Administrator.

Now that you have a mailbox to use, you can use it with the Set-CAS Mailbox cmdlet to set configuration information. For example, say you want to remove IMAPI4 support from user John's mailbox. In this case, you type **Set-CASMailbox -Identity John -ImapEnabled $false** and press Enter. When you view the IMAP4 setting on the Mailbox Features tab of the user's Properties dialog box, you see that it's disabled.

This cmdlet works much as you would expect. You must provide some type of identity. The easiest way to do this is to use the -Identity command line switch and provide the mailbox name you retrieved using the Get-Mailbox cmdlet. It's also important to provide some kind of configuration information.

The example uses the -ImapEnabled command line switch, but you can use any combination of supported command line switch. The only difference from working with any command line you used in the past is that you must pass a false Boolean value as $false.

Adding custom resources using the Set-ResourceConfig cmdlet

Any resources you manage using Exchange Server have resource configuration items that are part of a schema you define. For example, a room can have a network connection and seat 20 people. It may have a whiteboard, windows, and projection equipment. Another room may not have all these features, but it may seat 30 people instead of only 20. Although both objects are rooms, they differ in their characteristics, the resources they offer to the people who are in the room.

Unfortunately (or perhaps fortunately), no one at Microsoft is psychic yet, so they can't provide a schema for your rooms. You need to provide this information. The only way to create a schema is at the command prompt using the Set-ResourceConfig cmdlet. The first time you create a schema, you can use the Set-ResourceConfig cmdlet alone.

A schema is simply a key/value pair. For example, if you want to define the schema for a room that allows 20 people, you might use a key/value pair of room/20Seats. Because a key/value pair could contain spaces, you place the entire value in double quotes. The schema resides in a parenthesis and you separate multiple values using commas. Consequently, a two-value room schema might look like this: ("Room/NetworkConnection", "Room/20Seats"). The only two keys that you can use in a schema are Room and Equipment.

To create a new schema, you use the -ResourcePropertySchema command line switch. For example, if you want to add the schema defined in the previous paragraph to the default Exchange Server setup, you type **Set-ResourceConfig -ResourcePropertySchema ("Room/NetworkConnection", "Room/20Seats")** and press Enter. The result of this change is that you now have two options for describing a room.

The only time that the schema is blank is during the first time you create one. Because using Set-ResourceConfig removes all previous entries, you need to know what the previous entries are before you take any action. The Get-ResourceConfig cmdlet provides the answer to this need. All you need to do is type **Get-ResourceConfig** and press Enter to see the current schema, as shown in Figure 12-5.

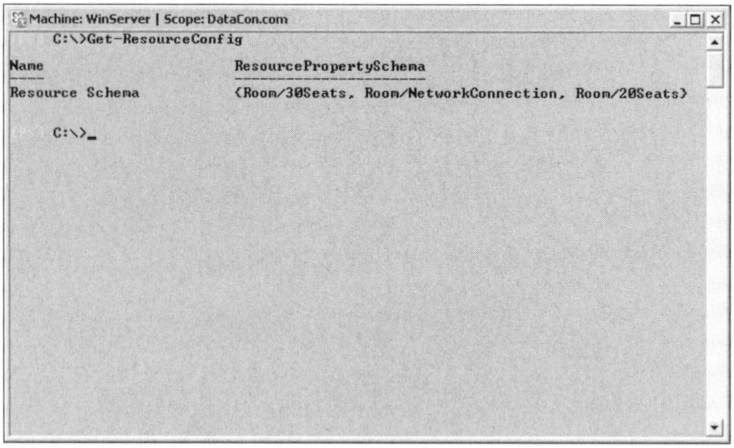

```
Machine: WinServer | Scope: DataCon.com                                    _□×
        C:\>Get-ResourceConfig                                              ▲
Name                            ResourcePropertySchema
────                            ──────────────────────
Resource Schema                 {Room/30Seats, Room/NetworkConnection, Room/20Seats}

        C:\>_
```

Figure 12-5:
Use Get-
Resource
Config to
determine
the current
schema.

As you can see from the output, the information isn't in the correct format to use as input to the `Set-ResourceConfig` cmdlet. Fortunately, Microsoft doesn't ask you to retype everything by hand either. The following process helps you modify the resource schema. Begin this process in Exchange Management Shell:

1. **Type** $MySchema = Get-ResourceConfig **and press Enter.**

   Nothing appears to happen. However, if you type **$MySchema** and press Enter, you see the same schema listing you see when using the `Get-ResourceConfig` cmdlet. The ability to create objects and modify them at the Windows PowerShell prompt is a new feature that makes Windows PowerShell extremely flexible. You often use objects when working with Exchange Server.

2. **(Optional) Type** $MySchema.ResourcePropertySchema+=("<Key/Value Pair>") **and press Enter to add new schema elements.**

   When a new schema element replicates an existing schema element, you see an error message saying the element already appears in the schema.

3. **(Optional) Type** $MySchema.ResourcePropertySchema-=("<Key/Value Pair>") **and press Enter to remove existing schema elements.**

   You won't see any error message if you try to remove a nonexistent element. Consequently, you may think you've removed an element when you haven't.

4. **Repeat Steps 2 and 3 as often as needed to modify the schema.**

5. **Type** $MySchema **and press Enter.**

6. **Verify that the resource schema is correct.**

7. **Type** Set-ResourceConfig -Instance $MySchema **and press Enter.**

   `Set-ResourceConfig` modifies the resource schema to match the new object you've provided.

Installing and configuring antispam agents

Any Exchange Server setup that provides Internet connectivity requires antispam functionality. However, Microsoft doesn't provide this functionality by default and you can't add it using Exchange Management Console. Fortunately, you can add antispam functionality using Exchange Management Shell. The following steps tell you how to accomplish this task. Begin this process in Exchange Management Shell:

1. **Type** CD "\Program Files\Microsoft\Exchange Server\Scripts" **and press Enter.**

   Exchange Management Shell changes directories to the Exchange Server Scripts *directory*, which is the command line name for *folder*. If you installed Exchange Server in a different location, provide the path to that location instead of using the default path of `\Program Files\ Microsoft\Exchange`.

2. **Type** Install-AntiSpamAgents.PS1 **and press Enter.**

   Exchange Management Shell runs the script as requested. You see the output shown in Figure 12-6. If you later decide that you don't want antispam support, you can remove it by running the `Uninstall- AntispamAgents.PS1` script.

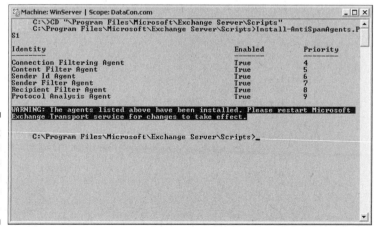

Figure 12-6: Running the script adds antispam support to your server.

3. **Type** Restart-Service MSExchangeTransport **and press Enter.**

   The `Restart-Service` cmdlet works with any service, so this is a handy cmdlet to keep in mind as you perform other management tasks. You see status messages as Windows restarts the MSExchangeTransport service. This process can require up to a minute to complete. Be sure you see the command prompt again before you do anything with Exchange Server.

4. **Open Exchange Management Console.**

   Close Exchange Management Console and reopen it if you already have it open. The new feature appears only after Microsoft Management Console reloads the required snap-in.

5. **Choose the Anti-spam tab of the Organization Configuration\Hub Transport folder.**

   You see the new Anti-spam tab contents, as shown in Figure 12-7, where you can modify the antispam settings.

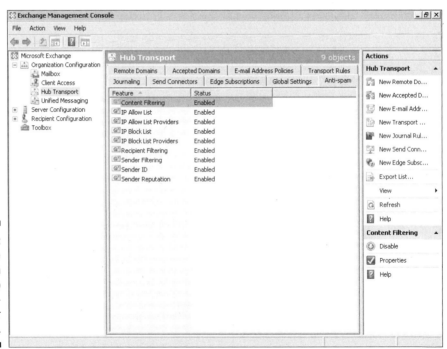

Figure 12-7:
Use the Anti-spam tab to provide protection for mailboxes.

Performing a multimailbox search

One of the most powerful features of Exchange Server is the ability to locate messages across mailboxes. You can look for messages using any search criteria that Exchange Server supports, such as sender, recipient, and subject. Before you can search the mailboxes, you need a list of mailboxes to search. The `Get-Mailbox` cmdlet helps in this case. It provides a means for locating messages throughout the organization or in a particular database. For example, if you type **Get-Mailbox -Database "Mailbox Database"** and press Enter, you see all mailboxes in Mailbox Database.

The `Export-Mailbox` cmdlet provides the means for locating a particular message in a mailbox. This cmdlet requires a mailbox as input. You must also specify what to do with the mailbox. When exporting a mailbox, you can send the content to a folder in another mailbox or to a PST file. It's also possible to delete messages within the mailbox by using the `-DeleteAssociated Messages` or `-DeleteContent` command line switches. However, let's say you want to export the messages from John's mailbox to the Administrator mailbox. In this case, you would type **Export-Mailbox John -Target Mailbox Administrator -TargetFolder "JohnsData"** and press Enter. You'll see a warning message that says that the transfer may take a long time. Type **Y** and press Enter. Now all of John's messages are also in the Administrator mailbox in a folder named `\JohnsData\Recovered Data - John - <Date> <Time>`. The date and time elements of the folder name let you perform the export multiple times.

Of course, you won't want to export all the messages, so you provide parameters that define what to export. For example, if you type **Export-Mailbox John -TargetMailbox Administrator -TargetFolder "JohnsData" -SubjectKeywords "Hello"** and press Enter, you export only the messages with the word *Hello* in the subject. You can see a complete list of command line arguments for filtering the data at `http://technet. microsoft.com/en-us/library/aa998579(EXCHG.80).aspx`.

Typing the mailboxes one at a time is awkward and error prone. To avoid these issues, you combine the `Get-Mailbox` and `Export-Mailbox` cmdlets using a feature called a pipe. Information flows from the `Get-Mailbox` cmdlet to the `Export-Mailbox` cmdlet through the pipe. To check for messages with the word *Hello* in the topic in all mailboxes, you type **Get-Mailbox -Database "Mailbox Database" | Export-Mailbox -TargetMailbox Administrator -TargetFolder "JohnsData" -SubjectKeywords "Hello"** and press Enter. Notice that you don't provide a mailbox name for the `Export-Mailbox` cmdlet because the `Get-Mailbox` cmdlet provides this information. The pipe symbol (|) provides the connection between the two cmdlets.

Now, let's say there's a virus and you want to delete it from all mailboxes. You can add to the command line that you've already used to perform this task. Simply type **Get-Mailbox -Database "Mailbox Database" | Export-Mailbox -TargetMailbox Administrator -TargetFolder "JohnsData" -SubjectKeywords "Hello" -DeleteContent** and press Enter to accomplish the task. This command line moves all messages found in the Mailbox Database that contain the word *Hello* in the subject line to the **JohnsData** folder in the Administrator mailbox and then deletes those messages in the user mailboxes. You may now examine the messages and send them back to the users if they're clean.

Working with Common Management Shell Cmdlets

You can perform most common management tasks using Exchange Management Console. However, you may find times where you want to work using Exchange Management Shell to perform tasks faster. Typing a command is often faster than using the mouse. In addition, you can combine commands by creating a text file in Notepad and saving it as a script. Simply place one command per line and save it with a PS1 file extension. (You can find a complete discussion of scripting with Windows PowerShell at http://www.microsoft.com/technet/scriptcenter/hubs/msh.mspx.)

All of these cmdlets require that you have administrator permissions. If you don't create an administrator command prompt as described in the "Opening an Administrative PowerShell Prompt" section of the chapter, UAC will hound you incessantly for permission to perform the simplest task. In addition to administrator permission, you must have permission to work with various objects. For example, if you want to work with data inside a mailbox, you need permission for that mailbox — administrator permission alone isn't good enough to perform the task. In some cases, the descriptions of cmdlets that follow provide additional security information you need to consider. The following sections describe techniques for performing common tasks at the command line. The list of cmdlets in these sections is by no means complete, but it will get you started.

Interacting with the user

Tasks that administrators perform relatively often are to add, remove, or otherwise manage users. Exchange Server is no exception to the rule. You must create and delete users as well as configure their e-mail. Exchange Management Shell provides access to the following user-related cmdlets:

- ✔ **New-MailUser:** Creates a new user and automatically defines a mailbox for them. Use the `Enable-MailUser` cmdlet instead if the user already exists in Active Directory.

- ✔ **Remove-MailUser:** Deletes a user from Active Directory. This cmdlet can also remove the associated mailbox. Use the `Disable-MailUser` cmdlet instead if you want to remove the mailbox without removing the user.

- ✔ **Enable-MailUser:** Defines a mailbox for a user who already exists within Active Directory.

- ✔ **Disable-MailUser:** Deletes the user's mailbox but doesn't remove the user from Active Directory. Use this option in place of `Remove-Mail User` when you want to maintain the user's other settings in Active Directory.

- ✔ **Get-MailUser:** Displays the user's mailbox information contained in Active Directory. Use this cmdlet with mail-enabled users. If you want to find users who aren't mail-enabled, use the `Get-User` cmdlet instead.

- ✔ **Set-MailUser:** Modifies mailbox-related attributes for a particular user in Active Directory. Use the `Set-User` cmdlet when you want to change other user attributes.

- ✔ **Get-User:** Obtains generic information about any user even if the user doesn't have an Exchange Server mailbox.

- ✔ **Set-User:** Modifies the generic attributes for any user even if the user doesn't have an Exchange Server mailbox. Use the `Set-MailUser` cmdlet if you want to modify mailbox-specific attributes.

Most user activities begin with the `Get-User` cmdlet. When you type **Get-User** and press Enter, you see a list of the users on the system, as shown in Figure 12-8. Notice that the list tells you whether or not a user has a mailbox. For example, the Administrator account has a mailbox but the Guest account doesn't.

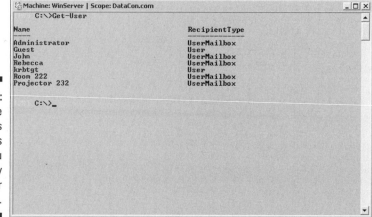

Figure 12-8:
Determine the user's status before you perform any other user tasks.

Knowing whether the user exists and has a mailbox tells you which of the cmdlets to use next. If the user doesn't exist, you can use the `New-MailUser` cmdlet to create the user and a mailbox for them. Likewise, when the user exists but doesn't have a mailbox, you use the `Enable-MailUser` cmdlet to perform the task.

It's easy to become confused about modifying user settings. When a user setting is mailbox-specific, use the `Set-MailUser` cmdlet. If you want to change a generic setting, you use the `Set-User` cmdlet. However, there's some crossover between the two utilities. For example, you can change a user's Windows e-mail address using either cmdlet with the `-WindowsEmailAddress` command line switch.

Removing a user is always a one-way process. Even if you create a user with precisely the same name and other characteristics, that user will have a different Security Identifier (SID), which means they're a different user as far as Windows is concerned. Unless you export that user's digital certificates, none of the user's access will work as before either. Consequently, remove users and their mailboxes carefully because you can't retrieve them. Unfortunately, the cmdlets aren't very good at reminding you about this potential problem.

Interacting with mail folders

The mailbox-related cmdlets are more numerous than any other area of Exchange Server. It's possible to find a cmdlet to perform nearly any task — everything from creating and deleting mailboxes to enabling mailboxes and modifying their settings.

Mailbox cmdlets are sensitive to the version of Outlook you use. In most cases, you should assume that you must have Outlook 2003 SP2 or later installed to use any of the mailbox-related cmdlets. Older versions of Outlook require special utilities. For example, if you want to import a PST file into an older version of Outlook, you need the Exchange Server Mailbox Merge wizard (`ExMerge.EXE`) utility, rather than using the `Import-Mailbox` cmdlet.

Almost all cmdlets require that you provide a mailbox name. The best way to obtain this name is using the `Get-Mailbox` cmdlet. If you type **Get-Mailbox** and press Enter, you see all mailboxes in an organization. Of course, most organizations have many mailboxes, so `Get-Mailbox` includes support for a number of filters. You can also sort the output using the `-SortBy` command line switch. For example, you might want to retrieve all user mailboxes, sort them in name order, and see unlimited details about them. In this case, you type **Get-Mailbox -RecipientTypeDetails UserMailbox -SortBy Name -ResultSize Unlimited** and press Enter. Figure 12-9 shows typical output.

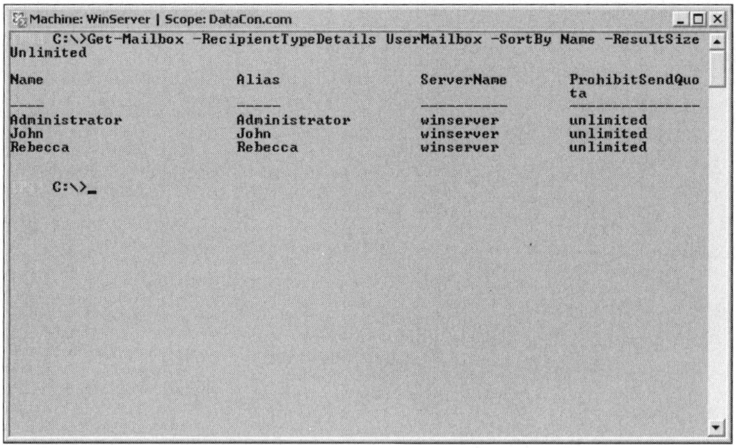

Figure 12-9:
Obtain a list
of mailboxes
you need to
manage.

Notice that the output contains the mailbox name, alias, hosting server, and sending message quota size. After you obtain this information, you can perform additional tasks. The following list provides an overview of the cmdlets for this area of Exchange Server:

- **New-Mailbox:** Creates a new user in Active Directory and then creates a new mailbox for that user. Use `Enable-Mailbox` when you want to create a mailbox for an existing user.

- **Enable-Mailbox:** Creates a new mailbox for an existing user.

- **Disable-Mailbox:** Removes a mailbox from active use. The mailbox and its user remain in Active Directory, but the mailbox no longer receives any messages. Use the `Enable-Mailbox` cmdlet to reactivate the mailbox. This cmdlet is useful when someone is on extended vacation and you want to disable his or her account without having to recreate it later. If you want to remove the mailbox permanently, use the `Remove-Mailbox` cmdlet in place of this cmdlet.

- **Remove-Mailbox:** Removes a user from Active Directory. After the user is removed, this cmdlet processes the resulting disconnected mailbox according to the command line arguments you provide. If you don't provide processing instructions, the mailbox remains in limbo in Exchange Server for 30 days, at which time Exchange Server deletes it.

- **Clean-MailboxDatabase:** Performs mailbox maintenance by scanning Active Directory for any disconnected mailboxes that aren't marked as disconnected. After a mailbox is marked disconnected, you have 30 days in which to reconnect it to another user with the `Connect-Mailbox` cmdlet; otherwise Exchange Server deletes it.

- **Connect-Mailbox:** Reconnects a disconnected mailbox to a user who appears in Active Directory. You can use this feature to recover from a `Remove-Mailbox` cmdlet error as long as you do so within 30 days.

✔ **Get-MailboxFolderStatistics:** Obtains and displays a wealth of information about the folders in a mailbox. The best use for this cmdlet is to locate user folders that are full or may require maintenance. You must supply a particular mailbox name to use this cmdlet. The output you receive has the following statistics:

- Date
- Name
- Identity
- FolderPath
- FolderId
- FolderType
- ItemsInFolder
- FolderSize
- ItemsInFolderAndSubfolders
- FolderAndSubfolderSize
- OldestItemReceivedDate
- NewestItemReceivedDate
- ManagedFolder

✔ **Get-MailboxStatistics:** Obtains and displays basic information about a particular mailbox. The information includes the number of items in the mailbox, whether the mailbox user has exceeded storage limits, and the user's last logon time. Use this cmdlet to locate unused mailboxes and mailboxes that are using too much disk space.

✔ **Move-Mailbox:** Changes the location of a mailbox to any other location, even an Exchange Server in another organization. You must have the permissions required on both the sending and receiving machines to make the move. SP1 adds a feature that lets you move mobile device mailboxes without requiring that the mobile device sync to the mailbox in the new location using Exchange ActiveSync. Exchange Server performs the required synchronization automatically.

✔ **Export-Mailbox:** Moves the content of a mailbox to a folder in another mailbox. To use this cmdlet, you must have full administrator permissions, as well as full access to both the source and target mailboxes. You can obtain access to a mailbox using the `Add-MailboxPermission` cmdlet. The export process transfers even empty folders in any of these special folders.

- Inbox
- Deleted Items
- Drafts

- Junk E-Mail

- Outbox

- Sent Items

- Journal

- Calendar

- Contacts

- Notes

- Tasks

✔ **Import-Mailbox:** Incorporates mailbox data found in a PST file into an existing mailbox. You must have permission to use the target mailbox. You can obtain access to a mailbox using the Add-MailboxPermission cmdlet.

✔ **Restore-Mailbox:** Retrieves a mailbox from a recovery storage group. In effect, this cmdlet moves a mailbox from the recovery storage group to an active storage group, making it accessible to the user who needs it. Use this feature with the replication features provided by Exchange Server to create a complete recovery solution.

✔ **Set-Mailbox:** Modifies the settings for the specified mailbox. You can use pipelining techniques to make the same change on a group of mailboxes.

✔ **Get-MailboxPermission:** Displays the permissions for a mailbox. The cmdlet lists the Active Directory identity, user, access rights, whether those rights are inherited, and whether the rights are denied or granted. Most of the user information you see is in the form of a domain and username. If you want to see the full mailbox permission information, pipe the output of this cmdlet to the Format-List cmdlet. For example, if you want to see the full permissions for mailbox John, type **Get-MailboxPermission John | Format-List** and press Enter.

Some user information is in the form of a Security Identifier. The "Converting a SID to a Username with User Info" section of Chapter 14 tells you how to overcome this issue. Unfortunately, the output truncates the SID, so you don't even have the full SID. Obtaining the full SID is a two-step process. First, place the Get-MailboxPermission output in an object by typing something like **$ThePermission = Get-MailboxPermission John** (where John is the name of the mailbox) and press Enter. Now, count the number of items displayed in the output starting with 0. Type **$ThePermission[0].User** and press Enter to retrieve the first item or any other number in the object list.

✔ **Add-MailboxPermission:** Grants a mailbox permission.

✔ **Remove-MailboxPermission:** Denies a mailbox permission.

✔ **Get-MailboxServer:** Obtains and displays a list of mailbox servers or displays the parameters for a specific mailbox server. In most cases, you type `Get-MailboxServer` and press Enter the first time, and then type `Get-MailboxServer <Server Name> | Format-List` and press Enter to obtain the mailbox parameters. Piping the output to the `Format-List` cmdlet makes it possible to see all output parameters, as shown in Figure 12-10.

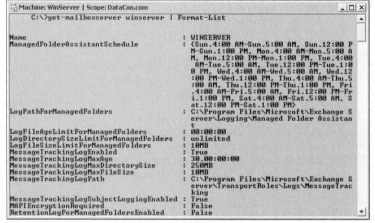

Figure 12-10: Some cmdlets show only partial output until you pipe it to Format-List.

✔ **Set-MailboxServer:** Modifies any mailbox server properties displayed by the `Get-MailboxServer` cmdlet. There's some overlap between this cmdlet and the `Set-TransportServer` cmdlet. If you have both the Hub Transport Server and Mailbox Server roles installed, you can use either cmdlet to configure the message tracking settings. When a server includes only the Hub Transport Server role, you must rely on the `Set-TransportServer` cmdlet to make any changes. Likewise, if you install only the Mailbox Server role, you must rely on the `Get-MailboxServer` cmdlet.

✔ **Get-MailboxDatabase:** Obtains and displays a list of mailbox databases or displays the parameters for a specific mailbox database. In most cases, you type `Get-MailboxDatabase` and press Enter the first time, and then type `Get-MailboxDatabase <Database Name> | Format-List` and press Enter to obtain the mailbox parameters. Refer to Figure 12-10 for an example of the `Format-List` cmdlet in action for the `Get-MailboxServer` cmdlet.

✔ **New-MailboxDatabase:** Creates or recovers a mailbox database. When creating a new mailbox database, you must provide the `-Name` and `-StorageGroup` command line arguments as a minimum. Exchange Server will create a new mailbox database using the default parameter. When recovering a mailbox database, you must provide the `-MailboxDatabaseToRecover` and `-StorageGroup` command line arguments as a minimum. The recovered database will use any default settings it used before.

✔ **Remove-MailboxDatabase:** Deletes an existing mailbox database. This cmdlet removes only the database entries from Active Directory; it doesn't remove the physical files. You must remove the files manually to complete the deletion process. The fact that the files still exist also means that you can recover from an accidental deletion by creating a new database and assigning the existing files to that database.

✔ **Set-MailboxDatabase:** Modifies any mailbox database settings displayed by the `Get-MailboxDatabase` cmdlet.

✔ **Get-ManagedFolderMailboxPolicy:** Obtains and displays a list of managed folder policies or displays the parameters for a managed folder policy. In most cases, you type `Get-ManagedFolderMailboxPolicy` and press Enter the first time, and then type `Get-ManagedFolder MailboxPolicy <Managed Folder Policy Name> | Format-List` and press Enter to obtain the mailbox parameters. Refer to Figure 12-10 for an example of the `Format-List` cmdlet in action for the `Get-MailboxServer` cmdlet.

✔ **New-ManagedFolderMailboxPolicy:** Defines a new managed folder mailbox policy. You need only define the managed folder mailbox policy name as part of creating a new managed folder mailbox policy.

✔ **Remove-ManagedFolderMailboxPolicy:** Deletes an existing managed folder policy.

✔ **Set-ManagedFolderMailboxPolicy:** Modifies any managed folder mailbox policy parameters displayed by the `Get-ManagedFolderMailbox Policy` cmdlet.

✔ **Get-CASMailbox:** Obtains and displays a list of Client Access Server (CAS) mailboxes or displays the parameters for a particular CAS mailbox. This cmdlet displays attributes for the OWA, Exchange ActiveSync, POP3, and IMAP4 settings you have in place. In most cases, you work directly with a single user's mailbox. The standard display doesn't show all the parameters, so you must pipe the output to the `Format-List` cmdlet. For example, if you want to find the settings for user John, you type `Get-CASMailbox John | Format-List` and press Enter. Refer to Figure 12-10 for an example of the `Format-List` cmdlet in action for the `Get-MailboxServer` cmdlet.

✔ **Set-CASMailbox:** Modifies any CAS mailbox settings displayed by the `Get-CASMailbox` cmdlet.

Working with a clustered mailbox server

Depending on how you configure Exchange Server, you may need to work with a clustered mailbox server configuration. Clustering is one of several server reliability features that you can use with Exchange Server. The following list describes the more important clustered mailbox server cmdlets:

✔ **Move-ClusteredMailboxServer:** Initiates a scheduled move of the clustered mailbox server from the active node to a passive node. This move differs from an unscheduled move when the server fails. Use this cmdlet when you need to move the server to perform maintenance or other tasks that require the server to be offline.

✔ **Start-ClusteredMailboxServer:** Restarts a server after you stop it using the `Stop-ClusteredMailboxServer` cmdlet. This feature is part of an explicit stop-to-start sequence where automatic failover doesn't occur. Use this cmdlet to restart the server after you perform maintenance tasks on it.

✔ **Get-ClusteredMailboxServer:** Displays the status of a clustered mailbox server as Partially Online, Online Pending, Offline, Offline Pending, or Failed. You can also use this cmdlet to display a list of computers that can host the clustered mailbox server. Use this cmdlet to determine whether a clustered mailbox server has potential problems. If you determine there's a need to move the clustered mailbox server, you also use this cmdlet to determine where to move a clustered mailbox server before using the `Move-ClusteredMailboxServer` cmdlet. SP1 provides additional details in the output of this cmdlet:

  • OperationalReplicationHostNames:{Host1,Host2,Host3}

  • FailedReplicationHostNames:{Host4}

  • InUseReplicationHostNames:{Host1,Host2}

✔ **Stop-ClusteredMailboxServer:** Causes the clustered mailbox server to stop processing messages without activating the passive node in the cluster. The result is that all clustered mailbox server operations stop. You use this cmdlet in an emergency, such as massive equipment failure, or when you need to perform specific kinds of maintenance that require a clustered mailbox server shutdown. Use the `Start-ClusteredMailboxServer` cmdlet to restart the clustered mailbox server.

Configuring distribution groups

Distribution groups are the basis for sending much of the e-mail in an organization. Instead of sending e-mail to individual group members, distribution groups make it possible to send the e-mail to a single location. From an Exchange Management Shell perspective, distribution groups are divided into three areas:

- ✔ Distribution groups
- ✔ Dynamic distribution groups
- ✔ Distribution group members

Each entity has its own get cmdlet, and you normally use the get cmdlet as a first step to working with other distribution group cmdlets. These three get cmdlets are

- ✔ Get-DistributionGroup
- ✔ Get-DynamicDistributionGroup
- ✔ Get-DistributionGroupMember

All three cmdlets display more information than the tabular format used by the cmdlet for output. Consequently, you usually use the get cmdlet by itself first to obtain a list of distribution group elements, and then use it a second time with a specific distribution group element. For example, you might begin by typing **Get-DistributionGroup** and pressing Enter. You see the My Group entry you want to know more about, so you type **Get-DistributionGroup "My Group" | Format-List** and press Enter. After you discover the distribution group or group member you want to work with, you can use the following cmdlets to perform modifications:

- ✔ **Enable-DistributionGroup:** Lets an existing Active Directory universal group receive mail. A universal group is one that has the Universal Group option selected in the group Properties dialog box, as shown in Figure 12-11 (accessible from the Users folder of the Active Directory Users and Computers console in the Administrative Tools folder of Control Panel). This is the distribution group equivalent of mail-enabling a user. The group must exist in Active Directory before you use this cmdlet. All you need to do is type the group name as input. For example, to mail-enable Project 221, you type **Enable-DistributionGroup "Project 221"** and press Enter.

- ✔ **Disable-DistributionGroup:** Removes the mail capabilities of a group without removing the group from Active Directory. You always use this option with groups that you want to keep. Otherwise, you must recreate the group in Active Directory and add members back into it. Use the Remove-DistributionGroup cmdlet when you want to remove the group from Active Directory.

- ✔ **New-DistributionGroup:** Creates a new distribution group. You must provide the -Name, -SamAccountName, and -Type arguments as a minimum. The -Name argument can contain spaces, but the -SamAccountName argument (Alias when using the graphical interface) is used for older systems and can't contain a space. The -Type argument can contain either Distribution or Security and corresponds to the Group Type field in Figure 12-11.

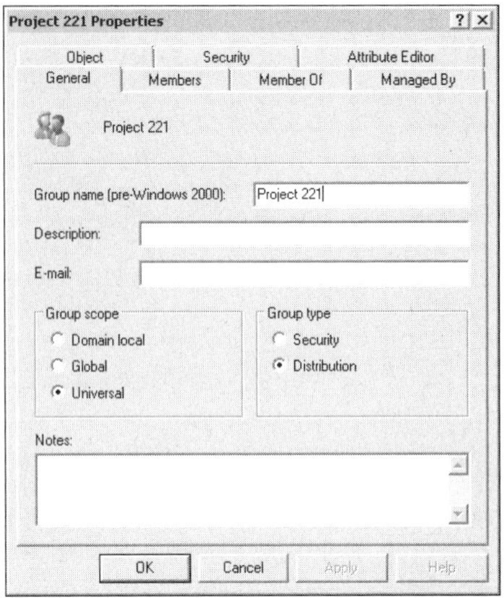

Figure 12-11:
You can
mail-enable
only univer-
sal groups.

✔ **Remove-DistributionGroup:** Removes the mail capabilities of a distribution group and deletes its entry in Active Directory. After you use this cmdlet, you can no longer access the distribution group.

✔ **Set-DistributionGroup:** Modifies any distribution group settings displayed by the `Get-DistributionGroup` cmdlet.

✔ **New-DynamicDistributionGroup:** Creates a new dynamic distribution group. You must provide the `-Name` and `-IncludedRecipients` or `-RecipientFilter` arguments as a minimum. The `-Name` argument can contain spaces. The `-IncludedRecipients` argument contains the kind of mailboxes in the group membership. For example, if you want to create a dynamic distribution group with user mailboxes as included recipients, you would type **New-DynamicDistributionGroup -Name "My Distribution Group" -IncludedRecipient "MailboxUsers"** and press Enter.

If you want to use the `-RecipientFilter` form of the command line syntax, you must create a logical statement that defines the conditions under which the dynamic distribution group becomes active. For example, if you want to create a group of everyone who lives in Wisconsin, you type **New-DynamicDistributionGroup -Name "My Distribution Group" -RecipientFilter {((StateOrProvince -eq 'WI'))}** and press Enter. It's more common to include an recipient type, even when creating a filter. If you want to add user mailboxes as a requirement to this command line, you type **New-Dynamic DistributionGroup -Name "My Distribution Group" -RecipientFilter {((RecipientType -eq 'UserMailbox') -and ((StateOrProvince -eq 'WI')))}** and press Enter. The `RecipientType` filter always appears first and its second parenthesis always surrounds the remaining filter elements.

✔ **Remove-DynamicDistributionGroup:** Removes the mail capabilities of a dynamic distribution group and deletes its entry in Active Directory. After you use this cmdlet, you can't access the dynamic distribution group any longer.

✔ **Set-DynamicDistributionGroup:** Modifies any of the dynamic distribution group settings displayed by the `Get-DynamicDistribution Group` cmdlet.

✔ **Add-DistributionGroupMember:** Adds a member to an existing distribution group. You must provide the group name and the name of the member you want to add using the `-Member` argument. For example, if you want to add John to My Group, you type **Add-Distribution GroupMember "My Group" -Member John** and press Enter.

✔ **Remove-DistributionGroupMember:** Removes a member from an existing distribution group. You must provide the group name and the name of the member you want to add using the `-Member` argument. For example, if you want to remove John from My Group, you type **Remove-DistributionGroupMember "My Group" -Member John** and press Enter. Type **Y** and press Enter when asked if you're sure you want to remove the member.

Using Calendar Attendant

Calendar Attendant provides a means of ensuring that meetings don't overlap and that the people who need to get to a meeting can get there without undo stress. In previous versions of Exchange Server, all calendar processing occurred on the client machine. Calendar Attention centralizes processing of meeting requirements, puts new meetings on the calendar, deletes out-of-date meeting entries, and updates existing meetings, all without user intervention. Most of the time this feature works without much administrator intervention too. You can always monitor the performance of Calendar Attendant using Performance Monitor. The following objects provide the information you need about the functionality of Calendar Attendant on your server:

✔ Average Calendar Attendant Processing Time

✔ Last Calendar Attendant Processing Time

✔ Lost Races

✔ Meeting Cancellations

✔ Meeting Messages Deleted

✔ Meeting Messages Processed

✔ Meeting Requests

✔ Meeting Responses

✔ Requests Failed

In some cases, you must interact with Calendar Attendant to ensure that it operates correctly. For example, you might decide that you want to disable out-of-date meeting deletion for a while because you need to track past meetings for some reason. It's possible to make configuration changes to Calendar Attendant that will make it perform better in a given circumstance. All Calendar Attendant settings focus on a mailbox, normally a room mailbox, rather than a user mailbox. The following list of cmdlets helps you perform Calendar Attendant management.

✔ **Get-MailboxCalendarSettings:** Obtains the current list of Calendar Attendant settings. If you type **Get-MailboxCalendarSettings** and press Enter, the cmdlet displays a list of applicable room and user mailbox accounts on the system. However, in most cases, you need to know about a particular mailbox, such as Room 222. In this case, type **Get-MailboxCalendarSettings Room222 | Format-List** and press Enter to display a complete set of properties, as shown in Figure 12-12.

✔ **Set-MailboxCalendarSettings:** Modifies any Calendar Attendant settings displayed by the Get-MailboxCalendarSettings cmdlet. You must specify the mailbox name and at least one property you want to change. For example, if you want to change the AutomateProcessing property to None, you type **Set-MailboxCalendarSettings Room222 -AutomateProcessing None** and press Enter.

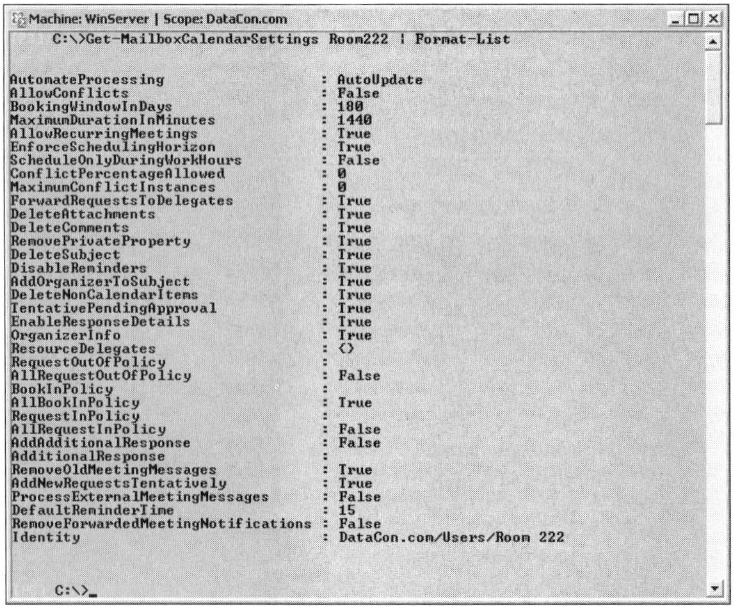

Figure 12-12:
Calendar
Attendant
settings tell
you how
a room
or user
mailbox is
configured
for appoint-
ments.

```
Machine: WinServer | Scope: DataCon.com                          _ □ ×
     C:\>Get-MailboxCalendarSettings Room222 | Format-List

AutomateProcessing                    : AutoUpdate
AllowConflicts                        : False
BookingWindowInDays                   : 180
MaximumDurationInMinutes              : 1440
AllowRecurringMeetings                : True
EnforceSchedulingHorizon              : True
ScheduleOnlyDuringWorkHours           : False
ConflictPercentageAllowed             : 0
MaximumConflictInstances              : 0
ForwardRequestsToDelegates            : True
DeleteAttachments                     : True
DeleteComments                        : True
RemovePrivateProperty                 : True
DeleteSubject                         : True
DisableReminders                      : True
AddOrganizerToSubject                 : True
DeleteNonCalendarItems                : True
TentativePendingApproval              : True
EnableResponseDetails                 : True
OrganizerInfo                         : True
ResourceDelegates                     : {}
RequestOutOfPolicy                    :
AllRequestOutOfPolicy                 : False
BookInPolicy                          :
AllBookInPolicy                       : True
RequestInPolicy                       :
AllRequestInPolicy                    : False
AddAdditionalResponse                 : False
AdditionalResponse                    :
RemoveOldMeetingMessages              : True
AddNewRequestsTentatively             : True
ProcessExternalMeetingMessages        : False
DefaultReminderTime                   : 15
RemoveForwardedMeetingNotifications   : False
Identity                              : DataCon.com/Users/Room 222

C:\>_
```

Chapter 13

Using the Command Line

*1*n the beginning of the personal computer, there was the Disk Operating System (DOS). DOS relied on a command line to perform every task. People wanted something better than DOS because remembering all those commands was confusing. Eventually, Microsoft introduced Windows with its GUI (graphical user interface) to make things easier. Now, legions of computer professionals have used the GUI to perform all their work and find it both slow and cumbersome. Consequently, Microsoft has reintroduced the command line in a big way to speed things up. In fact, you can now install Windows Server 2008 Server Core, which has nothing more than a command line and a hint of a GUI (imagine Windows without the Start menu, taskbar, notification area, or desktop). Of course, you still have to remember all those commands.

It's important to keep the command line separate from Exchange Management Shell. The command line is the native code environment that essentially appeared with DOS (the low-level details are different but don't worry about these differences because you won't see them). Exchange Management Shell is a form of Windows PowerShell, and it relies on the managed environment created using .NET Framework. The two environments are different and you can't execute commands in one that appear in the other, even though Windows PowerShell does provide some equivalent commands for compatibility. Chapter 12 tells you all about Exchange Management Shell.

In most cases, you use Exchange Management Shell to perform essential Exchange Server configuration, testing, and maintenance tasks. The command line offers access to ancillary utilities that help you perform monitoring or repair tasks. You also rely on the command line for compatibility, such as working with older versions of Exchange Server. The following sections describe how to work with the command line and also provide an overview of some command line utilities that come with Exchange Server.

Configuring the Command Line

It's possible to simply open a command line and use it for many tasks. All you need to do is type the command you want to use, along with any command line arguments it requires, and press Enter to execute the command. The problem is that many Exchange Server commands require administrator privileges. Like Exchange Management Shell, you need to open an administrator command window in newer versions of Windows to ensure that you can execute commands.

After you successfully open a command window, you can customize it. Many users start the command window, see the typical command prompt, and just assume that they'll never see anything else. However, you can easily configure the command window to appear as you want, at least within limits. You can access these features by clicking the box in the upper-left corner of the command window and choosing Properties from the context menu. You'll see a properties dialog box with four tabs. The following sections describe various configuration requirements for the command window.

Opening an administrator command line

The default command window that provides access to the command line provides standard user privileges. In most cases, these privileges limit what you can do with Exchange Server commands because these commands require administrator privileges. The following steps help you open an administrator command line:

1. **Choose Start➪Programs➪Accessories.**

   You see the Accessories menu.

2. **Right-click Command Prompt and choose Run As Administrator from the context menu.**

   Windows opens a command prompt that has Administrator in the title, as shown in Figure 13-1. The default title is Administrator: Command Prompt as shown, but you can use special commands to give the window other titles, such as Administrator: My Command Prompt. The important consideration is the word *Administrator* in the title.

Setting the window options

The Options tab shown in Figure 13-2 defines how the command window reacts when you open it. The Cursor Size option controls the size of the cursor, with small being the default. The Large option provides a block cursor that is very easy to see.

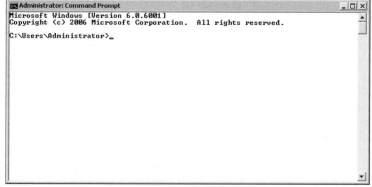

Figure 13-1:
An admin-
istrator
command
window has
the word
Admini-
strator in
the title.

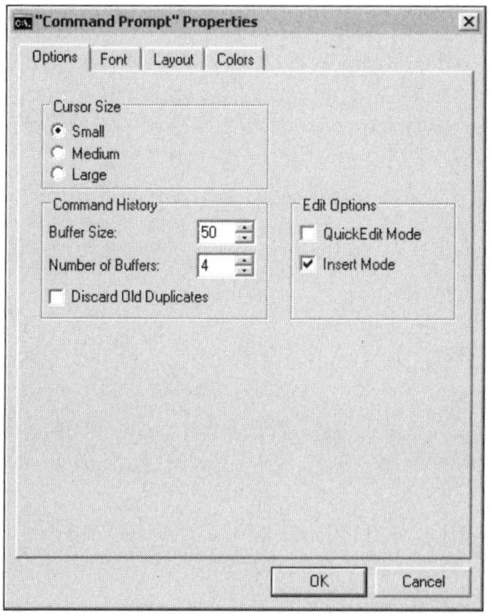

Figure 13-2:
The Options
tab helps
you control
the appear-
ance and
behavior
of the
command
window.

The Command History is especially important. The Buffer Size option determines the number of commands the buffer will store. Every command requires memory, so increasing this number increases the amount of memory the command prompt requires. Increase this number when you plan to perform a number of complex commands. A smaller number will save memory for larger command line applications. The Number of Buffers option controls the number of individual histories. You need one history for each process (application environment) you create. Generally, the default of 4 works fine. Normally, the command history includes every command you issue. You can save space in the history by checking Discard Old Duplicates, which removes duplicate commands from the list.

The Edit Options determine how you interact with the command window. Select the QuickEdit Mode option when you want to use the mouse to work with the entries directly. The only problem with using this feature is that it can interfere with some commands, such as Edit, that have a mouse interface of their own. The Insert Mode option lets you paste text into the command window without replacing the text that is currently there. For example, you might copy some information from a Windows application and paste it as an argument for a command.

If you have used the command line before, you'll notice that the Display Options group is missing from Figure 13-2. The Display Options determine whether you see the command window full screen or as a window. Windows Server 2008 doesn't let you run the command window in full-screen mode by changing the Display Options setting. Using the full-screen mode when you have a number of tasks to perform is easier on the eyes. Unfortunately, Windows Server 2008 appears to share this problem with the latest versions of Vista. The display drivers simply don't support a full-screen display, and using registry cheats to overcome this problem no longer works. You can read about the many command line changes in both Vista and Windows Server 2008 at http://www.trnicely.net/misc/vista.html.

Changing the font

The Font tab shown in Figure 13-3 controls the font used to display text. The font size automatically changes when you resize the window, but you can also control the font size directly using this tab. The raster fonts give the typical command line font appearance that works well for most quick tasks. The Lucida Console font works better in a windowed environment. It's easier on the eyes because it's smoother, but you might find that some applications won't work well with it if they create "text graphics" using some of the extended ASCII characters. The extended ASCII characters include corners and lines that a developer can use to draw boxes and add visual detail.

Choosing a window layout

The Layout tab shown in Figure 13-4 has the potential to affect your use of the command window greatly when working in windowed mode. The Screen Buffer Size controls the width and height of the screen buffer, the total area used to display information. When the Window Size setting is smaller than the Screen Buffer Size, Windows provides scroll bars so you can move the window around within the buffer area and view all it contains. Some commands require a great deal of space for display purposes. Adjusting the Screen Buffer Size and Window Size can help you view all the information these commands provide.

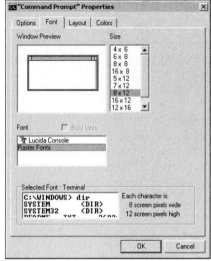

Figure 13-3:
Use the
Font tab to
control the
size of the
text in the
command
window.

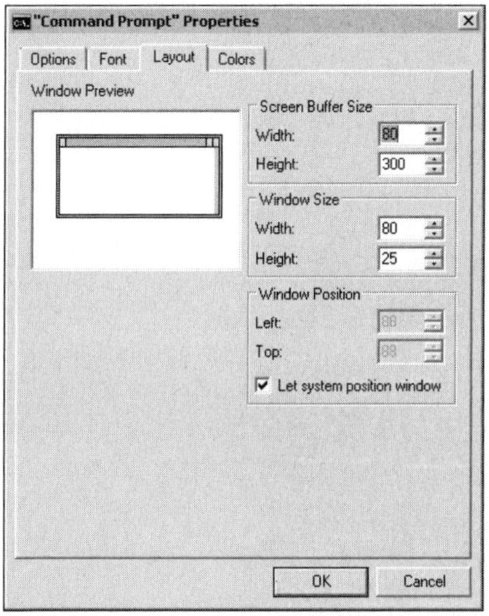

Figure 13-4:
Change the
size and
position-
ing of the
command
window
using the
Layout tab.

The Window Position determines where Windows places the command
window when you first open it. Some people prefer a specific position on the
screen so they always know where a new command window will appear.
However, it's generally safe to select Let System Position Window to allow
Windows to place the command window on screen. Each command window
will appear at a different, randomly chosen, position.

Defining text colors

Microsoft assumes that you want a black background with light gray letters for the command window. Although DOS used this setting all those years ago, many people today want a choice. The Colors tab lets you choose different foreground, background, and pop-up colors for the command window (even though Figure 13-5 doesn't show the colors, it does present the dialog box layout). You can modify the window to use any of the 16 standard color combinations for any of the text options. Use the Selected Color Values options to create custom colors.

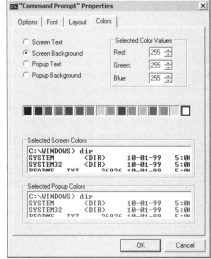

Figure 13-5:
Modify the
text colors
for an
optimal
display
using the
Colors tab.

Interacting with Exchange Server Databases Using ESEUtil

The most important task you can perform at the command line is maintaining the Exchange Server databases. The databases contain all of the user data, so managing these databases is of prime importance. Previous chapters have shown you some GUI methods for performing Exchange Server database maintenance. The Extensible Storage Engine Utility (ESEUtil) command performs Exchange Server database maintenance tasks at the command line.

Don't confuse the ESEUtil command with the Extensible Storage Engine Technology Utility (ESEnTUtl) command provided with Windows to maintain Windows databases. The two commands perform similar tasks with different kinds of databases. If the database has an EDB file extension, you must use the ESEUtil command. On the other hand, if it has an SDB file extension, you must use the ESEnTUtl command.

The first command line argument you provide to ESEUtil always determines its mode. For example, using /d configures ESEUtil for the defragmentation mode. You can also repair, restore, recover, display, and copy the database. In addition, ESEUtil provides access to tests that determine the integrity and checksum of the database.

All ESEUtil modes require a database name. The default location for these databases is the `\Program Files\Microsoft\Exchange Server\Mailbox\<Storage Group>\` folder of your system. For example, many of the screenshots in this book show the Mailbox Database found in the `\Program Files\Microsoft\Exchange Server\Mailbox\First Storage Group` folder as `Mailbox Database.EDB`. Many of the example commands in this section rely on the Mailbox Database. You can also use ESEUtil on other Exchange Server databases, such as queues, which have a QUE file extension.

Always change directories (using the CD command) to the directory containing the database file before you execute a command on that database. For example, to change directories to the First Storage Group, you type **CD "\Program Files\Microsoft\Exchange Server\Mailbox\First Storage Group"** and press Enter. Notice the use of the double quotes for the directory name since it contains spaces. In addition, you must dismount the database before you can perform maintenance on it. The easiest way to dismount the database is to right-click the database entry in the Database Management tab of the Server Configuration\Mailbox folder of Exchange Management Console, and choose Dismount Database from the context menu. The following sections describe each of these modes and tells how to use them.

Defragmenting the database

Databases become fragmented as Exchange Server adds and removes records. A new record appears in any space that can hold it within the database file unless there aren't any spaces large enough. In this case, Exchange Server adds the new record to the end of the database. Deleting records leaves holes in the database file that Exchange Server later fills with new records. The result is that a single user's records can appear all over the place within the database file and, consequently, on the hard drive. A fragmented database performs poorly because of the physics of moving the hard drive head looking for the right records — having records in order speeds up searches considerably.

Defragmenting reorders the records so that a single user's records appear in one place. In addition, defragmenting removes empty records — those left by a deletion. The removal of empty records reduces the size of the database on disk and greatly improves performance because there is less to search. Finally, defragmenting rebuilds the indexes, which are special search terms that Exchange Server uses to locate data you request. Rebuilding the indexes further improves performance by decreasing search times. Here is the basic command line syntax for the defragmentation mode:

```
ESEUtil /d <database name> [options]
```

If you want to defragment the Mailbox Database, you type **ESEUtil /d "Mailbox Database.EDB"** and press Enter. Notice that you must use double quotes to delimit the database name since it contains spaces. The database name must also include the file extension. Figure 13-6 shows typical results of a defragmentation. You can discover more about this mode at http://technet.microsoft.com/en-us/library/aa998863 (EXCHG.80).aspx.

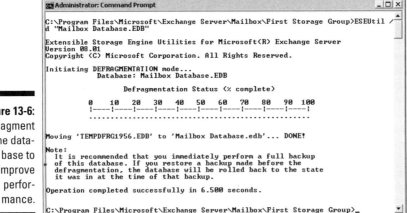

Figure 13-6: Defragment the database to improve performance.

Repairing the database

Exchange Server databases can suffer damage under adverse conditions. The repair mode searches the database for damaged pages and discards those pages, which means that this process causes data loss. No, you couldn't retrieve the data — it was lost before you performed the repair, but the bottom line is that the pages holding the data are gone now as well. The result of this process is a database that contains only useful pages.

A repair is only the first step of the process. The repair process doesn't check the relationships between tables for potential problems. In addition, the database is left in a fragmented state, which makes additional repairs time consuming. After you perform a repair, you must defragment the database as a second step. The third step is to use the ISInteg utility to check and repair the database integrity to ensure that all the tables work with each other. Here is the basic command line syntax for the repair mode:

```
ESEUtil /p <database name> [options]
```

Even though the Microsoft command line syntax lists options for this mode, the detailed usage information doesn't reveal any options. Consequently, if you want to repair the Mailbox Database, follow these steps:

1. **Type** ESEUtil /p "Mailbox Database.EDB" **and press Enter.**

   ESEUtil displays a message saying that you should run this mode only on a corrupted database. Remember that you always have other options for repairing the database, such as restoring a known good backup. The repair option is for situations where that database has contained corrupted information for a long time and none of your backups contain uncorrupted data.

2. **Click OK.**

   ESEUtil performs the check. You see a display similar to Figure 13-6 that shows the status of the check and provides details about errors that the repair mode found.

3. **Type** ESEUtil /d "Mailbox Database.EDB" **and press Enter.**

   ESEUtil defragments the database.

4. **Type** ISInteg -fix -s <Server Name> -test Folder **and press Enter.**

   ISInteg displays a list of databases and their status on the server you select. You can fix only offline databases.

5. **Type the number of the database you want to check and press Enter.**

   ISInteg asks whether you're certain that you want to perform the check.

6. **Type** Y **and press Enter.**

   ISInteg performs the integrity check on your database and corrects any integrity errors between tables. The integrity test can take a long time to complete.

Make sure you make a backup of the new database as soon as possible. Even though old backups still contain useful information, you can't use them to recreate the new database. You can discover more about this mode at http://technet.microsoft.com/en-us/library/aa998231 (EXCHG.80).aspx.

Restoring the database

Exchange Server maintains a transaction log — essentially a list of tasks it performs on the database. You use the restore mode after you restore a backup from an older streaming backup, such as a tape. A backup from an older copy of Exchange Server will contain a file named `Restore.ENV` that contains a log of the tasks that Exchange Server has to perform.

If you don't find `Restore.ENV`, you know that you don't need to use this mode because there aren't any transaction log entries to restore. Make sure you use the recovery mode described in the "Recovering the database" section when working with newer versions of Exchange Server. Here is the basic command line syntax for the restore mode:

```
ESEUtil /c[mode-modifier] <path name> [options]
```

The mode-modifier determines what kind of restoration ESEUtil performs. If you use the `/cc` command line switch, ESEUtil replays the transaction logs and restores the database to a known good state. Using the `/cm` command line switch merely displays the transactions in `Restore.ENV` so you can determine whether you want to replay the transaction logs. You can discover more about this mode at `http://technet.microsoft.com/en-us/library/aa998303(EXCHG.80).aspx`.

Recovering the database

The recovery mode works much like the restore mode described in the "Restoring the database" section of the chapter. However, recovery mode works with newer backup strategies. Microsoft calls this recovery strategy a soft recovery. You use a soft recovery to replay the transaction logs after an unexpected event such as a stop, when you transfer the transaction logs into an offline copy of the database, or when you transfer the transaction logs into a Volume Shadow Copy Service (VSS) backup set.

The essential requirement for a soft recovery is that the database and log files are intact. This technique relies on a checkpoint file to perform the recover process. These checkpoint files normally appear in the same folder as the database file and begin with the letter *E,* such as `E0000000079.LOG`. You tell ESEUtil to use a particular log file base name such as E00, which would replay all logs that begin with E00 in their name — `E0000000079.LOG` would replay but `E0100000079.LOG` wouldn't.

Use the `/L` option to change the location of the log files, such as `/LC:\Exchange\MyLogs` if the log file appears in the `C:\Exchange\MyLogs` folder. Here is the basic command line syntax for the recovery mode:

```
ESEUtil /r <logfile base name> [options]
```

If you want to recover the E00 files for a particular storage group, you change directories to that storage group's folder on the hard drive, type **ESEUtil /r E00**, and press Enter. You can discover more about this mode at http://technet.microsoft.com/en-us/library/bb123919 (EXCHG.80).aspx.

Performing an integrity check

Databases require integrity at several levels. The term *integrity* essentially means that the database contains good data and that Exchange Server can access it correctly. However, the term means a lot more than that to a programmer.

The integrity mode performs checks at two levels for Exchange Server databases. The first level verifies the integrity of the database pages, which are the basic unit of physical storage for the database. The second level verifies the Extensible Storage Engine (ESE) integrity of the database. This level ensures that ESE can interact with the database. You use the ISInteg utility to verify application-level integrity, so this mode doesn't provide a complete integrity check. Here is the basic command line syntax for the integrity check mode:

```
ESEUtil /g <database name> [options]
```

If you want to verify the integrity of the Mailbox Database, you type **ESEUtil /g "Mailbox Database.EDB"** and press Enter. The output simply says that the integrity check is successful or tells you about errors that the integrity check has found. You can discover more about this mode at http://technet.microsoft.com/en-us/library/aa998361 (EXCHG.80).aspx.

Displaying the database contents

At some point, you may want to see the contents of Exchange Server database files. You may want to verify that specific content appears in the file or may simply be curious about the content. The display mode has three submodes associated with it as shown here:

- ✔ **/mh:** Displays the database headers
- ✔ **/ml:** Validates the integrity and sequence for the database transaction logs, which helps you ensure you can recover from an error
- ✔ **/mk:** Displays the headers for the database checkpoint files

Of these three submodes, the most useful for most administrators is /ml because it helps you validate the integrity of the transaction logs. These transaction logs are essential for the soft recovery method described in the "Recovering the database" section of the chapter. Here is the basic command line syntax for the database contents display mode:

```
ESEUtil /m[mode-modifier] <filename>
```

If you want to view the headers for the Mailbox Database, you type **ESEUtil /mh "Mailbox Database.EDB"** and press Enter. This command can require a long time to complete, so don't worry if you see "Initiating FILE DUMP mode..." and then the screen seems to freeze for a while. You can discover more about this mode at http://technet.microsoft.com/en-us/library/bb125171(EXCHG.80).aspx.

Performing a checksum test

A *checksum* is a kind of mathematical method for verifying the integrity of any file. A checksum can be performed in a number of ways but the method isn't important here. The Exchange Server checksum validates all pages in the database, log files, and checkpoint files. In short, this check provides a very fast way for you to determine whether the database has any problems that require further action on your part. Here is the basic command line syntax for the checksum test mode:

```
ESEUtil /k <file name> [options]
```

If you want to perform a checksum test on the Mailbox Database, you type **ESEUtil /k "Mailbox Database.EDB"** and press Enter. You can discover more about this mode at http://technet.microsoft.com/en-us/library/bb123956(EXCHG.80).aspx.

Copying the database to another location

At some point, you may want to copy a database from one location to another. You may want to create a copy for the simple purpose of creating a quick backup of a large file. The ESEUtil doesn't do anything more than the Copy command that is already available at the command line. However, it does perform the task faster when working with large files because it uses larger blocks of memory. Here is the basic command line syntax for the copy mode:

```
ESEUtil /y <source file> [options]
```

ESEUtil assumes that you perform this task in the destination folder. Consequently, it doesn't provide a method for defining the destination as part of the command. Let's say you create a folder named `MyCopy` as a subdirectory of the folder that contains the Mailbox Database object. If you want to copy the Mailbox Database to `MyCopy`, you type **ESEUtil /y "..\ Mailbox Database.EDB"** and press Enter. Notice that you must specify the full or relative path for the folder that contains Mailbox Database.EDB. You can discover more about this mode at `http://technet.microsoft.com/ en-us/library/aa996409(EXCHG.80).aspx`.

Confirming Database Integrity Using ISInteg

You use the Information Store Integrity Checker (ISInteg) command to verify that the database has all the correct inner connections — that tables refer to each other in the correct way. It's important to verify that there aren't any reference problems within the database because these internal problems can cause a host of other problems, including lost data. Here is the basic command line syntax for ISInteg:

```
isinteg -s ServerName [-fix] [-verbose] [-l logfilename]
-test testname[[, test name]...]
```

As shown by the command line syntax, you must provide a server name and a test name. One of the most common tests is to check folders for errors, but you can perform other tests as well. The following list describes the command line options in greater detail:

- ✔ **-s *ServerName*:** Provides the name of the server you want to check. Tests verify the integrity of the entire server, not a single mailbox.

- ✔ **-fix:** Performs a repair of any problems that ISInteg encounters. Normally, ISInteg only tells you about problems in the database.

- ✔ **-verbose:** Displays additional information about the errors that ISInteg encounters.

- ✔ **-l *filename*:** Defines the name of the log used to store ISInteg results. The default log filename is `ISInteg.PRI` or `ISInteg.PUB`, depending on whether you perform a private or public check, respectively. You normally find the log file in the `\Program Files\Microsoft\ Exchange Server\Mailbox\MDBTEMP` folder of your system.

- ✔ **-t *refdblocation*:** Determines the location of the `Refer.MDB` file. This file stores the `Priv.EDB` or `Pub.EDB` file during testing and normally appears in the testing directory. The `Refer.MDB` file can cause an out-of-space condition on the hard drive, and using this command line switch provides a means to place the file in another location. See the Knowledge Base article at `http://support.microsoft.com/ kb/258301` for details.

✔ **-test** *testname*: Specifies the name of the test to perform. You can specify multiple -test command line switches on the command line. For example, if you want to check for both folders and messages, you can type **ISInteg -s <Server Name> -test folder -test message** and press Enter. The following table shows the tests you can run:

aclitem	dumpsterref	newsfeed (public only)
aclitemref	fldrcv (private only)	newsfeedref (public only)
acllist	fldsub	ooflist (private only)
acllistref	folder	peruser
artidx (public only)	global	rcvfld (private only)
attach	mailbox (private only)	replstate (public only)
attachref	message	rowcounts
delfld	morefld	search
dlvrto	msgref	searchq
dumpsterprops	msgsoftref	timedev

In addition to single tests, you can also run a number of group tests: allfoldertests and allacltests. If you want to perform every test that ISInteg can perform, use the alltests keyword.

Checking Best Practices Using ExBPACmd

Use ExBPACmd to perform best practices checks from the command line. Instead of using the graphical version of the utility described in the "Using Best Practices Analyzer" section of Chapter 4, you type a command at the command line to initiate the tests. Type **ExBPACmd** and press Enter to use all the default settings. The following list describes command line switches you can add to modify the way in which ExBPACmd works:

✔ **-cfg** *Filename*: Reads settings and rules for performing the best practices check from the specified files. The default settings rely on the ExBPA.Config.XML file found in the \Program Files\ Microsoft\Exchange Server\Bin\<Language> folder.

✔ **-dat** *Filename*: Writes the output data to the specified file. The default settings create a file with the name output.<label>.<timestamp>. xml in the EXBPA output folder. In most cases, you find the EXBPA folder in the user's documents folder. For example, the administrator will find this folder at \Users\Administrator\AppData\Roaming\ Microsoft\ExBPA\.

✔ **-in** *Filename*: Provides a means of sending data to Best Practices Analyzer. You can use this additional data to collect data from other scopes using a single file or to reanalyze previously collected data. If you supply a $ for the filename, ExBPACmd searches for a file with the name `output.<label>.<timestamp>.xml`.

✔ **-d** *Server*: Specifies the name of the global catalog server to use. If you don't include this command line switch, ExBPACmd binds to the nearest global catalog server.

✔ **-l** *Label*: Specifies the label for the output file. Otherwise, the label is blank in the filename.

✔ **-u** *Context [Domain\]Username (Password | *)*: Provides a method for supplying credentials for the analysis. The default setting relies on the current user's settings. If you supply * (asterisk) for the password, ExBPACmd will prompt you for the password.

✔ **-r** *Option[=Value][,...]*: Defines the kind of collection/analysis to perform. The default setting uses the Health Check option. You can specify multiple options on a single command line.

✔ **-th** *NumberOfThreads*: Defines the maximum number of threads to run at once. More threads lets ExBPACmd perform the tests faster but also uses more memory. The default setting is 1,000 threads, which works fine in most cases.

✔ **-to** *TimeoutValue*: Defines the amount of time in seconds that ExBPACmd accesses data on the server. A larger value can help in remote access scenarios. The default setting of 300 seconds works fine for most LAN setups.

✔ **-c**: Forces ExBPACmd to collect data specified in the configuration file. The default setting is to collect data when the configuration file contains no other operation steps.

✔ **-a**: Forces ExBPACmd to analyze data using the rules found in the configuration file.

✔ **-e**: Strips the values of any settings marked NotForExport in the configuration file.

✔ **-s**: Forces ExBPACmd to rely on settings found in the registry during scheduled runs. You add these settings using the graphical version of the product.

Part IV
The Part of Tens

The 5th Wave   By Rich Tennant

CLIENT/SERVER SOLUTIONS

"Oddly enough, this has been the least disruptive part of our move to Client/Server computing."

In this part . . .

This part of the book is all about tens. Chapter 14 presents you with ten tools that could make your job considerably easier. These tools helped me during the writing of this book, and they appear as a standard part of my Exchange Server toolbox. You should choose your tools carefully to avoid the overstuffed toolbox.

Everyone likes to have tools and resources that make things easier. Chapter 15 discusses ten tools or resources you can use to make working with Exchange Server significantly easier. Exchange Server has been in the marketplace for quite a while now, so third parties are working feverishly to make your job easier. Check out these tools and resources when you have a special need for administering Exchange Server.

Chapter 14

Ten Exchange Server Tools

*E*very administrator loves tools because they make life easier. When you get the right set of tools, you can see several orders of magnitude increase in personal performance. Of course, you want to tailor your toolbox to make it possible to perform all required organizational tasks, without overfilling it and making it inefficient. Having too many tools can be as bad as not having enough. Most administrators have personal tastes that determine the kind of tool that proves most useful. In addition, organizational requirements help define the environment in which the tool works.

This chapter provides ten useful tools. In fact, they're tools that I found useful for my needs. Not all of these tools will meet your needs, but some of them are almost certain to help in some way. Read each of the reviews and decide for yourself whether a particular tool is the right addition to your toolbox. I'd love to hear your feedback about these tools at `JMueller@mwt.net`. While you're at it, please let me know about the tools you like too. I'm always on the lookout for a new tool to fill a niche in my personal toolbox.

Upgrading to Windows PowerShell 2.0

Chapter 12 demonstrates the many Exchange Server management tasks that you can perform using Windows PowerShell. Windows PowerShell 1.0 provides adequate functionality for management tasks, but you may find that it doesn't provide everything you want from an automation or operating system access perspective. For this reason, and others, you may want to try Windows PowerShell 2.0. You find a host of features in Windows PowerShell 2.0, including those shown in this list:

- Background jobs
- Cmdlets (in addition to those found in Windows PowerShell 1.0)
- Data language
- Graphical PowerShell
- Language keywords `Data` and `Cmdlet`
- Metadata APIs for command and parameters
- Parser Tokenizer API
- PowerShell Hosting APIs (in addition to those found in Windows PowerShell 1.0)
- PowerShell remoting
- Restricted runspaces
- RunspacePools
- Script debugging
- Script internationalization
- ScriptCmdlets

Windows PowerShell 2.0 has a number of new cmdlets you can use to perform tasks. Many of these new cmdlets help you perform debugging tasks or start Windows PowerShell jobs, a kind of automation. The following list contains some, but not all, of the new cmdlets you can access with Windows PowerShell 2.0. Use the Get-Help cmdlet to obtain more information about any of these new cmdlets:

ConvertFrom-StringData	Invoke-WMIMethod	Remove-WMIObject
Disable-PSBreakpoint	New-PSBreakpoint	Set-WMIInstance
Enable-PSBreakpoint	New-Runspace	Start-PSJob
Get-PSBreakpoint	Out-GridView	Step-Into

Get-PSCallStack	Receive-PSJob	Step-Out
Get-PsJob	Remove-PSBreakpoint	Step-Over
Get-Runspace	Remove-PSJob	Stop-PSJob
Import-LocalizedData	Remove-Runspace	Wait-PSJob

Currently, Windows PowerShell 2.0 is still under development. However, you can obtain a Community Technology Preview (CTP) version at `http://www.microsoft.com/Downloads/details.aspx?FamilyID=60deac2b-975b-41e6-9fa0-c2fd6aa6bc89`. You must uninstall Windows PowerShell 1.0 and install a number other products, such as .NET Framework 2.0, to install Windows PowerShell 2.0. However, the new automation and debugging features are well worth the effort.

Creating Scripts Using Windows PowerShell Scriptomatic

Writing scripts can be difficult, especially when you haven't spent a lot of time memorizing the innermost secrets of Windows Management Instrumentation (WMI). The WMI interface is one of the more important scripting interfaces because it provides access to nearly every aspect of Windows. Many administrators interact with WMI using the WMIC command at the command line. However, you can also write scripts to interact with WMI and that's the purpose of the Windows PowerShell Scriptomatic application. You can download it from `http://www.microsoft.com/downloads/details.aspx?FamilyID=d87daf50-e487-4b0b-995c-f36a2855016e`.

After you download and install Scriptomatic, you can immediately begin creating scripts with it. Exchange Server administrators will commonly use the `root/directory/LDAP` (for Lightweight Directory Access Protocol) WMI namespace. Within this namespace is the `ads_exchangeadmin service` class that you use to interact with Exchange Server. If you choose the Display Class Properties option (click the drop-down arrow on the third button on the toolbar), you see a list of properties for this class, as shown in Figure 14-1.

Notice that as you select items in the drop-down list boxes, Scriptomatic begins building your script for you. Each selection helps you create another script element. You may also need to interact with the myriad `ads_msexch` classes, such as `ads_msexchaddressingpolicy`, when creating a script to manage Exchange Server.

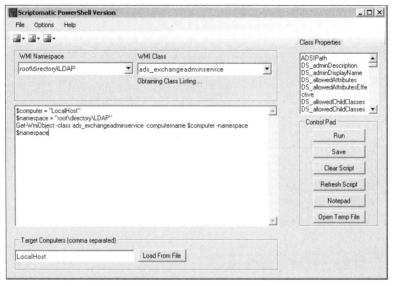

Figure 14-1:
Scripto-
matic
helps you
navigate
the complex
WMI
environ-
ment.

At some point, you'll need to begin writing a bit of your own code. By the time you reach this point, however, you'll have a significant amount of information available for locating what you need from Microsoft's online help services. For example, you can look up information about `ads_msexchaddressing policy` and research the use of the `DS_cn` property because Scriptomatic tells you that these items exist.

Once you finish your script, click Run. Scriptomatic opens a Windows PowerShell window and executes the script. You see any error messages that you normally see when building scripts completely by hand and can use the same debugging techniques as normal. When the script runs without error, click Save to save it to disk for future use.

The only problem with Scriptomatic is that it isn't as automatic as it could be at times. You may find that you need to click Refresh Script to see the result of changes you make to the IDE. For example, select Run with Parameters from the drop-down list for the second button on the toolbar and you see Scriptomatic add code for working with parameters. However, clear this option and the code doesn't return to its original state — you must click Refresh Script first to see the change.

Using Microsoft Forefront Security for Exchange Server

Microsoft Forefront Security for Exchange Server (called simply Forefront Security for the rest of this section) is the next step in security functionality for Exchange Server. The main page for this new product is `http://www.microsoft.com/forefront/serversecurity/exchange/en/us/default.aspx`. Forefront Security isn't just one product. You'll also find Forefront Security add-ons for products such as SharePoint Services. Microsoft is attempting to create a comprehensive suite of security features for their entire product line. Unfortunately, this product isn't out of beta yet, so you'll need to test it on something other than a production system (a developer or test server will work well).

You download Forefront Security at `http://www.microsoft.com/downloads/details.aspx?FamilyID=2CEB14D4-404B-4D8F-8A21-EBFC71B2E82B`. Microsoft requires that you fill out a registration form before you begin the download. Many administrators associate such registrations with snooping on Microsoft's part. However, in this case you receive three e-mails from Microsoft that help you work with Forefront Security:

- ✔ The first e-mail tells you about Forefront Security and helps you discover its features.
- ✔ The second e-mail helps you assess whether Forefront Security is the solution your organization requires.
- ✔ The third e-mail includes resources for deploying Forefront Security on your server.

The basic idea behind Forefront Security is to create a more secure server environment. Forefront Security begins by including multiple scan engines to detect and eradicate numerous threats to your server. It provides good performance through deep integration with Exchange Server. In fact, Forefront Security sounds like a perfect solution, but you have to remember the high cost usually attached to Microsoft products and the fact that Microsoft tends to focus on the needs of large Exchange Server customers. Make sure you set up and use the trial version before you buy. You can see a complete listing of Forefront Security features at `http://www.microsoft.com/forefront/serversecurity/exchange/en/us/features.aspx`.

Your server must meet some minimum requirements to use Forefront Security. These requirements are in addition to those required by Exchange Server 2007 except where a requirement for one would answer the need for both, such as having Windows Server 2008 as your server. The following list defines these requirements:

- ✔ A compatible 32-bit (x86) or 64-bit (Intel Xeon, Intel Pentium Family, AMD Opteron, or AMD Athlon 64) processor
- ✔ Windows Server 2003 or Windows Server 2008
- ✔ 1GB RAM (2GB recommended)

✔ 550MB hard drive space

✔ Microsoft Exchange 2007

Editing XML Files Using XML Notepad

Microsoft makes extensive use of XML with Exchange Server. For example, if you look in the `\Program Files\Microsoft\Exchange Server\ Logging\MigrationLogs\` folder, you see a series of XML files that contain migration logs for you system. Reading these logs can prove inconvenient unless you have an XML program designed for the purpose. (You can read them in a browser that has the required support, such as Internet Explorer.)

In many cases, the files don't even have an XML extension. Microsoft uses a wealth of file extensions for XML files today. Any configuration file (many have a CONFIG extension) is likely to use XML. For example, look at the `\ Program Files\Microsoft\Exchange Server\Bin` folder and you see all the configuration files for the Exchange Server executables.

You'll also find that many log files and even some lower-level operating system data files all rely on XML. With this change in mind, you really need a good XML utility to work at the command line, but many of the free products on the market come up lacking. XML Notepad provides a decent level of XML support and you'll find that it works just fine for most, if not all, Exchange Server administration needs. You can obtain this utility at `http:// www.microsoft.com/downloads/details.aspx?familyid=72d6aa49- 787d-4118-ba5f-4f30fe913628`.

Microsoft has produced a number of versions of XML Notepad. Old versions of XML Notepad won't install on Vista or Windows Server 2008. You must download and install XML Notepad 2007 from the Web site provided in this section to obtain a working copy of XML Notepad. Even XML Notepad 2006 fails to install on newer versions of Windows.

After you install XML Notepad, the setup program automatically opens an HTML page containing information about XML Notepad. You'll typically find this file at `\Program Files\XML Notepad 2007\Readme.HTM` or `\Program Files (x86)\XML Notepad 2007\Readme.HTM`. One of the links opens a sample XML folder. In this folder you'll find the `Basket.XML` file that appears in Figure 14-2. Right-click the file in Windows Explorer and choose Edit with XML Notepad to open the file.

The XML Notepad display color code entries by type and includes special icons to identify various types. For example, value entries appear with a special icon to differentiate them from elements.

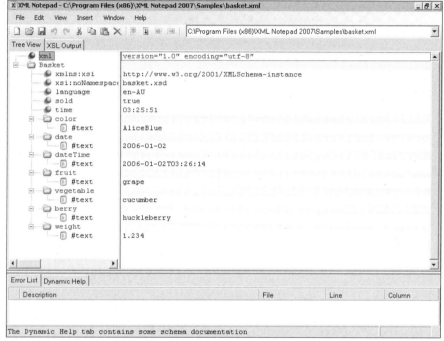

Figure 14-2:
XML
Notepad
provides a
safe editing
environment
for your
XML files.

You add a new entry by selecting it from the Insert menu. As an alternative, you can add new entries by right-clicking an existing entry and choosing the entry type from the context menu. In both cases, the new entry appears as a child of the currently selected entry in the left pane. You type a value for the new entry in the right pane. When you make a mistake in creating an entry, such as not adhering to a restriction in an XML Schema Definition (XSD) file, XML Notepad provides an entry in the bottom pane. Double-clicking the error entry takes you to that position in the file.

If your file has an eXtensible Stylesheet Language Transformation (XSLT) processing instruction, you can view the output by clicking the XSL Output tab. The RSS.XML file provides a sample of this XML Notepad feature, as shown in Figure 14-3. You can change XSL files by clicking the ellipses button (...) and choosing another XSL file in the Open dialog box. Click Transform to display the transformed XML file.

One of the more interesting features of XML Notepad is the ability to compare two XML files. You begin by loading the primary XML file into XML Notepad. Choose View➪Compare XML Files to display an Open dialog box. Select the secondary XML file and click Open. An XmlDiff window that has a complete comparison of the two files opens. This feature is helpful when you need to compare configuration settings or server events found in logs.

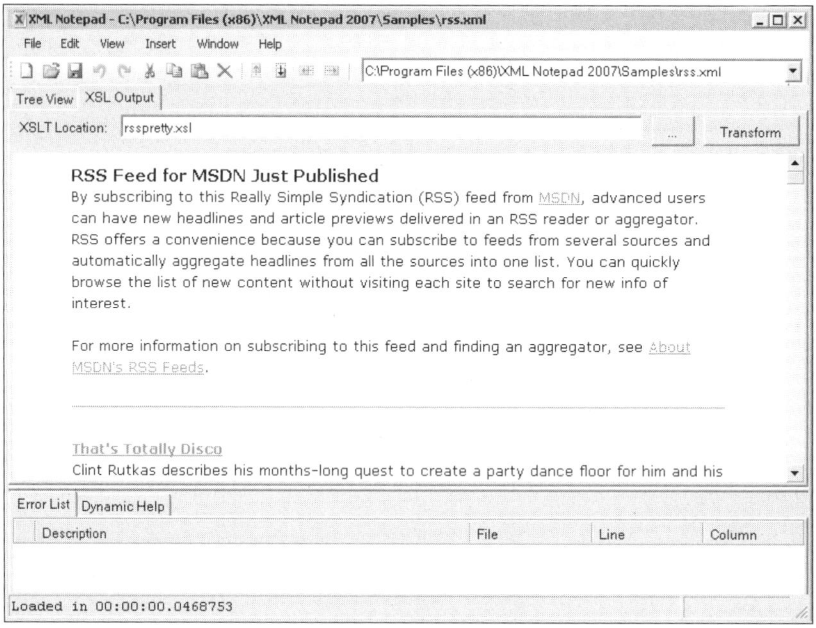

Figure 14-3:
Use XSLT
files to make
XML files
easier to
read.

Recovering a Lost Product Key Using ProduKey

ProduKey is an interesting utility that makes it possible to track the product keys for Microsoft applications anywhere on your network. Given the licensing requirements that companies must adhere to today, being able to gather all product keys on your network is beneficial. You can download ProduKey from `http://www.nirsoft.net/utils/product_cd_key_viewer.html`.

There isn't any installation for ProduKey. All you need to do is extract the ZIP file to a folder and start the ProduKey application. The application comes in both 32-bit and 64-bit versions, which means you can use it directly on a Windows Server 2008 setup. The output displays

- ✔ Application name
- ✔ Product identifier
- ✔ Project key
- ✔ Installation folder
- ✔ Service pack number
- ✔ Computer name

The default settings show the product keys for the local computer, as shown in Figure 14-4. However, you can set ProduKey to display the product keys on another machine or to display all products keys for every machine on a network. Simply click Select Source to display the Select Source dialog box where you can choose the ProduKey source. One of the interesting features of ProduKey is that you can also gather product keys from a specific domain or from a range of IP addresses regardless of domain.

The Options menu determines which product keys ProduKey gathers. You can choose to gather just Exchange Server product keys or those from a range of predetermined Microsoft applications. Once you gather the product keys you want, you can save the result to a text file on disk. An administrator can then refer to this list when restoring applications to a failed machine.

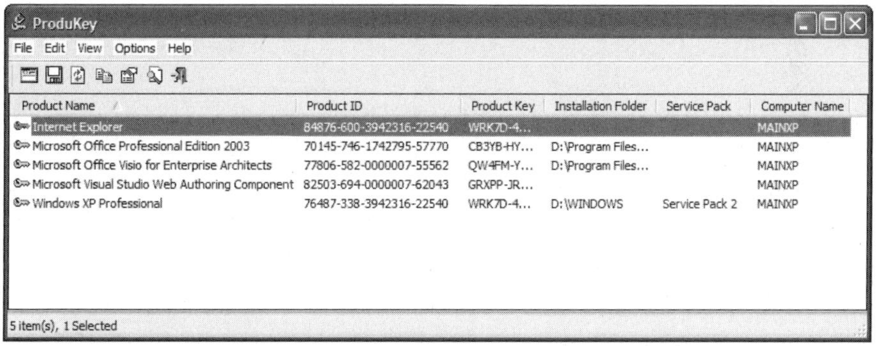

Figure 14-4:
ProduKey
makes it
easy to
locate and
manage
product
keys.

Converting a SID to a Username with User Info

Exchange Server often provides object identity as a Security Identifier (SID) rather than as a username (or object name, as the case may be). Using a SID is more accurate than any other identification means because SIDs are unique on a particular computer. Unfortunately, most people don't speak SID. People need a friendly name that helps them identify the object. The User Info utility, which you can download from `http://www.codeproject.com/KB/cpp/lkupuserinfo.aspx`, makes it possible to convert from SID to a friendly name and back. This is a must-have utility because Windows doesn't provide any means of performing the conversion, unless you want to delve into the registry — and most administrators would prefer not to do that.

The Web site offers two forms of the application. As an administrator, you want to download the demo project form rather than the source files, which you must compile into an application. After you download the file, simply extract the ZIP file and you're ready to go. Double-click LkupUserInfo.EXE and you see a display similar to the one shown in Figure 14-5.

Figure 14-5 shows the results for the well-known SID S-1-5-32-544, which is the Administrators group. Every Windows system has this SID, so you can try it out on your machine. Simply type the SID in the User Name/SID field, select Fetch User Name, and click OK. Microsoft supplies a list of well-known SIDs at http://support.microsoft.com/kb/243330. The process for finding any other SID is just as easy. You can also enter a user or group name, select FetchSid, and click OK to obtain the SID for that user or group.

User Info also works across machines. Simply type a value into the System Name field to access SIDs on another system. As long as you have administrator access on that system, User Info can obtain the SID information for you.

The developer of User Info assumes that everyone downloading it is also a developer, which means that you have a suitable development platform installed on your system. Unfortunately, administrators won't have such an application installed and the host system may therefore lack two files that User Info requires to execute, MFC71U.DLL and MSVCR71.DLL. Fortunately, you can download both files from DLL-files.com (http://www.dll-files. com/). After you download the two files, extract them into the same directory in which you have placed LkupUserInfo.EXE. The application will work as normal.

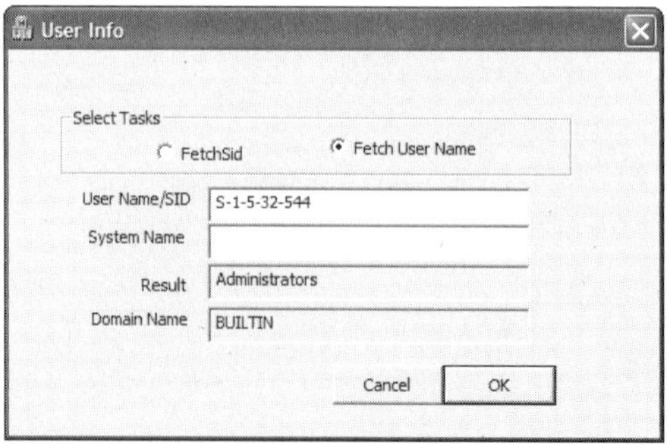

Figure 14-5:
Convert
between
username
and SID as
needed.

User Info

Select Tasks

○ FetchSid   ● Fetch User Name

User Name/SID | S-1-5-32-544

System Name |

Result | Administrators

Domain Name | BUILTIN

Cancel   OK

Obtaining Access to the SysInternals Tools

SysInternals is a toolbox of administrator tools that you use to maintain your system. The tools do everything from help you find potential root kits

on your system to working with processes. You can perform tasks such
as viewing streams within files and monitoring ports. In fact, it would be easy
to write several chapters about the wealth of tools you find in SysInternals.
The following list contains tool names (the titles tell you basically what
the tool does, but you can find a full description at `http://technet.`
`microsoft.com/en-us/sysinternals/0e18b180-9b7a-4c49-8120-`
`c47c5a693683.aspx`):

AccessChk	Junction	PsLogList
AccessEnum	LDMDump	PsPasswd
AdExplorer	ListDLLs	PsService
AdRestore	LiveKd	PsShutdown
Autologon	LoadOrder	PsSuspend
Autoruns	LogonSessions	RegDelNull
BgInfo	NewSid	RegJump
CacheSet	NTFSInfo	RegMon
ClockRes	PageDefrag	RootkitRevealer
Contig	PendMoves	SDelete
Ctrl2Cap	PortMon	ShareEnum
DebugView	ProcessExplorer	ShellRunas
Defrag (live connection only)	Process Monitor	SigCheck
DiskExt	ProcFeatures	Streams
DiskMon	PsExec	Strings
DiskView	PsFile	Sync
Disk Usage (DU)	PsGetSid	TCPView
EFSDump	PsInfo	VolumeID
FileMon	PsKill	WhoIs
Handle	PsList	WinObj
Hex2dec	PsLoggedOn	ZoomIt

You may remember these tools as part of a 70-tool suite originally offered by
Winternals Software. Microsoft acquired Winternals Software (`http://www.`
`microsoft.com/presspass/press/2006/jul06/07-18Winternal-`
`sPR.mspx`) and now offers the tools to you. The SysInternals suite is so
useful that *ComputerWorld* recently ran a review of it that you can read at
`http://www.computerworld.com/action/article.do?command=vie`
`wArticleBasic&articleId=9090778`.

Microsoft supplies two methods for accessing SysInternals. First, you can choose the live connection at `http://live.sysinternals.com/Tools/`. Simply click the tool you want to use. When you see the File Download – Security Warning dialog box, click Run to start the application or Save to save it to disk. However, some system firewalls may not allow the application to execute. In this case, you use the second option, which is to download the entire suite from `http://download.sysinternals.com/Files/SysinternalsSuite.zip`.

SysInternals is a work in progress. Microsoft constantly adds new utilities to the list. Consequently, you want to be sure to download the most current version when you obtain SysInternals. In addition, check back at the SysInternals Web site frequently to discover new tools added to the suite.

Making Sense of Error Codes Using Err

You receive one of those numeric errors from Exchange Server that lacks any explanation — what do you do? If you're like many administrators, you scratch your head for a bit and then head off to the Internet with only an error number in hand. In many cases, you come back without answers because you simply don't have enough information at the outset. The Microsoft Exchange Server Error Code Look-up (Err) utility works at the command line and can provide some additional information about the mysterious error codes that you receive when working with Exchange Server. Download this tool from `http://www.microsoft.com/downloads/details.aspx?familyid=be596899-7bb8-4208-b7fc-09e02a13696c`.

After you download the file, simply extract it to a directory on your machine. To use this tool, you must open a command prompt, change directories to the Err utility location, and type **Err** followed by the error number. For example, say you received error number 0x55f. You would type Err 0x55f and press Enter to see the results shown in Figure 14-6.

Figure 14-6: Err provides you with additional information you can use to resolve errors.

The results aren't precisely human readable, but you have more information than you did earlier. You can now use the error text to look for a potential solution. The `WinError.H` reference also tells you which Windows header file generated the error message, which can provide additional help in obtaining a fix for the problem.

You don't necessarily need a number to work with Err. You can provide error information in one of the following formats, so you can get information no matter which format Exchange Server uses for a particular error:

- ✔ Decorated hex (0x54f)
- ✔ Implicit hex (54f)
- ✔ Ambiguous (1359)
- ✔ Exact string (=ERROR_INTERNAL_ERROR)
- ✔ Substring (:INTERNAL_ERROR)

Obtaining Antivirus Support Using GFI MailSecurity

Microsoft has all kinds of plans for organizations when it comes to antivirus and spam support. However, to obtain this functionality, you must set up several servers and create a relatively complex setup that includes Edge Transport Server, which must reside outside your firewall. In short, you must have a large investment in hardware to make the Microsoft solution work, which means that this solution is essentially designed for large organizations. A small organization requires a different solution. GFI MailSecurity (`http://www.gfi.com/mailsecurity/`) is one of several third-party offerings that let you add both antivirus and spam support to a Hub Transport Server. Using a third-party solution saves money because you can use a single server to accommodate every need.

You can obtain a trial version of GFI MailSecurity for Exchange/SMTP in two forms: Exchange Server 2000/2003 or Exchange Server 2007. Make sure you download the correct version of the product. In addition to GFI MailSecurity, you can also try out GFI MailSecurity ReportPack, which provides reports on server security, during the 30-day trial stage.

Two requirements that GFI MailSecurity has that you won't have installed on a default Exchange Server setup are Microsoft Message Queuing Service and Microsoft Exchange MAPI Client and Collaboration Data Objects (version 1.2.1 is the minimum acceptable). You can address the first requirement by installing the Message Queuing Server element of the Message Queuing feature using Server Manager. Address the second requirement by downloading the add-on found at `http://www.microsoft.com/downloads/details.aspx?FamilyID=E17E7F31-079A-43A9-BFF2-0A110307611E` and installing it on your system. Double-click the `ExchangeMapiCdo.MSI` file and follow the installation instructions, which amount to approving the licensing agreement.

After you download the product, you need to install it on your system. The installation program is relatively straightforward. You can obtain installation instructions in English, German, Italian, and Spanish. In addition, GFI software provides an installation video in English and makes the complete user manual available for your use, so you have everything needed to perform the installation. The installation feature that administrators will like best is that the application constantly checks to make sure the system can support GFI MailSecurity. If the system lacks a particular prerequisite, the installation program will tell you, rather than attempt to forge ahead, only to fail later.

Even though you can use GFI MailSecurity for simple setups, don't sell it short by thinking it can't handle larger installations as well. This product can scale up to the same extent that the Microsoft offering can — it simply starts at a lower level. You can see a complete list of GFI MailSecurity features at `http://www.gfi.com/mes/mesfeatures.htm`.

Interacting with the Client Machine Using Remote Desktop

The Remote Desktop Connection application (or simply Remote Desktop) provides the means to connect to Windows Server 2008 for remote management. You need this application only when you want to access the server from your client machine, which may be the only option you have in some cases. The Remote Desktop Connection application is exceptionally useful because it lets you create a direct connection to the server. You can monitor events and manage the system directly, which reduces one potential cause of failure (making the remote connection every time you want to perform a task).

You must make any changes you want to the Remote Desktop configuration before you connect to the remote server. Once you make the connection, you can't change the configuration. Consequently, it's always a good idea to create a complete configuration first, save it to disk, and then reopen it as needed for a particular server. Otherwise, you spend a lot of time reconfiguring Remote Desktop Connection every time you want to use it. Choose Start⇔Programs⇔ Accessories⇔Communications⇔Remote Desktop Connection to start the Remote Desktop Connection application. The following sections describe how to use this application.

Enabling Remote Desktop

Before you can create a connection from a client to a Windows Server 2008 system, you must enable Remote Desktop on the server. To do so, right-click Computer, choose Properties, click Advanced Settings in the System window, and click the Remote tab of the System Properties dialog box. The screen shown in Figure 14-7 appears. To enable Remote Desktop, select one of the two connection options shown.

Remote Desktop allows two levels of connection. Select the first Allow Connections setting when you want to connect using an older Windows client, such as Windows XP. This setting is less secure because it doesn't provide the detailed security checks on the caller that newer versions of Windows can provide. Use the second Allow Connections setting when you want to connect using a Vista client. This option provides far greater security, and you should use it when you can. In all cases, the Administrators group automatically has access to the server using Remote Desktop. If you want to use Remote Desktop for administration tasks only, don't add any users to the list of people allowed to connect to the server.

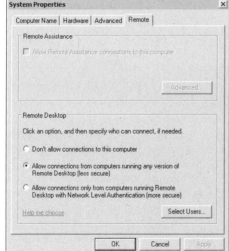

Figure 14-7:
Enable
Remote
Desktop
when you
want to
connect to
the server
from a
remote
location.

Creating a connection

The "Enabling Remote Desktop" section shows how to configure the server to use Remote Desktop. Once the server is ready for a connection, you must configure Remote Desktop to make the connection. The following procedure helps you make the connection:

1. **Start the application and click Options.**

   The General tab shows the connection options, as shown in Figure 14-8.

2. **Type the server name or select it from the drop-down list in the Computer field.**

3. **Type your account name on the server in the User Name field.**

4. **Type your password in the Password field.**

   Make sure you use the password for your account on the remote system.

5. **Type the name of the server in the Domain field when using a workgroup setup. If you're using a domain setup, type the name of the domain in the Domain field.**

6. **(Optional) Select the Save My Password option if you want Remote Desktop to save your password for future use.**

7. **(Optional) Click Save As.**

   • If you want to save this setup as the default connection, click Save.

   • Otherwise, type a name for the setup in the File Name field and click Save.

   You can save as many setups as needed for the servers you want to access. Use the default setup for the server you access most often.

Figure 14-8:
Set the connection parameters for the connection you want to normally make.

8. **Click Connect.**

   You see Remote Desktop performing all required connection tasks. Eventually, you see the Remote Desktop window, as shown in Figure 14-9.

After you create the initial connection, Remote Desktop opens with the default connection already set up. If you want to use the default connection, all you need to do is click Connect When Remote Desktop starts. Otherwise, you can click Options, click Open, choose the connection you want to use from the Open dialog box, click Open in the Open dialog box and, finally, click Connect to make the connection. You won't need to create a setup more than once if you save it to disk.

It's also possible to double-click the Remote Desktop Profile (RDP) file containing a connection in Windows Explorer to make the connection to the server, so you can simply place the RDP file on your desktop to make the connection instantly accessible.

Figure 14-9:
The remote connection appears in a special Remote Desktop window.

Setting the display

The display settings you use affect not only how much screen real estate you have for performing tasks but also performance. Using a larger screen size gives you more space to work. However, a larger screen size also requires more network bandwidth to transmit the data. Consequently, you must weigh the need to see as much as possible on the remote server against the performance requirements for your task. Figure 14-10 shows the display settings.

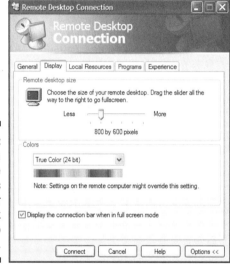

Figure 14-10: Define a display size that works best for the work you need to perform.

The Remote Desktop Size slider lets you change the size of the window. The smallest size is 640 x 480 pixels, which is normally too small to work with a GUI system. If you want to use your entire display to work with Windows Server 2008, move the slider all the way to the right. The size changes to Full Screen, and the display takes up your entire display area. In fact, it looks like you're working directly at the remote console rather than using Remote Desktop.

If you want to continue working with your local system while managing the remote system, make sure that you select the Display the Connection Bar When in Full Screen Mode option. Otherwise, you may need to log out every time you want to regain access to the local system.

Performance isn't affected by just the size of the screen. Notice that you can also modify the number of colors that Remote Desktop displays. More colors translate into a better display but also reduce performance because Remote Desktop has to transfer more data for the additional colors. Because Windows Server 2008 lacks much in the way of a GUI, you experience a performance gain by setting the number of colors to 256. In most cases, you won't even notice the difference in appearance, but you will notice the difference in performance.

Accessing local resources

Remote Desktop makes it possible to map your local hardware to respond to events on the remote machine. Figure 14-11 shows the settings you can use to map resources as needed. The following list describes each of the resource mapping areas:

- **Remote Computer Sound:** Lets you bring sounds from the remote machine to your local machine. This setting has three options: You can choose to play the remote sound locally, not play the remote sound at all (effectively muting the remote system), or play the sound at the remote location.

Figure 14-11: Perform automatic resource mapping to make local resources available for use.

- **Keyboard:** Controls the use of control-key combinations. For example, when you press Alt+Tab, this setting controls whether you switch between applications on the local machine or the remote machine. This setting affects Remote Desktop only when you have it selected when working in windowed mode. If you press Alt+Tab when Remote Desktop is working in a window and you don't have Remote Desktop selected, the Alt+Tab combination always affects the local machine even when you choose the On the Remote Computer option. Normally, any control-key combinations go to the remote machine only when you use Remote Desktop in full-screen mode.

- **Local Devices:** Determines which local devices you can access from the remote machine. This may sound like an odd consideration, but when you're working with the remote machine, Remote Desktop shuts off access to local resources, such as disk drives, printers, and serial ports. Only your display, keyboard, and mouse are active on the remote machine, unless you tell Remote Desktop to perform the required mapping. Check any of these options to make the resources on your local machine available when working at the remote machine.

Running a configuration program

You may find that you want to run a configuration program on the remote machine when you create the connection. This program can perform any task, and you can use both batch and script files, in addition to standard applications. Figure 14-12 shows the Programs tab. The options work very much like a remote profile. When you want to use a remote program, select Start the Following Program on Connection option, type the name of the application you want to use (including full path), and tell Remote Desktop which folder you want to use as a starting point.

Optimizing performance

The connection you use to create a Remote Desktop is important. You can't expect the same performance from a dial-up connection as you do from a high-speed internal network. Consequently, Remote Desktop provides a method for telling it what to expect in the way of connection, to optimize connection performance, as shown in Figure 14-13.

Choosing one of the default options, such as LAN (10 Mbps or higher), automatically sets the options that Remote Desktop uses — you don't need to do anything else. As an alternative, you can choose Custom from the list and configure the options you want to use. Windows Server 2008 works best with the Custom setting, even if you're working across a LAN.

Figure 14-12:
Use a configuration application as needed to automate Remote Desktop tasks.

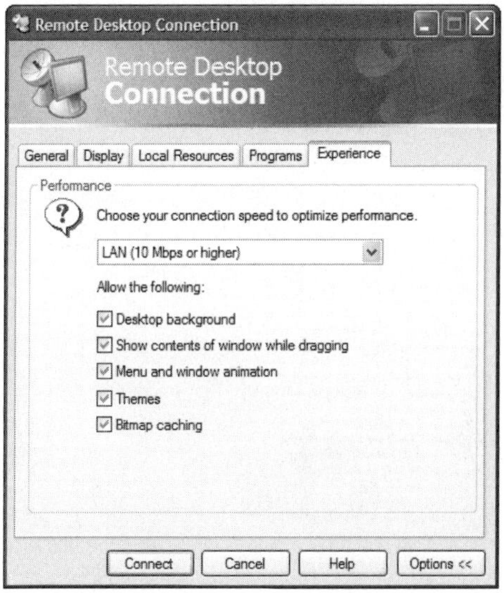

Figure 14-13:
Use only the resources you actually need to obtain good performance.

Chapter 15

Ten Exchange Server Resources

*I*t's always helpful to know where you can go for additional information, tools, and enhancements when working with Exchange Server. This book already contains a number of useful resources in other chapters. Chapter 14 contains the most additional tools, but you find other information, tool, and enhancement resources scattered throughout the book.

As nice as the lists in this book are, you probably need additional information about Exchange Server, which is the purpose of this chapter. In some cases, the information is for advanced setups not discussed in this book; in other cases, it provides help with a special organizational need. The point is that this chapter helps you find the information you need when you can't find it somewhere in this book.

This chapter is *my* list of ten helpful resources; I might have missed your favorite. Since I'm always looking for something better, please be sure to write me about your favorite resource at `JMueller@mwt.net`. I can't guarantee that I'll use the information you provide, but I do guarantee I'll at least check it out. It's amazing to see how many sources people provide me over time — many of which are indispensable at some point.

General questions wanted

Sometimes it's hard to know what to ask or your question is of such a nature that you need generalized help before you can get down to specific needs. In both cases, you want to visit a Web site that offers generalized help rather than specific help. People on a specific help site can sometimes get frustrated by the developer who has general needs, so you'll probably get better help on a general site. Two of the better general-question Web sites are MSExchange.org (`http://www.msexchange.org/`) and the Exchange Server TechNet forum (`http://forums.microsoft.com/ TechNet/default.aspx?Forum GroupID=235`).

Starting with TechNet

TechNet is one of the major sources of basic information for Exchange Server administrators. In fact, you find the most up-to-date documentation for Exchange Server at `http://technet.microsoft.com/en-us/library/ bb124558(EXCHG.80).aspx`. It's interesting to look around on this Web site because you sometimes find updates to documentation or topics that don't appear with the Exchange Server documentation on your machine. The display contains a table of contents on the left and help information on the right, as shown in Figure 15-1.

Beside the normal documentation, TechNet provides an interesting array of topics you might want to read. For example, *TechNet* magazine provides articles such as "Running Exchange with Windows Server 2008" (`http:// technet.microsoft.com/en-us/magazine/cc137736.aspx`). Some locations on TechNet simply provide access to software, such as the Evaluate Microsoft Exchange Server 2007 Service Pack 1 Today site at `http:// technet.microsoft.com/en-us/evalcenter/bb736128.aspx`.

You can access the vast majority of Exchange Server related information on TechNet through the Exchange Server TechNet site at `http://technet. microsoft.com/en-us/exchange/default.aspx`. However, in some rare cases you may not find what you need to get immediately. In this case, you can use the technique described in the "Finding your own MSDN resources fast" sidebar to locate information on either the `technet.microsoft. com` or `technet2.microsoft.com` domain. For example, you might use this technique to locate the Configure Outlook Anywhere in Outlook 2007 topic found at `http://technet.microsoft.com/en-us/library/ cc179036.aspx`.

Figure 15-1:
TechNet
provides the
ultimate in
Exchange
Server help.

Obtaining the Developer View with the Microsoft Developer Network

The Microsoft Developer Network (MSDN) has always provided the baseline material for all Microsoft development products. You may wonder why an administrator needs to know about development material. It turns out that the development material includes a wealth of information that administrators need to know, such as the error codes you might see in Exchange Server. In many cases, MSDN also provides an explanation for the error. Yes, it's an explanation that only a developer could love, but it still provides clues that you can use to locate problems on your Exchange Server setup.

In fact, you'll find a whole warehouse of information on MSDN — more than any one human being can probably read in a lifetime. Consequently, you need to sift the information carefully or you'll quickly become lost in the MSDN labyrinth. The main MSDN site for working with Exchange Server is at `http://msdn.microsoft.com/en-us/exchange/default.aspx`. The links on this site provide you with news, resources, and access to other information such as samples. You'll also want to check out these other locations on MSDN:

- ✔ What's New in Exchange Server 2007 SP1 Extensibility: `http://msdn.microsoft.com/en-us/library/bb608442(EXCHG.80).aspx`

- ✔ Exchange Server 2007 Technical Articles: `http://msdn.microsoft.com/en-us/library/bb332451(EXCHG.80).aspx`

- ✔ About MAPI Tools: `http://msdn.microsoft.com/en-us/library/ms528273(EXCHG.10).aspx`

- ✔ New Programmability Features in Exchange Server 2007: `http://msdn.microsoft.com/en-us/library/bb332450(EXCHG.80).aspx`

- ✔ Determining Exchange Server 2007 Storage Configuration: `http://msdn.microsoft.com/en-us/library/bb204051(EXCHG.80).aspx`

- ✔ Microsoft Exchange Server 2007 SP1 SDK: `http://msdn.microsoft.com/en-us/library/aa562613(EXCHG.80).aspx`

This list is only the tip of the MSDN iceberg when it comes to Exchange Server. You can find detailed technical information about Exchange Server on MSDN, and the topics discuss everything from configuration files to third-party add-ons. As an administrator, you need to know what is happening with your Exchange Server setup, and MSDN is often the only method to get that information. As the complexity of your Exchange Server setup increases, so does your need for MSDN. (You'll probably want to avoid the programming topics because they don't apply to administration requirements.)

Defining Search Techniques in the Microsoft Knowledge Base

Microsoft has a secret. They often add content to the Knowledge Base and then don't tell anyone about it. They know a problem exists with your Exchange Server setup and they provide a solution for it, but they don't want to publicize it for fear the media will pick up on the issue and write a major story about it. In fact, some newsletter writers make locating these hidden gems part of their task each newsletter submission. Knowing how to find these fixes can save you hours of research time.

You can find the Knowledge Base at `http://support.microsoft.com/search/?adv=1`. When you perform a search, select all the sources you want to use in the Where Do You Want to Search? list and select Exchange Server 2007 as the target product in the On What Product Do You Want to Search? field. Now, simply type the subject of the search in the supplied field and click Search. In most cases, you see a list of Knowledge Base articles you can use to discover a way around the Exchange Server problem you're having.

Finding your own MSDN resources fast

Trying to find something on MSDN can be difficult, especially considering the fact that Microsoft constantly moves things around, seemingly to annoy the administrators who use the site. The MSDN materials typically appear at two domains: `msdn.microsoft.com` and `msdn2.microsoft.com`. As a result, you can perform what is known as a site search with Google and locate information faster. Simply begin with your keywords at the main Google search site at `http://www.google.com/`, type the word *site* followed by a colon (:) and then the domain you want to use (`msdn.microsoft.com` or `msdn2.microsoft.com`). For example, if you want to find everything Microsoft has to offer on their newer MSDN site for Exchange Server 2007, you would type **Exchange Server 2007 site:msdn2.microsoft.com** in the Google Web page's search field.

Site searches work well for a number of other Microsoft resources. For example, you may have spent hours looking for a download, only to find that Microsoft has moved it yet again. To find the download fast, type the filename, followed by **site:download.microsoft.com** in the Google Web page's search field. You'll be amazed at how fast you can find whatever you need.

Let's say that you do find an interesting link on Google, but Microsoft insists that the link no longer exists. Google usually provides a special link called Cached. You see it at the end of the link description. Simply click this link and you'll see the cached version that Google provides of the Microsoft Web page.

If you're still stumped in finding that lost Microsoft Web page, you can rely on another resource. Go to the Internet Archive Wayback Machine site at `http://web.archive.org/collections/web/advanced.html`. Type the URL you want in the Find This URL field, choose the dates you want to see (optional), and click Go Wayback. The Web site shows you an archived copy of the Web page in question. In many cases, you can go back to Google with the title of the article or other MSDN resource you want and find the latest version of that Web page on MSDN. If you get too many hits, try enclosing your search terms in quotes. For example, if you want to find the site entitled, "What's New in Exchange Server 2007 SP1 Extensibility," you type **"What's New in Exchange Server 2007 SP1 Extensibility" site:msdn.microsoft.com** in the Google Web page's search field. A test of this search term during the writing of this chapter returned five results, making it a lot easier to find a particular Web site.

The problem with the Knowledge Base is that you often don't know what search term to provide. The key to using the Knowledge Base search is to keep the search terms short. If you want to find out more about a particular error number, try entering only the error number as your search term. The Knowledge Base search also tends to weight the terms you provide, with the first term receiving the greatest weight. Consequently, provide the terms in the order of greatest weight — an error number is of greater importance than the human readable text in most cases.

Sometimes a Knowledge Base article is so secret that even the search routine doesn't know about it. In this case, you can use the technique described in the "Finding your own MSDN resources fast" sidebar. Replace the MSDN domain with the Knowledge Base domain of `support.microsoft.com`.

Getting Tips from the Microsoft Blogs

Microsoft wants you to know how to work with Exchange Server. In the past, you'd find much of the information you needed on either TechNet or MSDN. These Web sites are still good places to go, but many administrators complained that using these Web sites was too formal (the articles are difficult to understand in some cases) and there wasn't any opportunity to interact with the authors. The Microsoft blogs (`http://blogs.msdn.com`) provide a friendlier environment for obtaining information where you can correspond with the author. Here are some of the blogs you'll definitely want to visit when working with Exchange Server 2007:

- ✔ Evan Dodds - Microsoft Exchange Server Blog: `http://blogs.technet.com/evand/default.aspx`
- ✔ Jason Langridge's WebLog - MR Mobile!: `http://blogs.msdn.com/jasonlan/default.aspx`
- ✔ Le Café Central de DeVa - Deva's Café: `http://blogs.msdn.com/deva/default.aspx`
- ✔ Microsoft Enterprise Search Blog: `http://blogs.msdn.com/enterprisesearch/default.aspx`
- ✔ Microsoft Higher Education - Mid-Atlantic: `http://blogs.msdn.com/hied_mid-atlantic/default.aspx`
- ✔ Microsoft SharePoint Team Blog: `http://blogs.msdn.com/sharepoint/default.aspx`
- ✔ Nick MacKechnie: `http://blogs.msdn.com/nickmac/default.aspx`
- ✔ OpsMgr, SCE And MOM Blog: `http://blogs.technet.com/cliveeastwood/default.aspx`
- ✔ SGriffin's MAPI Internals: `http://blogs.msdn.com/stephen_griffin/default.aspx`
- ✔ //steve clayton: geek in disguise: `http://blogs.msdn.com/stevecla01/default.aspx`
- ✔ The Industry Insiders: `http://blogs.technet.com/industry_insiders/default.aspx`
- ✔ VolkerW's WebLog: `http://blogs.msdn.com/volkerw/default.aspx`
- ✔ You Had Me at EHLO: `http://msexchangeteam.com/`

Most of these blogs are generic — they all discuss Exchange Server issues of some kind. Consequently, you'll find a mix of topics in each blog. The author may discuss the mailboxes on one day and the Hub Transport server on another. Each has Exchange Server-specific entries that you can use to improve your Exchange Server experience. The You Had Me at EHLO blog is the best place to go for a wealth of general Exchange Server information.

Some blogs are more technical than others are. For example, The Industry Insiders blog tends to cover advanced topics. If you ask a novice-level question at this blog, you might be ignored (or worse, ridiculed). The author will try to help, but these blogs are open to everyone else on the Internet who is looking for the answer to a technical question. It's important to remember that the same rules apply to blogs as apply to forums — ask the appropriate questions in the appropriate blog. To gauge whether your question is appropriate on a particular blog, read not only the blog entries but the responses the author gets to those entries. The responses often tell you what kind of audience reads the blog entries.

If you don't think that you're getting enough interaction with Microsoft through a blog, Microsoft employees often frequent the Microsoft forums as well. Uploading a message to the correct forum can net you some professional help or at least some knowledgeable help from another forum member. The Exchange Server forums appear at `http://forums.microsoft.com/ TechNet/default.aspx?ForumGroupID=235&SiteID=17`. Simply choose the most appropriate forum for your question and submit a new question there. Give the forum a day or two to provide a response before you upload the question to another forum. Most forum users view multiple forum entries of the same question from a single participant as a breach of etiquette and will ask you about it.

Locating Exchange Server Tips and Techniques Using Google

Exchange Server 2007 is a popular product and many Web sites provide support for it. Not only do you need to consider informational Web sites, but there are a host of third-party Web sites to consider as well. If you type **Exchange Server 2007** into the Google search field and press Enter, you'll currently see 11,100,000 hits, and that number is growing daily. You'd spend the rest of your life searching that many hits. The "Finding your own MSDN resources fast" sidebar in this chapter gives you one method of reducing that number by using a site search, but the site search technique works only when you know which site to search. This section discusses some techniques for finding what you want when you don't really know where to find it.

Part of the problem you encounter is that there are many versions of Exchange Server. If you place Exchange Server 2007 in quotes, you find that the number of search results is lower — 9,450,000 at the time of this writing. Of course, you want to provide a specific search term to go with that entry. Consequently, if you want to discover more about Hub Transport server, you would type **Hub Transport Server "Exchange Server 2007"** in the Google Search field and press Enter. In this case, you end up with 178,000 hits, which is still too many to search but far better than the millions you normally see.

You have other ways to reduce the number of results. For example, SP1 didn't arrive on the scene until 11/29/2007. It's reasonable to assume that anything older than that date is probably based on a beta or doesn't apply to SP1. If you set the Date field of the Advanced Search page to Last 6 Months, the number of hits for the previous search drops to 10,500. It pays to view the URL at this point. The `&as_qdr=m6` part of the URL tells you that Google is looking for information from the last six months. Each new item you add on the Advanced Search page adds another query term to the URL. Interestingly enough, if you set Safe Search to On (`&safe=active`), the number of hits drops to 10,400. Setting the language, English in my case (`&lr=lang_en`), further reduces the hits to 4,310, many of which are at least mildly useful.

The point of this section is that Exchange Server searches tend to produce a lot of results, most of which are unusable at the outset. If you want to find information quickly using Google, you'll need to rely on new techniques to do the job. Otherwise, you'll spend hours looking for that one site that might help.

Finding Help in Third-Party Web Sites

When you work with a Microsoft resource, you get the Microsoft view of Exchange Server, which is fine, but it's also biased. For example on a Microsoft Web site, you won't find out that some Exchange Server processes fail due to, ahem, bugs in Microsoft's software. In addition, you're unlikely to find a workaround for that bug unless Microsoft finally owns up to it and publishes a fix in the Microsoft Knowledge Base. Third-party administrators also have a different view of Exchange Server than Microsoft does and you'll find some interesting ideas if you scout around to the right places. With this in mind, you'll definitely want to check out these third-party sites:

- MSExchange.org: `http://www.msexchange.org/`
- Petri IT Knowledgebase: `http://www.petri.co.il/`
- Pro-Exchange: `http://www.pro-exchange.be/`

✔ SearchExchange.com: `http://searchexchange.techtarget.com/`

✔ Tech Republic: `http://www.techrepublic.com`

✔ WindowsITPro: `http://windowsitpro.com/microsoftexchange outlook/`

Many of these third-party Web sites also provide a newsletter. For example, you can subscribe to the MSExchange.org newsletter, which gives you the latest information about Exchange Server updates at `http://www. msexchange.org/pages/newsletter.asp`. Make sure you also check out the forums at MSExchange.org (`http://forums.msexchange.org/`). A few of the Web sites also have discussion forums and other resources you can use to discover more about Exchange Server.

Don't forget to check sites that offer computer courses. For example, Learning Tree (`http://www.learningtree.com/`) offers a host of Exchange Server classes. Other places to consider looking for course include SeekLearning (`http://www.seeklearning.com.au/`), Business Connect (`http://www. connect-utah.com/`), and Microsoft E-Learning (`https://www.micro softelearning.com/`). Taking a course can be an expensive way to discover new information about Exchange Server, but it can also save you time. Whether a course makes sense for you depends on how fast you have to get a Exchange Server setup up and running — courses often make it possible to fulfill those need-it-yesterday requirements.

Exchange Server information appears in the most interesting places. For example, you might not expect to see Exchange Server mentioned on a Sun Web site, but you can find it here: `http://www.sun.com/storagetek/ exchange/index.jsp`. In this case, you're looking at an interoperability solution that might fix problems within your organization.

Finding Help in Third-Party Newsletters and Blogs

Third-party newsletters are helpful because they provide you with tidbits of information and tips on how to get the most out of Microsoft technology. In addition, newsletters often provide a forum for you to voice questions or concerns and get a published response from the author.

One of the better selection of newsletters for Exchange Server administrators is at MSExchange.org. All of these newsletters are Exchange Server specific, so you don't spend any time looking at other topics trying to find the one bit of information you need. You can sign up for as many of these newsletters as you like at `http://www.msexchange.org/pages/newsletter.asp`.

WindowsITPro also provides a weekly newsletter for administrators that work with both Outlook and Exchange Server. This newsletter contains a variety of information, including news, strategies, and products. You can sign up for this newsletter at `http://windowsitpro.com/email/`.

Newsletters are nice, but they're also a one-way communication. As with the Microsoft blogs, third-party blogs can contain a wealth of information, only some of which is Exchange Server-specific. Following is a list of a few third-party blogs that contain some Exchange Server topics:

- Aaron Tiensivu's Blog: `http://blog.tiensivu.com/aaron/`
- Exchange Server Blog: `http://exchangeserverinfo.com/`
- Exchange Server Disaster Recovery Studies: `http://exchangeserver disasterrecovery.blogspot.com/`
- Exchangepedia Blog: `http://exchangepedia.com/blog/`
- MS Exchange Blog: `http://hellomate.typepad.com/`
- MSExchange.org: `http://blogs.msexchange.org/`
- Stealthpuppy: `http://blog.stealthpuppy.com/`
- Subject: Exchange: `http://msmvps.com/blogs/ehlo/default.aspx`
- Technically Speaking: `http://blog.shijaz.com/`

Many blogs aren't dedicated to Exchange Server but still provide you with good information. For example, the VoIP & Gadgets Blog (`http://blog.tmcnet.com/blog/tom-keating/`) has an article telling you how to synchronize your iPhone with Exchange Server. It's a useful article, even though it doesn't appear on a Web site that normally discusses Exchange Server. If you want to see another perspective on the same topic, check out the article at `http://computerrepairservice.net/blog/bling-bling-iphone-3gwell-worth-the-wait/`. Although it can be time consuming to find these nondedicated blogs, they often contain tidbits that Exchange Server aficionados don't consider because they aren't working with that particular technology.

Some of these nondedicated blogs are also focused and technical. For example, if you need a script to make Entourage work with Exchange Server, look no further than @ the Entourage Help Blog at `http://blog.entourage.mvps.org/2007/05/exchange_server_setup_script_u.html`. From the content of the blog listing, it's obvious that the author provides continuous updates of the script so you can be sure that any bugs will eventually get fixed.

A few of the blogs are extremely proactive about requesting your input. In fact, Exchange Server Disaster Recovery Studies posts an e-mail address on each page (`bizopps@dtidata.com`) asking for your questions. The author obviously wants to hear from you and enjoys answering your disaster recovery questions online so the answers can help everyone.

 This section doesn't discuss every third-party newsletter or blog out there. If you want to see a list of additional blogs, check out the article at `http://searchexchange.techtarget.com/news/column/0,294698,sid43_gci1302421,00.html`. The article's author takes time to tell you why you want to visit each of these blogs and helps you understand the kind of information you can expect to find.

Obtaining Whitepapers to Help with Management Tasks

The main source of whitepapers for Exchange Server is from Microsoft. You can find some of these offerings on the Exchange Server TechCenter at `http://technet.microsoft.com/en-us/exchange/default.aspx`. You also find a wealth of Exchange Server specific whitepapers at `http://technet.microsoft.com/en-us/library/cc164340(EXCHG.80).aspx`. Don't forget to look for whitepapers associated with other technologies. For example, Office yields more than a few whitepapers, such as the one entitled, "Configure Outlook Anywhere in Outlook 2007" at `http://technet.microsoft.com/en-us/library/cc179036.aspx`.

Whitepapers need not come from Microsoft. In many cases, you find helpful whitepapers on third-party Web sites, such as those found on ZDNet: `http://whitepapers.zdnet.com/abstract.aspx?docid=338803`. Notice that these whitepapers come from sources outside Microsoft, such as Citrix Online, Symantec, and Intel.

Another good place to look for white papers is Tech Republic. In this case, you use their search to locate appropriate materials using `http://search.techrepublic.com.com/search/Microsoft Exchange Server 2007.html` as an URL.

MSExchange.org is another good place to find whitepapers. You can see the entire list at `http://whitepapers.msexchange.org/platforms/microsoft-exchange/`. It appears that this Web site puts out at least one new whitepaper each month, so you'll want to keep checking back if you don't see the whitepaper you want.

Discovering Migration Techniques for Your Current Setup

Microsoft wants your migration to Exchange Server 2007 to go smoothly, so they provide a number of resources to make this task easier. The main Web site for migration needs is Upgrading to Exchange 2007 at `http://technet.microsoft.com/en-us/library/bb124008(EXCHG.80).aspx`. However, Microsoft provides a number of additional sites such as the Plan for Exchange Server 2007 site at `http://technet.microsoft.com/en-us/exchange/bb288462.aspx`.

Very few Web sites seem to provide a complete Exchange Server migration plan — a course you can follow when migrating your Exchange Server setup. One exception to the rule is the Vancouver Network Support site at `http://www.vancouver-network-support.com/exchange-server-resources.html`. A particularly helpful aspect of this Web site is that it discusses non-Microsoft issues, such as moving from Lotus Notes to Microsoft Exchange.

Planning is certainly part of the migration process. A number of Web sites provide planning tips for migrating your Exchange Server setup. For example, you can find a Webcast on the topic of preventing e-mail outages at `http://webcasts.techrepublic.com.com/abstract.aspx?docid=360573`.

Considering the Requirements for a Third-Party Add-in

For many administrators, it's not whether their organization will require an Exchange Server add-in, but when the organization will require it. In some cases, an organization requires an add-in simply because of the special needs of that organization. Microsoft didn't cover every contingency with Exchange Server, so you often find that you need to add a little something to make your setup work efficiently. Of course, the need to obtain an add-in begs the question of how you can determine that the add-in will be both useful and reliable.

The first place you should look for add-ins is on the Microsoft Web site at `http://www.microsoft.com/exchange/partners/default.mspx`. Even though this Web site doesn't list every third-party vendor supplying Exchange Server add-ins, you know that the vendor had to prove that the product works as advertised before Microsoft placed them on the Web site. If you ever do find that one of these vendors doesn't perform as expected, you might want to contact Microsoft about it so that someone with a little more clout can work with the vendor to correct the problem.

Another place to look for reliable vendors is the MSExchange.org site at `http://www.msexchange.org/software/E-mail-Anti%20Virus/`. In this case, you get a review to go along with the recommendation. Reading the reviews can help you determine when you should take the next step in working with a particular vendor.

No matter how many recommendations and reviews you see about a particular product, you can't make a choice on what others tell you. When you think about adding a new add-in to your Exchange Server setup, always set up a test server that replicates your production environment, install the trial version of the product, and see for yourself how it works. Yes, this approach is time consuming, but it's the only way you can be sure that a product will work with your setup.

When reviewing a vendor Web site for a third-party add-in, make sure you check the completeness of the add-in documentation. If the vendor doesn't do a good job of documenting the add-in while trying to sell it to you, you can be sure that the vendor will also fall short after the sale. As an example of a well-documented site, check out Kaspersky Security for Microsoft Exchange Server 2007 (`http://www.kaspersky.com/security_ms_exchange_07`). The vendor provides a clean display that makes it easy to discover information about the add-in. More information is always better when searching for an add-in, but the information must also appear in a form that you can understand.

Another good indicator on the vendor's site is the presence of a Gold Certified Partner stamp. A vendor has to pass stringent requirements to obtain this stamp. You can find out more about the Gold Certified Partner requirements at `https://partner.microsoft.com/40013031`. Although the Gold Certified Partner stamp doesn't prevent a vendor from selling you something you'd rather not have, it does reduce your risk significantly and gives you an avenue for working with the vendor through Microsoft. The vendor worked hard to become a Gold Certified Partner and will usually fulfill any requirements to maintain that certification.

Index

• F •

• *K* •

• *L* •

• P •

BUSINESS, CAREERS & PERSONAL FINANCE

Accounting For Dummies, 4th Edition*
978-0-470-24600-9

Bookkeeping Workbook For Dummies†
978-0-470-16983-4

Commodities For Dummies
978-0-470-04928-0

Doing Business in China For Dummies
978-0-470-04929-7

E-Mail Marketing For Dummies
978-0-470-19087-6

Job Interviews For Dummies, 3rd Edition*†
978-0-470-17748-8

Personal Finance Workbook For Dummies*†
978-0-470-09933-9

Real Estate License Exams For Dummies
978-0-7645-7623-2

Six Sigma For Dummies
978-0-7645-6798-8

Small Business Kit For Dummies, 2nd Edition*†
978-0-7645-5984-6

Telephone Sales For Dummies
978-0-470-16836-3

BUSINESS PRODUCTIVITY & MICROSOFT OFFICE

Access 2007 For Dummies
978-0-470-03649-5

Excel 2007 For Dummies
978-0-470-03737-9

Office 2007 For Dummies
978-0-470-00923-9

Outlook 2007 For Dummies
978-0-470-03830-7

PowerPoint 2007 For Dummies
978-0-470-04059-1

Project 2007 For Dummies
978-0-470-03651-8

QuickBooks 2008 For Dummies
978-0-470-18470-7

Quicken 2008 For Dummies
978-0-470-17473-9

Salesforce.com For Dummies, 2nd Edition
978-0-470-04893-1

Word 2007 For Dummies
978-0-470-03658-7

EDUCATION, HISTORY, REFERENCE & TEST PREPARATION

African American History For Dummies
978-0-7645-5469-8

Algebra For Dummies
978-0-7645-5325-7

Algebra Workbook For Dummies
978-0-7645-8467-1

Art History For Dummies
978-0-470-09910-0

ASVAB For Dummies, 2nd Edition
978-0-470-10671-6

British Military History For Dummies
978-0-470-03213-8

Calculus For Dummies
978-0-7645-2498-1

Canadian History For Dummies, 2nd Edition
978-0-470-83656-9

Geometry Workbook For Dummies
978-0-471-79940-5

The SAT I For Dummies, 6th Edition
978-0-7645-7193-0

Series 7 Exam For Dummies
978-0-470-09932-2

World History For Dummies
978-0-7645-5242-7

FOOD, GARDEN, HOBBIES & HOME

Bridge For Dummies, 2nd Edition
978-0-471-92426-5

Coin Collecting For Dummies, 2nd Edition
978-0-470-22275-1

Cooking Basics For Dummies, 3rd Edition
978-0-7645-7206-7

Drawing For Dummies
978-0-7645-5476-6

Etiquette For Dummies, 2nd Edition
978-0-470-10672-3

Gardening Basics For Dummies*†
978-0-470-03749-2

Knitting Patterns For Dummies
978-0-470-04556-5

Living Gluten-Free For Dummies†
978-0-471-77383-2

Painting Do-It-Yourself For Dummies
978-0-470-17533-0

HEALTH, SELF HELP, PARENTING & PETS

Anger Management For Dummies
978-0-470-03715-7

Anxiety & Depression Workbook For Dummies
978-0-7645-9793-0

Dieting For Dummies, 2nd Edition
978-0-7645-4149-0

Dog Training For Dummies, 2nd Edition
978-0-7645-8418-3

Horseback Riding For Dummies
978-0-470-09719-9

Infertility For Dummies†
978-0-470-11518-3

Meditation For Dummies with CD-ROM, 2nd Edition
978-0-471-77774-8

Post-Traumatic Stress Disorder For Dummies
978-0-470-04922-8

Puppies For Dummies, 2nd Edition
978-0-470-03717-1

Thyroid For Dummies, 2nd Edition†
978-0-471-78755-6

Type 1 Diabetes For Dummies*†
978-0-470-17811-9

INTERNET & DIGITAL MEDIA

AdWords For Dummies
978-0-470-15252-2

Blogging For Dummies, 2nd Edition
978-0-470-23017-6

Digital Photography All-in-One Desk Reference For Dummies, 3rd Edition
978-0-470-03743-0

Digital Photography For Dummies, 5th Edition
978-0-7645-9802-9

Digital SLR Cameras & Photography For Dummies, 2nd Edition
978-0-470-14927-0

eBay Business All-in-One Desk Reference For Dummies
978-0-7645-8438-1

eBay For Dummies, 5th Edition*
978-0-470-04529-9

eBay Listings That Sell For Dummies
978-0-471-78912-3

Facebook For Dummies
978-0-470-26273-3

The Internet For Dummies, 11th Edition
978-0-470-12174-0

Investing Online For Dummies, 5th Edition
978-0-7645-8456-5

iPod & iTunes For Dummies, 5th Edition
978-0-470-17474-6

MySpace For Dummies
978-0-470-09529-4

Podcasting For Dummies
978-0-471-74898-4

Search Engine Optimization For Dummies, 2nd Edition
978-0-471-97998-2

Second Life For Dummies
978-0-470-18025-9

Starting an eBay Business For Dummies, 3rd Edition†
978-0-470-14924-9

GRAPHICS, DESIGN & WEB DEVELOPMENT

Adobe Creative Suite 3 Design Premium All-in-One Desk Reference For Dummies
978-0-470-11724-8

Adobe Web Suite CS3 All-in-One Desk Reference For Dummies
978-0-470-12099-6

AutoCAD 2008 For Dummies
978-0-470-11650-0

Building a Web Site For Dummies, 3rd Edition
978-0-470-14928-7

Creating Web Pages All-in-One Desk Reference For Dummies, 3rd Edition
978-0-470-09629-1

Creating Web Pages For Dummies, 8th Edition
978-0-470-08030-6

Dreamweaver CS3 For Dummies
978-0-470-11490-2

Flash CS3 For Dummies
978-0-470-12100-9

Google SketchUp For Dummies
978-0-470-13744-4

InDesign CS3 For Dummies
978-0-470-11865-8

Photoshop CS3 All-in-One Desk Reference For Dummies
978-0-470-11195-6

Photoshop CS3 For Dummies
978-0-470-11193-2

Photoshop Elements 5 For Dummies
978-0-470-09810-3

SolidWorks For Dummies
978-0-7645-9555-4

Visio 2007 For Dummies
978-0-470-08983-5

Web Design For Dummies, 2nd Edition
978-0-471-78117-2

Web Sites Do-It-Yourself For Dummies
978-0-470-16903-2

Web Stores Do-It-Yourself For Dummies
978-0-470-17443-2

LANGUAGES, RELIGION & SPIRITUALITY

Arabic For Dummies
978-0-471-77270-5

Chinese For Dummies, Audio Set
978-0-470-12766-7

French For Dummies
978-0-7645-5193-2

German For Dummies
978-0-7645-5195-6

Hebrew For Dummies
978-0-7645-5489-6

Ingles Para Dummies
978-0-7645-5427-8

Italian For Dummies, Audio Set
978-0-470-09586-7

Italian Verbs For Dummies
978-0-471-77389-4

Japanese For Dummies
978-0-7645-5429-2

Latin For Dummies
978-0-7645-5431-5

Portuguese For Dummies
978-0-471-78738-9

Russian For Dummies
978-0-471-78001-4

Spanish Phrases For Dummies
978-0-7645-7204-3

Spanish For Dummies
978-0-7645-5194-9

Spanish For Dummies, Audio Set
978-0-470-09585-0

The Bible For Dummies
978-0-7645-5296-0

Catholicism For Dummies
978-0-7645-5391-2

The Historical Jesus For Dummies
978-0-470-16785-4

Islam For Dummies
978-0-7645-5503-9

Spirituality For Dummies, 2nd Edition
978-0-470-19142-2

NETWORKING AND PROGRAMMING

ASP.NET 3.5 For Dummies
978-0-470-19592-5

C# 2008 For Dummies
978-0-470-19109-5

Hacking For Dummies, 2nd Edition
978-0-470-05235-8

Home Networking For Dummies, 4th Edition
978-0-470-11806-1

Java For Dummies, 4th Edition
978-0-470-08716-9

Microsoft® SQL Server™ 2008 All-in-One Desk Reference For Dummies
978-0-470-17954-3

Networking All-in-One Desk Reference For Dummies, 2nd Edition
978-0-7645-9939-2

Networking For Dummies, 8th Edition
978-0-470-05620-2

SharePoint 2007 For Dummies
978-0-470-09941-4

Wireless Home Networking For Dummies, 2nd Edition
978-0-471-74940-0